CLASSICAL LITERARY CRITICISM

D. A. RUSSELL is an Emeritus Fellow of St John's College and Professor of Classical Literature in the University of Oxford.

MICHAEL WINTERBOTTOM is Corpus Christi Professor of Latin in the University of Oxford.

OXFORD WORLD'S CLASSICS

*For almost 100 years Oxford World's Classics have brought
readers closer to the world's great literature. Now with over 700
titles—from the 4,000-year-old myths of Mesopotamia to the
twentieth century's greatest novels—the series make· available
lesser-known as well as celebrated writing.*

*The pocket-sized hardbacks of the early years contained
introductions by Virginia Woolf, T. S. Eliot, Graham Greene,
and other literary figures which enriched the experience of reading.
Today the series is recognized for its fine scholarship and
reliability in texts that span world literature, drama and poetry,
religion, philosophy and politics. Each edition includes perceptive
commentary and essential background information to meet the
changing needs of readers.*

OXFORD WORLD'S CLASSICS

Classical Literary Criticism

Edited with an Introduction and Notes by
D. A. RUSSELL
and
MICHAEL WINTERBOTTOM

Oxford   New York
OXFORD UNIVERSITY PRESS

Oxford University Press, Great Clarendon Street, Oxford OX2 6DP

Oxford New York

Athens Auckland Bangkok Bogotá Buenos Aires Calcutta
Cape Town Chennai Dar es Salaam Delhi Florence Hong Kong Istanbul
Karachi Kuala Lumpur Madrid Melbourne Mexico City Mumbai
Nairobi Paris São Paulo Singapore Taipei Tokyo Toronto Warsaw

and associated companies in Berlin Ibadan

Oxford is a registered trade mark of Oxford University Press

© Oxford University Press 1972, 1989

Classical Literary Criticism is a revised edition, with a new
introduction, of Ancient Literary Criticism, first published 1972
First published as a World's Classics paperback 1989
Reissued as an Oxford World's Classics paperback 1998

All rights reserved. No part of this publication may be reproduced,
stored in a retrieval system, or transmitted, in any form or by any means,
without the prior permission in writing of Oxford University Press.
Within the UK, exceptions are allowed in respect of any fair dealing for the
purpose of research or private study, or criticism or review, as permitted
under the Copyright, Designs and Patents Act, 1988, or in the case of
reprographic reproduction in accordance with the terms of the licences
issued by the Copyright Licensing Agency. Enquiries concerning
reproduction outside these terms and in other countries should be
sent to the Rights Department, Oxford University Press,
at the address above

This book is sold subject to the condition that it shall not, by way
of trade or otherwise, be lent, re-sold, hired out or otherwise circulated
without the publisher's prior consent in any form of binding or cover
other than that in which it is published and without a similar condition
including this condition being imposed on the subsequent purchaser

British Library Cataloguing in Publication Data

Data available

Library of Congress Cataloging in Publication Data

Classical literary criticism / edited by D. A. Russell and
M. Winterbottom.—Rev. ed.
p.   cm.—(Oxford world's classics)
Bibliography: p.
Includes indexes.
1. Classical literature—History and criticism—Theory etc.
2. Criticism—Greece.   3. Criticism—Rome.   I. Russell, D. A.
(Donald Andrew)   II. Winterbottom, Michael.   III. Series.
PA3013.A47   1989   89–9369
801.95′0938—dc20

ISBN 0–19–283900–4

1 3 5 7 9 10 8 6 4 2

Printed in Great Britain by
The Bath Press, Bath

CONTENTS

INTRODUCTION

THE modern literary critic characteristically inhabits a university. He studies printed books, and writes others of his own, passing on the fruits of his labours, as he hopes, to a wider audience of intelligent readers than he commands among his own pupils. If he is a popular reviewer, he may have a very large readership indeed. Such a figure, however familiar to us today, was more or less unknown before, say, 1900, and finds no counterpart whatever in the ancient world. Higher education did not then concern itself with literature for its own sake, but with philosophy and rhetoric. If there were any professional critics, they contributed nothing to the distinguished critical literature whose peaks are arranged in the present volume. That was largely a side-product of the work of poets, philosophers, and historians who saw that literature was a crucial part of a world they wished to describe, reflect, and even reform.

In 405 BC the comic poet Aristophanes won the first prize before a large popular audience at Athens for a play, the *Frogs*, whose main point lay in the contrast of the styles and attitudes of two great tragedians, Aeschylus and Euripides. That contrast is not always conducted at any high level of sophistication, but familiarity of some kind with great literature is presupposed in the audience. That familiarity was the product not of reading, for at this time books were rare and expensive, but of hearing, especially by frequent presence at the festivals where both comedy and tragedy were produced.

The same sort of thing is true of the other genre which found a large audience: epic. It is a little unclear from Plato's *Ion* what the rhapsode in reality did beyond his primary task of reciting epic poetry. Perhaps an Ion would not do much more than give an introductory encomium of Homer and the passage to be presented. What is clear is that such a rhapsode would perform at a festival, and in the presence of 'twenty thousand or so persons' (p. 6). He is, in fact, closely parallel to the actor, with whom Socrates indeed classes him.

In Classical Greece only a minority would study literature at school. But tragedy and epic reached large numbers of ordinary people, and had on them an effect that went beyond the immediate emotional impact. It is in this sense that Aristophanes, again in the *Frogs*, was able to make Euripides claim that a poet was to be admired 'for his expertise and his sound advice and because we improve by our teaching / mankind's civic sense and their natures too', and Aeschylus, a little further on, that 'the poets alone are the teachers of youth'. The Aristophanic Aeschylus even asserts that the poets taught more than moral values: 'from Hesiod / field-work we have learned, when to reap, when to plough'; and as for Homer 'battle-order he showed and the deeds that excel and the way to bear arms'.

It is difficult for us to think that a Hesiod or a Homer consciously meant to be so informative, and that Aristophanes can have seriously supposed that audiences would have listened to them in that spirit. And it is tempting, too, to think that Plato is aware of his own fallacy when he makes Socrates challenge Ion about his knowledge of arts like charioteering and medicine, driving him into a corner where he has to admit that a rhapsode has little to contribute to the interpretation of Homer, which can properly be left to charioteers, doctors, and other specialists. But even in the *Republic* Plato makes Socrates represent Homer as 'trying to speak' of 'wars, strategy, government, education' (p. 41), and as doing it less expertly than masters of those fields. The view of the poet as an instructor in practical matters seems to have died hard.

The moral effect of poetry was a different matter, and here the critics were perhaps on firmer ground. No doubt Euripides' plays were a symptom of the new mood abroad in late fifth-century Athens rather than a cause of that mood. It remained true that his tone of voice could and would influence his audience, if not perhaps so deeply or so deleteriously as Aristophanes would have us believe. Nor was it only a matter of tragedy. A thoroughgoing critic of poetry like Plato felt that epic too was an evil teacher. His quarrel, in fact, was with Greek mythology as a whole, with 'all the tales of how gods war, plot, and fight against gods' (p. 15), and, even more fundamentally, with the proposition that 'god, who is good, is the cause of evil to anyone' (p. 18). It was only a logical deduction from such premises that in Plato's ideal city 'the only poetry admissible . . . is hymns to the gods and encomia to good men' (p. 49). Plato's solution is an extreme one; but the problem was genuine, and continued to exercise those concerned with the education of children, who by now were exposed to literature from an early age. Allegorization was tried, and found wanting. Later, in the first century AD, Quintilian was to recommend what no doubt happened in practice, a grading of literature according to age, so that, for instance, the dangerous love elegy would be left for older pupils. Among the Greeks, Plutarch devoted a whole treatise (pp. 192–216) to the sort of guidance that needed to be given to the young confronted with Homer and other poets.

The condemnation of most current poetry was perhaps a reaction to particular Greek circumstances. But Plato's two other quarrels with poetry arise more directly from his philosophical presuppositions. First we have his views on imitation. The foundations for these are laid in *Republic* 3, where Plato sees not only tragedy but epic too as a matter of the 'imitation', or representation, of words and action. Indeed, from the literal sense of *mimesis*, Plato seems to draw a general distrust of the whole activity of imitating. However that may be, epic and tragedy presented obvious dangers for Plato, for the words and actions they portrayed might so easily be immoral or emotional. But in Book 10 more esoteric considerations surface as well. In a disastrous though familiar analogy Plato likens poems to pictures. At the top of the hierarchy of beds is the 'idea' of the bed, constructed by God; next comes the physical example, this actual bed, constructed by a carpenter; lowest of all is the picture of a bed, made by a painter. Even the proposition that a painting is less 'real' and valuable than what it depicts is questionable enough, though it may have seemed natural in a civilization that placed great store by representational accuracy in art. But that poems, no less than paintings, are somehow inferior to what they represent was a catastrophic extension of a doctrine that could do little harm when kept in the metaphysical realm to which it belonged.

Even more basic to Plato's thought—and indeed to that of the Stoics and Epicureans later—was the proper control of the emotions. Rational man should be controlled by his reason, just as the ideal city was to be governed by the reasoning. Emotions like pity, fear, and grief were to be kept under rigid control. Yet it was precisely such emotions that were portrayed and aroused by both tragedy and epic. The rhapsode Ion remarks that 'when I recite a pathetic passage, my eyes fill with tears; when it is something alarming . . . my hair stands on end in terror' (p. 6). As for his audience, 'I can see them from up on the platform, weeping and looking fierce and marvelling at the tale'. Worse still, such communication of emotion gave pleasure to the hearers: 'when the best of us,' Socrates says in the *Republic*, 'hear Homer or some other tragic poet imitating a hero in mourning . . . we feel pleasure and give ourselves up to it' (p. 48). That was how the imitative poet did his damage: 'he rouses and feeds this part of the mind [the non-rational, that is] and by strengthening it destroys the rational part' (p. 47). Epic and tragedy (and Plato draws only a formal distinction between them) are, then, based on a corrupting mythology, encourage feelings that we should strive to tame, and in any case give us only at second remove a world that is itself somehow inferior to the ultimate realities of the Forms.

Plato's pupil Aristotle reacts firmly to all of these criticisms, though with varying degrees of emphasis. One pregnant sentence overthrows the Platonic picture of the poet as instructor, whether of charioteering or morality: 'correctness in poetry is not the same thing as correctness in morals, nor yet is it the same as correctness in any other art' (p. 84). This crucial perception is not much developed in the *Poetics*, but part of Plutarch's *On listening to poets* forms an intelligent commentary on it (p. 198). It is not the prime duty of poetry to put over a favoured view of human behaviour (though tragedy has a certain bias towards the morally good), nor is it of the first importance that a poet should represent the world (for example, the way a horse runs) correctly, for 'this does not involve the essential nature of poetry' (p. 85). If mythology is unsatisfactory, 'well,' one can answer, 'that is what people say' (ibid.), and the poet is not responsible for it. Equally curt, and for us not unmysterious, is the answer to Plato on emotion. It is made part of the definition of tragedy that it is productive of pity and fear, and through them it produces 'the *catharsis* of such emotions' (p. 57). A certain distrust of the feelings remains, but Aristotle is convinced that, in some way we cannot be sure of, tragic performances have a good effect on minds too prone to emotion. Finally, Aristotle makes 'imitation' (*mimesis*) the foundation of his view of poetry. The desire to 'imitate', far from being somehow undesirable, is basic in man, and provides pleasure to the imitator and his audience. Tragedy, and in a rather different way epic too, produces *mimesis* of an action: it is a representation 'not of people but of their actions and life' (p. 59). The terminology and some of the presuppositions are an inheritance from the *Republic*. But, as one might expect from Aristotle's philosophical standpoint generally, there is no opprobrious contrast of 'real' life and its pale imitation in art. 'Life' and 'art' have their own independent values. There is even a sense, not fully explained by Aristotle, in which 'poetry is at once more like philosophy and more worthwhile than history' (p.62).

The *Poetics*, which can hardly be more than a series of working notes from which Aristotle would have lectured at far greater length and with far superior lucidity to his pupils, is a work that does not so much describe the genres of tragedy and epic as analyse them to see what makes them what they are, with some admixture of historical information to show how they have developed. It gives not so much prescriptions as judgements. We learn what kind of play Aristotle likes and dislikes, and there is some polemic against modern trends; for by this time the great age of poetry was long over. It was left to a much later and infinitely different world to try to use Aristotle's dicta as rules: though French neo-classicists and others tended to look for what they wanted there—and if they could not find it, to supply the deficiencies from Horace's *Art of Poetry*.

That poem (a 'letter', not to be judged in principle differently from Horace's other Epistles) is in the Aristotelian tradition, though it seems to draw on the *Poetics* only at second hand. Unlike the *Poetics*, it has an openly prescriptive stance, for it is addressed to a family of Pisones who are assumed to be interested in producing tragedies (and even the associated satyr-plays). But like any other 'didactic' poem—Lucretius' *De Rerum Natura* and Virgil's *Georgics* are distant relations—it can hardly

serve as more than a protreptic to its theme. For all the show of
technical detail, for instance on neologism or metre, brought with
great virtuosity into verse form, this is no handbook to the writing
of tragedy.

Horace was not a tragedian, and tragedy was only a minor part
of the repertory of the Augustan poet. Naturally enough the *Art of
Poetry*, for all its superficial concern with tragedy, looks far wider
for its subject matter. The Romans had over a couple of
centuries slowly built up a literature that looked for its inspiration
almost exclusively to Greek models. That literature was in
Horace's time at its finest flower. But the conservative Roman
public still hankered after the older poets, perhaps partly because
an Ennius or a Plautus seemed more truly Latin in inspiration
than, say, Virgil's *Eclogues* or Horace's own *Odes*. In the *Art*, as in
his epistle to Augustus, Horace tries to woo the public away from
the old writers. They showed, to his taste, insufficient care for
technical detail: 'Latium would have been as famous for
literature as for valour and deeds of arms if the poets had not,
one and all, been put off by the labour and time of polishing their
work' (p. 105). Horace sounds a clarion call for cultivated poetry,
and thereby shows his affinity to the 'Hellenistic' period of Greek
poetry rather than to what had preceded it. And his views were,
of course, applicable far beyond tragedy. They are the key to
Horace's own lyric poetry.

In his quirky way Horace portrays a Rome in which everyone
thinks he can be a poet. But poetry for him is a professional
matter, to be essayed only by gifted writers who are prepared to
take trouble. Nor are cliques and mutual admiration societies the
best milieu for a poet. He needs a friend who will criticize his
verse without flattery. Here, incidentally, we are given a hint as to
where the ancients practised their truest literary criticism: in
careful discussion of each other's work, particularly before
publication.

All this might make it seem that poetry is a private matter,
written for the satisfaction of the poet himself and a few favoured
friends. That indeed is the impression given by an early satire,
where Horace reels off the names of a number of famous friends,
including Virgil, whose approval is all he feels the need to win.
But there is another side to Horace's view of the poet. In the *Art*

he gives us the traditional picture of the influence of poets on the development of civilization. In the wake of Aristophanes he remarks that Homer 'sharpened masculine hearts for war'. But there is more: 'The path of life was pointed out in verse. Kings' favours were won by the Muses' tunes' (p. 108). Both themes were relevant to Horace's own poetry, and he develops them in the *Letter to Augustus*. There the poet's educational, religious, and moral role is stated, and the relationship of a court poet with his patron explored. Poetry had not lost its public role, and in Horace's own *Odes* public themes jostle with private matters. Even more deeply, Horace's constant concern with 'philosophy'—in particular moral—represents a firm if unconscious reaction to Plato's doubts about poetry. 'Wisdom is the starting-point and source of correct writing. Socratic books will be able to point out to you your material' (p. 106).

'It is not enough for poetry to be beautiful; it must also be pleasing *and lead the hearer's mind wherever it will*' (p. 100). Horace does not forget the emotional impact of the tragedian on the audience. In Plato's *Ion* Socrates is made to speak of a chain of magnetized rings linking the inspired poet with his audience by the mediation of the rhapsode or actor (p. 5). A similar process was visualized in oratory, which, in ever-changing ways, always rivalled tragedy as a public spectacle in Greece and the Greek East, and which played a significant political role in the last centuries of the Roman republic. Cicero, just like Horace, speaks of the orator's need to lead an audience where he will, and both he and Quintilian believed that if an orator was to communicate an emotion he must, like Plato's inspired poet, feel it himself. And techniques for arousal of feelings were a key part of the elaborate system of precept developed from the fifth century onwards. By Plato's time rhetoric was something at once to be ridiculed for its pedantry and lambasted for its amorality. Aristotle, following up a Platonic hint, wrote a substantial book in which rhetoric was given a philosophical and psychological basis. In Cicero, orator, philosopher (of a sort), and composer of treatises on rhetoric, the old quarrel between philosophy and rhetoric might seem to have reached a compromise.

Rhetoric naturally gave rise to and had an impact on literary criticism. It was the basis of secondary education both in the

Hellenistic Greek world and at Rome after 100 BC, for the child who had had a grounding in literature at the school of the *grammaticus* or grammarian proceeded at around 14 to the school of the *rhetor* to learn precepts and to put them into practice in 'declamations' on themes set to him (Tacitus' *Dialogus* comments sharply on this kind of education: p. 136). To Quintilian, whose *Institutio Oratoria* ('Education of the orator') is our fullest picture of this educational system, it was important what the pupil read at primary as well as secondary level; and the famous chapter 10.1, after sketching what different genres of literature had to contribute to the trained orator, lists Greek and Latin authors with comments, sometimes very terse, on their appropriateness to the budding speaker's reading-list. Much of the comment on Greek literature is inherited from Dionysius of Halicarnassus, and Dionysius' treatise *On Imitation* will lie behind another important chapter of Quintilian (10.2). Imitation now means not the representation of people and action, as in Plato and Aristotle, but the following and emulation of earlier writers, something as common in classical oratory as in every other genre. Another old theme of the critic, morality, is not forgotten. Quintilian's Book 12 contains deeply serious discussion of the moral problems facing the lawyer-orator: just as in the *Dialogus* Maternus recoils from the profiteering of some modern oratory.

At some date perhaps not far removed from Quintilian's the man we think of as Longinus (and that he shall be called here) wrote a short book which, merging in a wholly novel way the Platonic and rhetorical strands we have examined, brought ancient literary criticism to a striking climax. *On Sublimity* is not a textbook in the ordinary sense, but it was intended to be of practical use: Longinus expresses the possibility that there may be something 'in my observations which may be thought useful to public men' (p. 143), that is, presumably, to lawyers and politicians. A good deal of the material used is the sort of thing that is familiar to us from rhetorical handbooks. In particular, Longinus has a long section on figures. On the other, philosophic side, there is, to begin with, a profound feeling of the crucial importance of Plato. Using a simile that is in itself entirely in the Platonic manner, Longinus describes a form of imitation of the great writers of the past that is no mere plagiarism, but rather possession 'by a spirit not [one's] own . . . The genius of the ancients acts as a kind of oracular cavern, and effluences flow from it into the minds of their imitators' (p. 158). Longinus pictures Plato as a 'young aspirant' challenging the admired Homer, and tells us that we should try to imagine how Plato (or Demosthenes or Thucydides) would have treated our subject. Longinus admires Plato's style and defends it against its critics. But more crucially he answers and transcends Plato in holding up the ideal of a great literature based on the great thoughts of an uncorrupt writer. And his book ends with an eloquent statement of the reasons for the decline of letters in his day: not despotism, as a philosopher friend had suggested (and we remember the argument of Maternus in Tacitus' *Dialogus*), but slavery to pleasure and greed. That is not unPlatonic. But Longinus' book, taken as a whole, is far from Plato's pessimism. He shows us that great thoughts *have* been uttered by great men in the past; perhaps they could be uttered again.

Longinus looks at literature as a whole, and for its own sake. Grammarians, and rhetoricians in their wake, had exemplified figures and other stylistic devices from poetry as well as prose. Longinus goes far beyond them in promoting 'sublimity' to be 'the source of the distinction of the very greatest poets and prose writers' (p. 143), something that could strike, like a thunderbolt, *anywhere*. It is easy to cavil at the terminology, and to feel, as Hugh Blair put it in the eighteenth century, that Longinus often departs from the 'just and proper meaning' of sublimity, substituting, 'in the place of it, whatever, in any strain of composition, pleases highly'. Indeed it is not at all clear in what sense some of the passages Longinus commends are sublime at all. But the great thing is that he *does* quote them, and that he is himself pleased by them. He discusses, often in some detail, individual passages of a very wide variety of literature. He is not concerned merely to label a writer with a facile phrase or categorize a device by giving a stock example. He is at his best highly alert to the effect of a passage on the reader or the imagined hearer.

Longinus writes memorably when he generalizes, as on the contrast of *Iliad* and *Odyssey* or Cicero and Demosthenes. But the real glory of his book lies in his discussion of cited passages.

None of the other authors anthologized here, with the possible exception of Plutarch, made it his business to get down to texts in this way. Even Dio, in his unique comparison of the three plays by different tragedians on the subject of Philoctetes (pp. 189–91), quotes only one line of poetry. If we look else-where, we find something similar in Dionysius of Halicarnassus and Demetrius. But they cannot match Longinus' perceptive illuminations. Still less can we turn to commentators on ancient texts, whether in Greek or Latin, to give us anything comparable. No doubt the great Alexandrian *grammatici* had high aims. But their successors, the scholiasts on the *Iliad*, or Servius on Virgil, were writing for young students needing merely to understand allusions and label devices. Longinus wrote for adults. At his best, as in the great request of Ajax to Zeus that he be killed in the light, he matches the grandeur of the texts he cites.

It is worth making two remarks about Longinus' detailed criticism. Both concern those magic rings that connect author and audience. First, Longinus is concerned, as the rhetorical preceptors only occasionally are, to go beyond the categorization of figures. Thus in discussing hyperbaton, or distortion of the natural order of words, he remarks that 'it is a very real mark of urgent emotion. People who in real life feel anger, fear, or indignation . . . often put one thing forward and then rush off to another, irrationally inserting some remark, and then hark back again to their first point. . . . Thus hyperbaton is a means by which, in the best authors, imitation approaches the effect of nature.' The speaker who employs hyperbaton gives the appearance of suffering under strong emotion, because those who do feel such emotion do employ hyperbaton. There is an inference from words to state of mind. And that state of mind was communicable: Demosthenes, speaking hyperbatically, 'throws the hearer into a panic lest the sentence collapse altogether, and forces him in his excitement to share the speaker's peril' (pp. 165–7).

Cicero and Quintilian, as we have seen, thought that to communicate emotion a speaker must himself feel it. Earlier Aristotle had remarked that 'the person who most realistically expresses distress is the person in distress' (p. 72). And perhaps Longinus did not mean to imply that Demosthenes, in such a passage, was only pretending to feel. At any rate—and this brings us to our second point—one of Longinus' deepest convictions is of the importance of the mental processes of the author. In the Ajax passage, Homer is said to 'enter into the greatness of his heroes' (p. 152). Again, in the *Phaethon* of Euripides, Longinus remarks that 'the writer's soul has mounted the chariot, has taken wing with the horses and shares the danger' (p. 160). Compounds in *syn-* ('with') are characteristic of Longinus' vocabulary of verbs. He holds that in an almost mystical way the composer is identified with what he describes; and it is because of the excitement of that moment of inspiration that the hearer or reader too is stunned by a sudden conviction of the sublimity of the passage.

Longinus' book was translated by Boileau in 1674, and was for 150 years highly influential, even playing a part in shaping the preconceptions of the Romantic movement. Ironically enough, its popularity was brought to an end precisely by the Romantics, who simultaneously, though for rather different reasons, rejected Aristotle's *Poetics*. Since then, ancient literary criticism has inevitably lost some ground. Yet its great landmarks still stand up impressively. It was Plato and Aristotle who first raised critical problems that remain important, and Longinus who first brought passion to the study of literature.

The editors are most grateful to Dr Catherine Whistler for suggesting the attractive cover illustration.

medium thru C divine works
divine possession
raising status painters as intellectual
medium thru which gods work
born genius

PLATO: *ION*

'Welcome, Ion! Where have you arrived from? Have you been 530 home to Ephesus?'

'No, Socrates; I've come from Epidaurus, from the Asclepieia.'*

'Oh, do the Epidaurians hold a competition for rhapsodes* too in honour of the god?'

'Yes indeed, and for other musical arts.'

'Did you compete then? And how did you get on?'

'We won the first prize, Socrates.'

'Splendid! Mind we win the Panathenaea* too!'

'God willing, we shall.'

'I have often envied you rhapsodes your profession, Ion. It is an enviable lot, to find it always professionally appropriate to be beautifully dressed and look as handsome as possible, and at the same time to find it essential to occupy oneself with so many good poets, and Homer above all, the best and divinest of all, and learn not only his words but his meaning. No one can be a good rhapsode who fails to understand what the poet says; the rhapsode has to be an interpreter of the poet's meaning, and this can't be done properly unless he understands what the poet says. It's all most enviable.'

'Quite right, Socrates. Anyway, that is what gives me most work in my profession, and I believe I can speak about Homer better than any man. Neither Metrodorus of Lampsacus nor Stesimbrotus of Thasos nor Glaucon* nor anybody else has ever had so many fine thoughts to utter about Homer as I have.'

'Splendid, Ion! I'm sure you won't grudge me a demonstration.'

'Well, Socrates, my embellishments of Homer really are worth hearing. I deserve a golden crown from the Homeridae,* I fancy.'

'I shall make leisure to hear you yet; but for the moment just tell me one thing. Are you good only at Homer, or at Hesiod and 531 Archilochus too?'

'Only at Homer; I think that is quite enough.'

'But is there anything about which Homer and Hesiod say the same?'

'Many things, surely.'

'Then can you expound what Homer says about these things better than what Hesiod says?'

'Equally well, Socrates, as far as the things about which they both say the same are concerned.'

'And what about things where they don't say the same? For instance, Homer and Hesiod both speak of divination.'

'Yes.'

'Well, would you or a good diviner give a better explanation of the similarities and differences between what these two poets say about divination?'

'The diviner.'

'And if you were a diviner, would you not know how to expound the things which they say differently, if you were able to expound those of which they give a similar account?'

'Certainly I should.'

'Why then are you good at Homer but not at Hesiod or any other poet? Is it that Homer talks about different things from all other poets? Does he not for the most part talk of war, dealings of men—good and bad, laymen and craftsmen—with one another, the dealings of gods with one another and with men, the phenomena of the heavens, Hades, the genealogies of gods and heroes? These are the subjects of Homer's poetry, are they not?'

'Indeed, Socrates.'

'And what about other poets? Don't they handle the same subjects?'

'Yes, but not like Homer, Socrates.'

'Worse?'

'Much.'

'Homer's better?'

'Yes, indeed.'

'My dear Ion, when many people speak about number, and one talks best, the good speaker can be recognized, can't he?'

'Yes.'

'By the same person who will recognize the bad speakers?'

'Yes.'

'In fact, by the possessor of the skill of arithmetic?'

'Yes.'

'Take another example. When a number of people discuss healthy food and one speaks best, will it be the same critic or a

different one who will be able to recognize the best speaker and
the worse?'

'The same, obviously.'

'Who? What is he called?'

'A doctor.'

'So to sum up, it will always be the same person who, in a given
group of speakers, will know who is speaking well and who badly;
if he doesn't recognize the bad, he won't recognize the good
either, so long as the subject is the same.' 532

'Yes.'

'Then the same man is clever at both tasks?'

'Yes.'

'Now you say that Homer and the other poets, including
Hesiod and Archilochus, talk about the same subjects, but not all
equally well?'

'Yes, and it's true.'

'Then if you know the good speaker, you will also know that
the bad speakers are in fact worse.'

'So it would seem.'

'Then we shall not be wrong if we say that Ion is clever both
about Homer and about other poets, since you admit yourself
that the same person is an adequate judge of all who speak about
the same subject, and that poets, generally speaking, all
compose on the same subjects.'

'Then why is it, Socrates, that when someone talks about any
other poet I don't attend and I can't contribute anything at all
worth while—I just doze off—but as soon as someone mentions
Homer, I wake up and attend and find I have something to
say?'

'It's not hard to make a guess about that, my friend. It's plain
to anyone that you are not capable of talking about Homer out of
skill (*technē*) and knowledge; because, if you were, you would
have been able to talk about all the other poets as well; the whole
thing is poetry, isn't it?'

'Yes.'

'Then, when one takes some other complete art, the inquiry
will take the same form, whatever the art? Do you want to
understand what I mean, Ion?'

'Indeed I do, Socrates. I love listening to you clever people.'

'I wish you would tell the truth, Ion; it's you rhapsodes and actors and those whose poems you recite who are clever; I simply tell the truth, like a plain man. To take the question I asked you just now; see how easy and unspecialized it is—anyone can understand the point—to see that when one takes any art as a whole the manner of inquiry is the same. For instance, take painting; it's an art as a whole, isn't it?'

'Yes.'

'And there are and have been many painters, good and bad?'

'Yes.'

'Well, have you ever seen anyone good at explaining what is well done and what badly in the work of Polygnotus the son of Aglaophon, but incapable of doing this for other painters? 533 Anyone who dozes and is at a loss and can make no contribution when shown the work of other painters, but wakes up and attends and has something to say when he has to give an opinion about Polygnotus or some other one, individual painter?'

'Good gracious, no.'

'Take sculpture too. Have you ever seen anybody good at explaining the good things in Daedalus son of Metion or Epeus son of Panopeus or Theodorus of Samos* or some other one individual sculptor, but dozes and is at a loss and has nothing to say about the works of other sculptors?'

'No, I've never seen anyone like that either.'

'Nor yet, I imagine, have you ever seen, in connection with flute- or lyre-playing or singing to the lyre or being a rhapsode, anyone who is good at expounding Olympus or Thamyras or Orpheus or Phemius the rhapsode from Ithaca,* but at a loss about Ion of Ephesus, with no contribution to make as to what he recites well and what badly?'

'I can't oppose you, Socrates. But I do know that I speak about Homer better than anyone else, and I have much to say, and everyone says I am good; but not about the others. Please see what this can mean.'

'I do see, Ion, and I am going on to explain to you what I think it is.

'This ability of yours to speak well about Homer is, as I was saying just now, no art (*techne*). It is a divine force which moves you. It is like the force in the stone Euripides calls a magnet, and most people "the Heraclean stone". This not only attracts iron rings, but induces in the rings the power to do the same themselves in turn—namely to attract other rings, so that sometimes a long chain of iron rings is formed, suspended from one another, all having the force derived from the stone. Thus the Muse herself makes people possessed, and from these possessed persons there hangs a chain of others, possessed with the same enthusiasm. All good epic poets produce all their beautiful poems not by art but because they are inspired and possessed. So too with good lyric poets: just as Corybantic dancers* perform when they are not in their right mind, so the lyric poets compose these beautiful songs when they are not in their right mind; once involved in harmony and rhythm, they are in a state of possession and it is then—just as women draw honey and milk from the rivers when under Bacchic possession, but not when they are in their right mind—it is then that the lyric poets have the experience they describe to us. They say, you see, that it is from fountains flowing with honey, in groves and gardens of the Muses, that they cull, like bees, the songs they bring us; and they too do it on the wing. Now this is perfectly true: a poet is a light, winged, holy creature, and cannot compose until he is possessed and out of his mind, and his reason is no longer in him; no man can compose or prophesy so long as he has his reason. So, because it is not art but divine dispensation that enables them to compose poetry and say many fine things about the world, as you do about Homer, every individual poet can only compose well what the Muse has set him to do—one dithyrambs,* one encomia,* one hyporchemata,* one epic, one iambics.* They are no good at anything else. This is because their utterances are the result not of art but of divine force. If they could utter on any one theme by art, they would also be able to do so on every other. This is why god takes away their senses and uses them as servants, as he does divine prophets and seers, so that we who hear may realize that it is not these persons, whose reason has left them, who are the speakers of such valuable words, but god who speaks and expresses himself to us through them. There is good evidence for this in Tynnichus of Chalcis, who never composed a poem worth remembering except the paean* which everybody sings, perhaps the most beautiful of all lyrics, a real "windfall of

534

the Muses", as he says himself. Herein god seems to me to have
shown, to prevent us being in any doubt, that these beautiful
poems are not human and of men, but divine and of the gods,
poets being merely *interpreters* of the gods, each possessed by his
own peculiar god. To demonstrate this, the god deliberately sang
the most beautiful song through the mouth of the worst poet.
535 Don't you think I'm right, Ion?'

'Indeed I do. You touch me in the heart, Socrates, by what you
say, and I believe it is by a divine dispensation that good poets
interpret these messages to us from the gods.'

'And you rhapsodes then interpret the messages of the poets?'

'That's right too.'

'So you are interpreters of interpreters?'

'Just so.'

'Well now, tell me this, Ion, and don't hide what I ask you.
When you recite well and most amaze your audience—say when
you sing Odysseus leaping on the threshold, revealing himself to
the suitors and pouring the arrows out at his feet, or Achilles
advancing against Hector, or some pathetic passage about
Andromache or Hecuba or Priam*—are you at that time in your
right mind, or are you beside yourself? Does your mind imagine
itself, in its state of enthusiasm, present at the actual events you
describe—in Ithaca or at Troy or whatever the poem requires?'

'That's a very clear indication you've given me, Socrates; I'll
tell you without concealment. When I recite a pathetic passage,
my eyes fill with tears; when it is something alarming or
terrifying, my hair stands on end in terror and my heart jumps.'

'Well, now, Ion: can we call a man sane who, when elaborately
dressed and wearing a gold crown, and not having lost any of this
finery, nevertheless breaks into tears at a sacrifice and festival, or
feels frightened in the company of twenty thousand or so friendly
persons, not one of whom is trying to rob him or do him any
harm?'

'To tell you the truth, Socrates—no.'

'You know then that you people have the same effect on many
of the spectators?'

'Certainly I do. I can see them from up on the platform,
weeping and looking fierce and marvelling at the tale. Indeed, I
am obliged to attend to them; for if I can set them crying, I shall

laugh when I get my money, but if I make them laugh, I lose my money and it's I who'll be crying.'

'You know then that the spectator is the last of the rings which I described as taking their force from the Heraclean stone? You—the rhapsode or the actor—are the middle link, and the poet himself is the first. Through all these, the god draws the human mind in any direction he wishes, hanging a chain of force from one to the other. Just as with the stone, there is a huge chain of dancers, producers, and under-producers, hanging sideways from the rings which hang down from the Muse. Poets are suspended from different Muses—we say "possessed by", but it is much the same thing—a matter of being held—and from this first set of rings, the poets, are suspended—or possessed—other persons, some from one and some from another, some from Orpheus, some from Musaeus—but most are possessed and held by Homer. You are one of these, Ion. You are possessed by Homer. When something by any other poet is performed, you fall asleep and have nothing to say, but the moment anyone utters a song of Homer, you wake up, your heart dances, and you have a lot to say; this is because your talk about Homer comes not from knowledge or art, but from divine dispensation and possession. Like the Corybantic dancers, who are keenly aware only of the tune that belongs to the god who possesses them and can dance and give utterance to this alone, taking no notice of others, so you, Ion, are ready enough when Homer is mentioned, but at a loss with everything else; and the reason for this, which is what you're asking, the reason why you are ready on the subject of Homer but not of the others, is that it is not art but divine dispensation that makes you a good encomiast of Homer.'

'You *do* speak well, Socrates; but I should be surprised if you were eloquent enough to persuade me that I am possessed and mad when I praise Homer. I don't believe you'd think so yourself if you heard me speaking about Homer.'

'I want to hear you very much, but not before you have answered one question. Which of the subjects Homer speaks of do you speak well about? It can't be *all*, surely.'

'Every single one, Socrates.'

'But not surely about things which Homer speaks of but of which you are ignorant?'

'And what is there, pray, that Homer speaks of and I don't know?'

'Well, doesn't Homer often say a good deal about various arts? For example, chariot-driving. If I can remember the lines, I'll say them.'

'No, I will: I remember.'

'Well, then, repeat what Nestor says to his son Antilochus, advising him to take care at the turn in the chariot race in honour of Patroclus:*

> Lean over yourself in your polished chariot
> gently, to the left; goad on the right-hand horse,
> and let him have the reins.
> Let the left-hander graze the post,
> so the wheel-hub seems just to touch,
> but beware of hitting the stone.'

'That'll do. Now, Ion, who would know best whether Homer is right here—a doctor or a charioteer?'

'A charioteer, of course.'

'Because he possesses the art, or for some other reason?'

'Because he possesses the art.'

'Then god has granted every art the power of knowing some one thing? What we know by the pilot's craft, we shan't know by medicine, for instance.'

'Indeed not.'

'And what we know by medicine, we shan't know by carpentry.'

'No.'

'And so with all other arts: what we know by one, we shan't know by another? But first answer me this: do you say there are *different* arts?'

'Yes.'

'When one is knowledge of one set of things, and another of another, I go by that, and call them different arts: is that what you do?'

'Yes.'

'Now if there were a science which dealt with one set of things, how could we say that there are two *different* sciences, at least if the same facts were to be learned from both? For example, I know that these fingers are five in number, and you know so too; and if I were to ask you whether you and I both knew this by the

same art, namely arithmetic, or a different one, you would reply
"by the same".'

'Yes.'

'Then tell me now what I was going to ask you just then. Do
you think it applies to all arts that the same art must necessarily
have knowledge of the same things, and a different art of
different things?'

'Yes I do, Socrates.'

'Then anyone who doesn't possess a certain art will not be able
to know properly the words or actions which belong to that art?'

'True.'

'Then consider the lines you recited. Will you or a charioteer
know better whether Homer is right or not?'

'The charioteer.'

'Because you are a rhapsode, not a charioteer?'

'Yes.'

'And the rhapsode's art is different from that of the
charioteer?'

'Yes.'

'Therefore, since it is different, it is knowledge concerned with
different things?'

'Yes.'

'And what about the place where Homer* says that
Hecamede, Nestor's concubine, gave the wounded Machaon a
draught to drink?—

. . . with Pramnian wine;* and she grated goat's cheese upon it
with a bronze grater; and an onion went with the drink?

Is it the business of the rhapsode's art or that of the doctor to tell
properly whether Homer is right?'

'The doctor's.'

'And when Homer says:

> Like a lead weight she went to the bottom,
> that, mounted on the horn of an ox of the field,
> goes to bring trouble to the ravenous fish,

is it the business of the rhapsode's art or the fisherman's to judge
the correctness of this?'

'The fisherman's, obviously, Socrates.'

'Then suppose you were to put a question to me in these

538

terms: "Socrates, since you are discovering what there is in Homer which each of these arts ought to determine, go on now, please, to prophets and divination—of what ought the prophet to be able to judge the correctness or incorrectness?" See how readily I shall give you an answer. In the *Odyssey*, there is a lot of this: for instance the words of the Melampodid* prophet Theoclymenus to the suitors:

539

Gentlemen, what's wrong? Your heads are covered in darkness and your face and your bodies:
wailing I hear, and cheeks are wet with tears;
the hall and the courtyard are full of ghosts
hastening hellwards in the dark;
the sun has gone from the sky and an evil gloom has come over
    everything.

And there's a lot in the *Iliad*, too: for example, in the battle for the wall:

> A bird came towards them as they made to cross,
> an eagle flying high, flanking the host on the left.
> He carried a huge snake in his claws,
> alive, still writhing—it had not yet forgotten its fight,
> for it bent back and bit the eagle by the neck,
> and he felt the pain and dropped it to the ground,
> dropped it in the middle of the army,
> and flew off screaming on the wind.

This and similar passages, I shall maintain, are for the prophet to examine and criticize.'

'You are quite right, Socrates.'

'Well, you say it's right too, Ion. Now what I want you to do for me is this: just as I picked out for you passages in the *Iliad* and the *Odyssey* which belong to the prophet, the doctor, and the fisherman, you pick out for me, since you know Homer better than I do, passages which belong to the rhapsode and his art— things which the rhapsode ought to be able to examine and criticize better than other people.'

'In my view, Socrates, that means everything.'

'That's *not* your view, Ion: or are you so forgetful? A rhapsode has no business being forgetful.'

540   'What am I forgetting?'

Don't you remember that you said that the rhapsode's art was different from the charioteer's?'

nothing genuinely there's

'I remember.'

'And you admitted that, being different, it would have knowledge of different things?'

'Yes.'

'Then, on your view, the rhapsode and his art will not have knowledge of everything.'

'No; they will, Socrates, except perhaps for such exceptions.'

'And by "such exceptions" you mean the fields of other arts. But what *will* the rhapsode know, since it won't be everything?'

'I think it would be what a man *ought* to say, or a woman, or a slave, or a free man, or a subject or a ruler.'

'You mean that the rhapsode will know better than the pilot what the ruler of a ship ought to say in a storm at sea?'

'No; the pilot will know that better.'

'And the rhapsode will know better than the doctor what the ruler of a sick patient ought to say?'

'No.'

'He knows what a slave ought to say, does he?'

'Yes.'

'The rhapsode will know better than the cowherd, will he, what a slave cowherd ought to say to quieten his cattle when they are excited?'

'Oh no.'

'And what about what a woman woolworker ought to say about the treatment of wool?'

'Not that either.'

'But he will know what a man ought to say as a general exhorting his troops?'

'Yes; that's the sort of thing the rhapsode will know.'

'Then is the rhapsode's art the same as the general's?'

541

'Well, I should know what sort of thing a general ought to say.'

'Perhaps because you have the talents of a general, Ion. If you were both a horseman and a lyre-player, you would know good horsemanship from bad, but if I asked you which of your arts it was that enabled you to recognize good horsemanship, what would you answer?'

'The horseman's art.'

'And if you recognized good lyre-playing, that, you would admit, would have been by virtue of your being a lyre-player, not by virtue of your being a horseman?'

'Yes.'

'Then since you understand military matters, is this so because you have military talents or because you are a good rhapsode?'

'I don't think there's any difference.'

'What? No difference? Are the rhapsode's art and the general's one or two?'

'One, I believe.'

'Then the man who is a good rhapsode is in fact a good general?'

'Certainly, Socrates.'

'And the good general is a good rhapsode?'

'Well, no.'

'But the good rhapsode—you still think this?—is a good general?'

'Yes.'

'And you're the best rhapsode in Greece?'

'By a long way, Socrates.'

'Are you the best general in Greece, too, then?'

'Of course, Socrates, I've learned it from Homer.'

'Then why on earth, Ion, being the best rhapsode *and* the best general in Greece, do you go round performing as a rhapsode but not commanding as a general? Do you think Greece has need of a rhapsode with his gold crown but not of a general?'

'My city, Socrates, is under the government and military leadership of yours and needs no general, and your people and the Spartans would never elect me, for you think you are good enough yourselves.'*

'My dear Ion, don't you know Apollodorus of Cyzicus?'

'Who do you mean?'

'The foreigner whom the Athenians have often elected general. And there's Phanosthenes of Andros and Heraclides of Clazomenae, whom this city advances to generalship and other offices, though they are foreigners, because they have shown that they are men of worth. Won't it then elect Ion of Ephesus general, and honour him, if *he* seems to be a man of worth? Anyway, aren't you Ephesians Athenians by old tradition? Isn't

Ephesus a city as great as any? The fact is, Ion, that if you are right in saying that your capacity for praising Homer comes from art and knowledge, you are not playing fair: you professed to know many fine things about Homer, and you said you would demonstrate your knowledge, but now you deceive me and are far from making the demonstration; why, you won't even say what it is you're clever at, despite all my insistence, but twist about and turn yourself into all sorts of shapes like a veritable Proteus, until in the end you escape me altogether and turn up as a general! Anything to avoid demonstrating how good your Homeric scholarship is. As I say, if you are a man of art and are deceiving me with your undertaking to give a demonstration about Homer, you are not playing fair; but if you are no man of art, but are possessed by Homer by some divine dispensation and say many fine things about the poet without having any knowledge—this is the account I gave of you—then you're not being unfair. So choose which you would rather be thought—an unfair man or an inspired one.'

542

'That's a very unequal choice, Socrates; it's much more honourable to be thought inspired.'

'Then, so far as I am concerned, the more honourable part is yours, Ion; it is not art that makes you praise Homer as you do, but divine inspiration.'

sarcasm?

'Then what is this education? Or is it difficult to invent one any better than that which long ages have evolved? In other words, gymnastics for the body and "music" for the mind.'

'Indeed it is.'

'Then shall we begin with music before gymnastics?'

'Naturally.'

'And do you regard words as part of music or not?'

'I do.'

'And there are two kinds of words, the true and the false?'

'Yes.'

377 'Education is in both kinds, but first in the false.'

'I don't understand what you mean.'

'Don't you understand that we first of all tell children fables? Now these are, taken over all, falsehood, though there are true things in them. And we give children fables before we give them physical exercises.'

'That's true.'

'Well, that's what I meant by saying that we must tackle music before gymnastics.'

'You were right.'

'Well, you know that the beginning is the biggest part of any work, especially where the young and tender are concerned; for that is the most malleable age, when any mark you want can best be stamped on the individual.'

'Exactly.'

'So shall we lightly allow our children to hear *any* fables, no matter who made them up, and to take them to heart, though they are in fact, generally speaking, contrary to the opinions we shall expect them to hold when they grow up?'

'We shan't allow that at all.'

'Then, it would seem, we must begin by controlling the fable-makers, and admit only the good fables they compose, not the bad. We shall then persuade nurses and mothers to tell children the admitted fables, and mould their minds with fable much more than they now mould their bodies with the hand. Most of the tales they tell now will have to be thrown out.'

'Which?'

'If we look at the big fables, we shall also see the little ones. Big and little need to be of the same type and have the same effect. Don't you agree?'

'Yes: but I don't see what you mean by the big ones.'

'Those that Hesiod and Homer told, and the other poets. For it's the poets who told men, and still tell them, the false stories they themselves compose.'

'What stories? And what fault do you find with them?'

'The fault one must find, first and foremost, especially when someone tells falsehoods wrongly.'

'But what is it?'

'Making bad verbal likenesses of gods and heroes—just like a painter making a picture unlike the object he wants to paint.'

'Well, it's certainly right to find fault with that sort of thing. But just what do we mean?'

'To begin with, the greatest falsehood, involving the greatest issues, was wrongly told by the person who said that Ouranos did what Hesiod said he did, and that Kronos took his revenge upon him.* What Kronos did and what happened to him at his son's hands is something I should not want to be told without precaution to the young and foolish, even if it had been true. If possible, it should have been veiled in silence; but if there had been great need to tell it, it should have been made a secret, for as small an audience as possible—and they should have had to sacrifice not a pig,* but some expensive and inaccessible victim, so that as few people as possible should hear the tale.'

'These stories are indeed difficult.'

'They are not to be repeated in our city, Adimantus. Nor is it to be said in a young man's hearing that if he committed the most outrageous crimes, or chastised an erring father by the direst means, he would be doing nothing remarkable, but only what the first and greatest of the gods have done.'

'I don't myself think that these are suitable stories.'

'It's the same with all the tales of how gods war, plot, and fight against gods—not that they're true anyway—if our future city-guardians are to believe that readiness to hate one another is the

greatest scandal. Still less must they be told elaborate fables of
battles of giants, and all the other various hostilities of gods and
heroes towards their kith and kin. If we are somehow to convince
them that no citizen has ever been the enemy of another, nor is it
right that he should be, then *that* is the lesson that older men and
women must impress on the children from the start, the lesson
(more or less) that poets too must be forced to impress on the
adult population. Hera tied up by her son, Hephaestus thrown
out by his father because he was proposing to defend his mother
against a beating, Homer's battles of gods—all this is inadmissible,
whether it was composed allegorically or not. Young people can't
distinguish the allegorical from the non-allegorical, and what
enters the mind at that age tends to become indelible and
irremovable. Hence the prime need to make sure that what they
first hear is devised as well as possible for the implanting of
virtue.'

'That makes sense. But if we were to be asked what these
things are, what the stories are, what should we say?'

379   'You and I, Adimantus, are not poets, at the moment: we are
founders of a city. Founders have to know the patterns within
which poets are to be made to construct fables, and beyond
which they must not be allowed to go, but they don't have to
make up fables themselves.'

'True enough: but just what *are* the patterns for an account of
the gods?'

'Something like this, I fancy. God must always be represented
as he is, whether in epic or in lyric or in tragedy.'

'Yes indeed.'

'Now God is in truth good and must so be described.'

'Of course.'

'And nothing good is harmful, is it?'

'No.'

'Does the non-harmful harm?'

'No.'

'And does what doesn't harm do any evil?'

'No.'

'And what does no evil is cause of no evil?'

'Of course.'

'Now again. The good is useful?'

'Yes.'

'Therefore the cause of felicity?'

'Yes.'

'The good therefore is not the cause of everything, but only of what is well.'

'Certainly.'

'God therefore, being good, cannot be responsible for everything, as is the common opinion, but only of some few things in human life. There is much for which he bears no responsibility. Our blessings are far fewer than our troubles, and, while none but God is responsible for the blessings, we must seek other causes for the troubles.'

'That seems perfectly right.'

'We must therefore not allow Homer or any other poet to make this foolish mistake about the gods, and to say that

> by Zeus's door stand two jars full of dooms,
> one good, one bad,*

and that if Zeus gives a man a mixture of the two,

> sometimes he is in trouble, sometimes in luck,

while if he gives him the one kind unmixed,

> grim famine drives that man over the earth.

Nor can we allow that Zeus is "steward of our goods and ills". Nor shall we approve anyone who says that the breach of the oaths and truce, committed by Pandarus,* was due to the agency of Athena and Zeus—or that the quarrel and judgement of the goddesses was the work of Zeus and Themis. Young people must   380 not be allowed to be told, in Aeschylus' words, that

> god breeds a crime in men
> when he would utterly overthrow a house.

If a poet does write about the story of Niobe, or the House of Pelops, or Troy, or anything like that, then either he must be allowed to say that they are not the works of god, or if they are, he must concoct some such account as the one we are now seeking, and say that what god did was just and good, and the victims profited from their punishment. What the poet mustn't say is that god did it, and the victims were wretched. It is all right to explain that the wicked were wretched because they needed punishment, and profited from receiving that punishment at the god's hands. But that god, who is good, is the cause of evil to anyone is a proposition to be resisted at all costs. No one must say such a thing in the city, if it is to be well governed. No one must hear it said. This goes for young and old, for verse fables and prose. Such tales, if told, would be wicked, unprofitable and self-contradictory.'

'I shall vote with you for that law. I like it.'

'Then that's *one* of the laws and patterns relating to the gods, which speakers and poets will have to observe: god is responsible only for the good things.'

'That suffices.'

'What about the second one then? Do you think that god is a magician and appears, as it were deliberately, in different shapes at different times, sometimes in person, changing himself into many shapes, and sometimes deceiving us and making us think this of him? Or is he single and least likely of any being to depart from his own form?'

'I can't say, just at the moment.'

'Well. If he *were* to depart from his own form, must he not do so either by his own act or under the influence of another?'

'Yes.'

'But things which are in a very good condition are not changed or moved by other things. Consider the effect of food, drink, and exercise on bodies, or of exposure to sun and wind and other circumstances on plants; the healthiest and strongest are changed least.'

'Of course.'

381 'Then the mind which external happenings are least likely to disturb and change is the bravest and wisest?'

'Yes.'

'And, similarly, manufactured tools, houses, and clothing are least altered by time and other circumstances if they are well constructed and in good condition?'

'Yes.'

'Then, in general, whatever is in a good condition, as a result of nature or art or both, admits the minimum change from external influence?'

'So it seems.'

'But god and what is god's is in every way exceedingly good?'

'Of course.'

'So from this point of view god can't have "many shapes"?'

'No.'

'But might he change and vary himself?'

'He must, if he varies at all.'

'Well, then, does he change himself for better or for worse?'

'For worse, inevitably, if he does vary: for we can't say that god is defective in beauty or goodness.'

'Quite right. And that being so, Adimantus, do you think any god, or man, would voluntarily make himself worse in any way?'

'Impossible.'

'Impossible therefore for god to want to vary himself. Every god, being exceedingly beautiful and good, remains always simply, so far as possible, in his own shape.'

'Necessarily so.'

'So let none of the poets tell us that

> in guise of foreign strangers
> gods visit cities in every manner of shape.*

Let us have no tales against Proteus and Thetis; let us not have Hera brought in, in tragedy or any other poem, disguised as a priestess begging

> to the life-giving children of Inachus, river of Argos.*

There are a lot of other false tales we must not hear. Mothers must not be persuaded by these people into frightening their children with horrid fables of how the gods go about at night in the shape of strangers of all kinds. We can't have them blaspheming the gods and making cowards of their boys at the same time!'

'No, they mustn't do that.'

'Can it be then that, though the gods themselves can't change, they make us think they appear in various guises, deceiving and bewitching us?'

'Maybe.'

'Indeed? Might a god want to give a false impression in word
382 or deed by exhibiting a phantom?'

'I don't know.'

'You don't know that all gods and men abhor the true
falsehood, if I may use such an expression?'

'What do you mean?'

'That no one deliberately wants to be false in the most
important part of his being or in relation to the most important
subjects. Everyone is afraid of having falsehood *there*.'

'I still don't understand.'

'Because you think I'm saying something grand. But all I'm
saying is that everybody will refuse to continue or to be put into a
state of falsehood, or to be ignorant, in relation to reality in the
mind, or to have or acquire falsehood in that department. This is
something they detest.'

'Indeed.'

'But it's the mental ignorance of the deceived that is rightly
called, as I was saying, true falsehood. Verbal falsehood is a
representation of the mental situation, a subsequent image, not
real, undiluted falsehood. Agreed?'

'Yes.'

'So real falsehood is abhorred by men as well as by gods?'

'I think so.'

'What about verbal falsehood? When is it useful, and not
deserving of detestation? Is it not useful in dealing with enemies,
and, as a medicine, against some supposed friends, to deter them
when they try to do something bad through madness or folly? Or
again, falsehood can surely be made useful in mythology, such as
we have been discussing, because we don't know the truth about
antiquity: what we do is to make the falsehood as like the truth as
possible.'

'That's right.'

'Then in which of these ways is falsehood useful to god? Will
he produce falsehoods of the likeness type because he doesn't
know the past?'

'Ridiculous idea!'

'So there's no false poet in god?'

'No.'

'Will he lie then for fear of enemies?'

'Certainly not.'

'Or because of his friends' folly or madness?'

'No lunatic or fool is god's friend.'

'So god can have no reason for falsehood?'

'No.'

'So the superhuman and divine is altogether free from falsity?'

'Yes.'

'God, therefore, is simple and true in deed and word. He neither changes nor deceives in visions or words or significant signs, in waking or in sleep.'

'That is how it seems to me as I listen to you.'

383

'You agree, then, that this is the second pattern within which tales and poetry about gods are to be constructed: they are not wizards to change themselves nor do they trick us with falsehoods in word or deed.'

'Agreed.'

'There is much in Homer we must praise: but we shall not praise the dispatch of the Dream by Zeus* to Agamemnon. Nor, in Aeschylus, shall we praise the passage where Thetis tells of Apollo's song at her marriage:

> he hymned my happy children,
> a long and healthy life;
> he told it all, sang of god's love, my good fortune,
> heartening me, and I thought his holy lips,
> so skilled in prophecy, could speak no falsehood;
> but he who sang the hymn, he who was at the feast,
> he who said all this, he is my boy's killer.*

When a poet says things like this about gods, we shall be angry and shall not let his play be produced. Nor shall we allow teachers to use it for education, if our guardians are to be god-fearing and divine, in so far as human powers can be.'

'I agree completely with these patterns. I shall regard them as laws.' . . .

'To conclude, then: men who are to honour the gods and their parents and set a high value on mutual friendship must keep to some such rules as these about what may and may not be listened to concerning the gods.'

3.386

'And I think our view is right.'

'But what about their being brave? Must we not also say things of a kind to make them unafraid of death? Or do you think a man can be brave if he has this fear in him?'

'I do not.'

'Do you think that anyone who believes that Hades exists and is terrible will be unafraid of death, or will prefer death in battle to defeat and slavery?'

'No.'

'We must therefore exercise control over these myths too, and ask those who essay them not to speak ill of Hades but to praise it: otherwise what they say will be neither true nor useful to future warriors.'

'Right.'

'So we shall delete all such passages, beginning with:

> Rather would I be bound to the soil, a thrall to another,
> to a poor man at that, with no land to his portion,
> than be king of all the nations of the dead.*

And:

> And to mortals and immortals the house be revealed,
> dreadful and gruesome, that even gods abhor;

and:

> Truly indeed, even in the house of Hades
> there is soul and phantom, but no consciousness therein;

and:

> He alone has understanding, the rest are flitting shadows;

and:

> The soul flew from the limbs and went to Hades,
> lamenting its fate, leaving youth and manhood behind it;

387 and:

> The soul disappeared under ground, like smoke, squeaking;

and:

> They all went squeaking, as bats fly squeaking about

in the depths of a wonderful cave, when one of them falls
from the bunch on the rock, where they cling to each other.

We shall ask Homer and the other poets not to be angry if we
strike out these and similar lines. Not that they're not poetical
and pleasant hearing for the general public: indeed, the more
poetical they are, the less they should be presented to boys and
men who ought to be free, and more afraid of slavery than of
death.'

'Certainly.'

'Then all the awful and frightening words connected with
these things should be rejected—Cocytus, Styx,* "those below",
"the withered", and all such names as make the hearer shiver.
Perhaps they may be all right for some purposes; but *we* fear for
our guardians, lest these shivers make them more fevered and
softer than we would like them.'

'We are quite right to fear, too.'

'So these things must be got rid of?'

'Yes.'

'The pattern to be followed in stories and poetry is therefore
the opposite of these.'

'Clearly.'

'We shall therefore excise lamentations and expressions of pity
by men of note.'

'Inevitably, if we excluded what we have already discussed.'

'Well, consider whether we shall be doing right or not. We say,
I think, that the good man will not think death a terrible thing for
another good man, whose friend he is.'

'We do.'

'So he won't lament for him as though something dreadful had
happened to him.'

'No.'

'We also say that such a man is particularly self-sufficient for
living a good life, and needs other people less than anyone
does.'

'True.'

'So it's least dreadful for him to be deprived of a son or a
brother or money or anything like that.'

'Yes.'

'So he grieves least, and endures most placidly, when such a disaster overtakes him.'

'Yes.'

388 'So we should be right to remove the laments of notable men, and give them to women—but not to good women—and to bad men, so that the guardians whom we claim to be educating are disgusted at the idea of doing likewise.'

'Right.'

'So we shall again ask Homer and the other poets not to represent Achilles, the son of a goddess, as

> lying now on his side, now on his back, and again
> face-downwards,*

and then again getting up, wandering aimlessly on the beach of the unharvested sea, taking the brown dust in his hands and pouring it over his head—nor yet crying and moaning in the ways that Homer represents him. Nor should he represent Priam, who was near kin to the gods, as begging for mercy and

> rolling in the dung,
> calling on every man by name.

Still more shall we ask him not to represent gods as mourning or saying

> Unhappy me, unhappy mother of a hero!

Worse still is his venturing to represent the greatest of the gods in so unrealistic a fashion as to make him say,

> Alas, I see a man I love
> chased round the city, and my heart is grieving,

and

> Alas, alas, that Sarpedon whom I dearly love
> is doomed to be killed by Patroclus, Menoitios' son.

For, my dear Adeimantus, if our young men heard things like this in earnest and did not laugh at them as unworthy remarks, they would be most unlikely to think themselves, being but men, below this sort of thing, or to check themselves if it occurred to

them to say or do anything of the kind. They would mourn and
lament freely, without shame or restraint, at small accidents.'

'Very true.'

'But they ought not to do so, as our argument just now
showed—and we ought to be convinced by it, until someone
convinces us with a better one.'

'Indeed they ought not.'

'Nor must they be fond of laughter. If you indulge a violent fit
of laughter, you're looking for a violent change.'

'I agree.'

389

'So we mustn't allow anyone to represent serious men as
overcome by laughter, must less gods.'

'Much less.'

'So, on your argument, we mustn't admit Homeric passages
about the gods like

> then unquenchable laughter arose among the blessed gods,
> as they saw Hephaestus bustling about the room.'*

'Call it my argument if you like. Anyway, we mustn't admit
that.'

'But we *must* attach great value to truth. If we were right just
now, and falsehood is useless to gods and useful to men only as a
remedy, it can be allowed only to doctors, not to the layman.'

'Clearly.'

'Rulers of the city, therefore, may, if anybody may, appropriately
use falsehoods, because of enemies or fellow citizens, to help the
city. No one else can be allowed to touch such things. For a
private person to employ falsehood towards rulers like ours is
wrong: it is the same mistake, only on a bigger scale, that a
patient makes if he doesn't tell his doctor the truth about his
physical condition, or an athlete his trainer, or a sailor if he
doesn't give the helmsman a proper account of what he or his
fellow sailors are doing.'

'True'.

'So if the ruler finds anyone else in the city telling lies—

> any of those who work for the public,
> prophet or healer of ills or craftsman of timber*

—he will punish him for introducing into the ship of the city,
as it were, a subversive and destructive practice.'

'Yes he will, if deeds follow his words.'

'Well, then. Won't our young man need self-control? And doesn't the main element in self-control, for the mass of mankind, consist in their being obedient to the rulers and themselves being in command of the pleasures of drink, sex, and food?'

'I think so.'

'Then shall we think well of lines like that which Homer gives to Diomedes:

> Sit quietly, friend, and do as I say*

or what follows:

> On went the Achaeans, breathing strength,
> In silence, afraid of their leaders

and the like?'

'Yes.'

'But what about things like:

> You drunken sot, with dog's eyes and deer's heart*

and what follows that? Are these well said? Or any other
390 impertinence of a private person to the authorities, whether in prose or in poetry?'

'Not at all.'

'No, for they are not suitable for young persons to hear from the point of view of acquiring control. They may well give some pleasure, I shouldn't be at all surprised. What do you feel?'

'The same.'

'Well, then, do you think it is suitable, from the point of self-control, for young persons to hear it said of the wisest of mankind that he thinks the fairest thing of all is when

> the tables are laden with bread and with meat
> and the wine-pourer draws the drink from the bowl and
>   goes round with it
> pouring it into the cups?*

Or:

> the bitterest way to die and meet your end is by starving?*

And what about the story of Zeus? All the plans he had laid when he kept awake when all men and gods slept, he then forgets* because of sexual desire, and is so smitten when he sees Hera that he doesn't want to go indoors but to copulate with her there on the ground, saying he was not so possessed with desire for her even when they first went to see each other, unknown to their parents. What about all that? And what about the imprisonment of Ares and Aphrodite* by Hephaestus for similar reasons?'

'I don't think it's at all suitable.'

'On the other hand, if there are instances of endurance of any hardship in what is said of or done by notable men, these should be watched and listened to. For example:

> He beat his chest and reproved his heart, saying:
> "Heart, bear up; you have once borne worse than this."'*

'Yes, indeed.'

'But we mustn't let our men be takers of bribes or lovers of money.'

'Certainly not.'

'Nor sing to them that:

> Gifts convince gods, gifts convince respected kings.*

Nor ought we to commend Achilles' tutor Phoenix* and say he was right to advise him to help the Achaeans if he got gifts in return, but otherwise not. Nor again shall we think it worthy of Achilles* or indeed agree that he was so fond of money as to take gifts from Agamemnon or again be willing to release Hector's body for a price but not otherwise.'

391

'It certainly wouldn't be right to approve such sentiments.'

'I feel somewhat afraid, however, because of Homer, to declare that it is actually impious to say these things of Achilles, or to believe them when others say them. Similarly with what he said to Apollo:

> You have wronged me, far-darter, of all gods most dreadful:
> and if I had the power, I would surely take my revenge.*

Again, we should not believe the story of his disobedience* to the river-god and willingness to fight him, or of his saying of the locks that were sacred to the other river, Spercheios, that he would "offer them to the hero Patroclus", who was dead, and then actually doing this. We shall altogether deny the truth of the dragging of Hector round Patroclus' tomb and the massacre of captives on the pyre. We cannot allow our guardians to believe that Achilles, son of a goddess and of the wise and temperate Peleus, himself third in line from Zeus, and brought up by the wise Chiron, was in such a state of confusion as to have in himself two contrary diseases—meanness and love of money on the one hand, and contempt for gods and men on the other.'

'You are right.'

'Then there are other things also we shouldn't believe or allow to be said: how Theseus the son of Poseidon and Pirithous the son of Zeus* set off to carry out terrible acts of kidnapping, or how any other hero or child of a god could have ventured on the kinds of dreadful impieties that are now falsely alleged of them. Let us oblige the poets to say either that these persons did not do these deeds or that they are not children of gods. They must not say both, or try to persuade our young people that the gods breed evils and heroes are no better than men. As we said above, these things are neither pious nor true. We demonstrated, of course, that evil cannot come from the gods.'

'Of course we did.'

'They are also damaging to the hearers. Everyone will find excuses for his own wickedness, if he believes that such actions were and are done by

> the gods' near relatives,
> those near to Zeus, whose altar to their ancestor
> is high in heaven upon Ida's hill,
> and in whose veins divine blood does not fade.*

This is why we must put a stop to such stories, lest they induce
392 in our young people a ready inclination to bad conduct.'

'Precisely so.'

'In our attempt to define what kind of stories should be told, and what not, what class of story still remains? We have discussed gods, demigods and heroes, and Hades.'

'Yes.'

'The subject of men remains.'

'Clearly.'

'Well, we can't legislate for that at the moment.'

'Why not?'

'Because, I imagine, we shall say that poets and prose-writers make serious bad statements about men—that there are many unjust men who are happy and just men who are miserable, that secret wrongdoing is profitable, that justice is the good of others and our own loss—and so on. We shall have to forbid them to say this, and command them to compose songs and fables to the opposite effect.'

'I'm sure we shall.'

'Then if you agree I am right, shall I say you have agreed to what we have long been seeking?'

'Yes, that's right.'

'Then we shall come to our agreement that this is the sort of thing to be said about men only when we have discovered what justice is and what is its natural advantage to its possessor, whether or not he *appears* just.'

'True.'

'So much for what is said. We must next consider its expression. When that is done we shall have covered the whole subject of what is to be said and how.'

'I don't understand what you mean.'

'You ought to; but perhaps you'll know better if I put it like this. Everything that fable-tellers or poets say is a narrative of past or present or future.'

'Of course.'

'And they execute it either by simple narrative or by narrative conveyed by imitation (*mimēsis*) or by both.'

'I should like a clearer account of that too, please.'

'I must be a ridiculously obscure teacher. I'll try to do what incompetent speakers do and show you what I mean by taking a little bit, and not the whole topic. Tell me: you know the beginning of the *Iliad*, where the poet says that Chryses asked Agamemnon to release his daughter, Agamemnon was angry, and Chryses, unsuccessful, cursed the Achaeans to the god?'   393

'I know.'

'Then you know that as far as the lines

and he begged all the Achaeans,
and especially the two Atridae, the generals of the host,*

the poet speaks in his own person, and does not try to turn our attention in another direction by pretending that someone else is speaking. But from this point on he speaks as though he were Chryses himself and tries to make us think that it is not Homer talking, but the old priest. And he does practically all the rest of the narrative in this way, both the tale of Troy and the episodes in Ithaca and the whole *Odyssey*.'

'Yes.'

'Now it is narrative both when he makes the various speeches and in the passages between the speeches.'

'Of course.'

'But when he makes a speech pretending to be someone else, are we not to say that he is assimilating his expression as far as possible to the supposed speaker?'

'Certainly.'

'And to assimilate oneself in voice or gesture to another is to imitate him?'

'Yes.'

'So in this sort of thing Homer and the other poets are conveying their narrative by way of imitation (*mimēsis*)?'

'Yes.'

'Now if the poet never concealed himself, his whole poetry and narrative would be free of imitation. Don't say you don't understand again—I'll explain how it would be. If Homer, having said that Chryses came with his daughter's ransom to be a suppliant of the Achaeans, and particularly of the kings, had gone on not as Chryses but as Homer, it would have been pure narrative, not imitation. It would have gone something like this— I'll do it without metre, for I'm no poet. "The priest came and prayed that the gods might grant them to capture Troy and return home safely, if they accepted ransom, respected the god, and freed his daughter. Most of them respected his words and were ready to agree, but Agamemnon was angry, telling him to go away and never come back, lest his staff and the god's garlands might prove of no avail to him; before the daughter was freed, she would grow old in Argos with him. And he told the old man

to be off and not stir up trouble, if he wanted to get home safe.
Hearing this, Chryses was frightened and went silently away, but   394
when he had left the camp he prayed long to Apollo, calling on
him by his special names, reminding him and begging him, if he
had ever given him before an acceptable gift in temple-building
or sacrifice; in return for this, he prayed to him to avenge his
tears on the Greeks with his arrows."—That's pure narrative
without imitation.'

'I understand.'

'Then understand that the opposite happens when the poet
removes the passages between the speeches and leaves just the
exchange of conversation.'

'I see: that's what we have in tragedies.'

'Quite right. I think I'm making clear to you now what I
couldn't before, namely that there is one kind of poetry and fable
which entirely consists of imitation: this is tragedy and comedy,
as you say; and there's another kind consisting of the poet's own
report—you find this particularly in dithyrambs;* while the
mixture of the two exists in epic and in many other places, if you
see what I mean.'

'Yes: I understand now what you meant then.'

'Remember also what we said before that—that we've dealt
with the question *what* to say, but have still to consider *how*.'

'I remember.'

'Well, what I meant was, that we must come to an understanding
as to whether we are to allow our poets to narrate by imitation,
or partly by imitation (and if so, what parts), or not to imitate at
all.'

'I have an inkling that you are asking whether we should admit
tragedy and comedy into the city or no.'

'Perhaps—or perhaps more than that. I don't know yet: we
must go where the wind of the argument blows.'

'That's right.'

'Well then, consider whether our guardians ought to be
imitative people or not. Or does this follow from our previous
argument that an individual can do one thing well but is liable to
fail in everything, so far as acquiring real note is concerned, if he
tries to do many things?'

'Bound to follow.'

'Similarly with imitation—one individual can't imitate many things well, though he can one?'

'Yes.'

'So still less will one man be able to pursue some worthwhile pursuit and also imitate many things and be an imitator. Even 395 apparently closely related imitations cannot be practised well by the same person—tragedy and comedy for example. You called these two imitations, didn't you?'

'Yes; and you're quite right, the same people can't do both.'

'Nor can people be both rhapsodes and actors.'

'True.'

'Nor even tragic actors and comic actors. All these things are imitations, aren't they?'

'Yes.'

'Now it seems to me as if human nature is specialized even more minutely than this. It is unable to imitate many things well, or to do well the things of which the imitations are likenesses.'

'True.'

'So if we are to preserve our first conclusion, that our guardians ought to be exempt from all other crafts and be craftsmen of freedom in the city, and perfect craftsmen, and ought to practise nothing that does not conduce to this end, they *must* not do or imitate anything else. If they do imitate, the subject of their imitation, from childhood onwards, must be what is appropriate to them: the brave, the self-controlled, the righteous, the free, and so on. They must neither display in action nor be good at imitating the illiberal, or any other disgraceful quality, lest the fruit of their imitation be the reality. Haven't you observed that imitations, if persisted in from childhood, settle into habits and fixed characteristics of body, voice, or mind?'

'I have indeed.'

'So we shan't allow those whom we profess to care for, and who we say ought to be brave men, to imitate a woman, young or old, in the act of reviling her husband or boastfully competing with the gods, full of the conceit of her own felicity, or possessed by misfortune or mourning or lamentation. And as for illness, love, or childbirth*—God forbid!'

'Yes indeed.'

'Nor slaves, male or female, performing slavish tasks.'

'No.'

'Nor bad men, cowards, and people doing the opposite of what we have just described, people abusing or ridiculing one another or using filthy language, drunk or sober, or committing any of the other errors of word or deed against self or others that such people incur. Nor must we allow them to form the habit of likening themselves to madmen by word or action. Of course they must be able to recognize mad or wicked men or women—but they're not to do or imitate any of these things.' 396

'True.'

'Well then, what about smiths or other workmen doing their work, or rowers in triremes or their officers? Is anything like this to be imitated?'

'How could it be? None of them is going to be allowed even to think of these things.'

'Well, horses neighing? Bulls lowing? Rivers babbling? The roar of the sea? Thunder? Are they to imitate this sort of thing?'*

'They have been forbidden to be mad or to make themselves like the mad.'

'If I understand what you're saying, there is a kind of expression and narrative which the really good man would use, if he had to say anything, and there is another and very different kind which the person of opposite breeding and education would consistently use for his narratives.'

'What are these kinds?'

'As it seems to me, the decent man, when he comes in his narrative to the words or action of a good man, will want to report it by identifying himself with that good man, and will not be ashamed of such imitation. Especially will he imitate the good man secure and sane: less readily, the good man tripped up by sickness, love, drink, or some other accident. But when he comes to a man unworthy of himself, he will not want seriously to liken himself to his own inferior, except momentarily, when he's acting well. He will be ashamed. For one thing, he will have had no practice in imitating such characters. For another, he will feel disgust at modelling himself on, and inserting himself into, the patterns of the inferior. He will have an intellectual contempt for them, except as a game.'

'Probably so.'

'He will therefore use the style of narration that we described in connection with Homer's epic. His expression will have elements both of imitation and of narrative, but with very little narrative to a long story. Right?'

'Yes: that must be the pattern of a speaker of this kind.'

397 'But consider the other kind. The worse he is, the readier he will be to imitate everything. He won't regard anything as beneath him. He will try to imitate everything, seriously and in public—even what we were speaking of just now, thunder and the noise of wind and hail, axle and pulley, the sound of trumpets, oboes, pipes, and all kinds of instruments, the cries of dogs, sheep, and birds. His expression will be entirely imitative, in voice and gesture—or at most it will have a little narration in it.'

'Necessarily so.'

'Then this is what I meant by the two kinds of expression.'

'I see.'

'In one of them, the variations are not great. If you give the expression its appropriate harmony and rhythm, a correct speaker is able to deliver the piece practically in one and the same harmony—the variations are small—and in very much the same rhythm.'

'Quite so.'

'The other performer's type, on the other hand, needs the very opposite—all harmonies and all rhythms—if it is to be delivered appropriately, because of the manifold forms of its variations.'

'Certainly.'

'Then all poets and speakers fall into one or other pattern of expression or into one arising from their combination of the two.'

'Inevitably.'

'What shall we do then? Shall we admit all these patterns into the city, or one or other unmixed, or the mixed one?'

'If my vote is allowed to prevail, the imitator of the good, unmixed.'

'But the mixed pattern is pleasing—while to children and their attendants and to the multitude it's the one that's opposite to your choice that gives by far the most pleasure.'

'Yes, it is.'

'But perhaps you would say it didn't suit our "republic", for we have no double or multiple men, because everybody performs one function.'

'Well, it doesn't suit.'

'So this is the only city where we shall find the cobbler a cobbler and not a ship's pilot as well, the farmer a farmer and not a juryman as well, and the man of war a man of war and not also a man of money. Isn't it?'*

'It is.'

'Suppose then there arrived in our city a man who could make himself into anything by his own skill, and could imitate everything. Suppose he brought his poems and wanted to give a display. We should salute him as divine, wonderful, a pleasure-giver: but we should then say that there is no one of his sort in our city and it is not allowed that there should be. We should therefore pour ointment on his head, give him a garland of wool, and send him off elsewhere. Meanwhile we should employ the more austere and unpleasing poet and tale-teller, for use not pleasure: he would imitate the expression of the good man and tell his tales within the patterns for which we legislated at the beginning, when we were trying to educate the soldiers.'

'Indeed we should, if it were in our power.'

595 'There are many respects in which I feel convinced, when I reflect on it, that we founded our city rightly—and not least in this business of poetry.'

'In what way?'

'In our refusing to admit imitative poetry. It is even clearer, I think, that we ought not to admit it, now that we have distinguished the elements in the mind.'

'How so?'

'Between ourselves—and I know you're not going to denounce me to the writers of tragedy and all the other imitators—all this kind of thing is ruination to the listeners' minds, unless they are protected by the knowledge of what it really is.'

'What are you thinking of?'

'I shall have to be frank—though my lifelong liking and respect for Homer inhibits me, for he is the prime teacher and leader of all these fine folk. Still, persons mustn't be put before the truth. As I say, I shall have to be frank.'

'Indeed you will.'

'Listen then—or rather answer.'

'Ask away.'

'Can you tell me what imitation in general is? I can't see myself what it means.'

'Then it's hardly likely that I should.'

'There would be nothing surprising if you did. Duller eyes 596 often see sooner than sharp ones.'

'I dare say. But with you there I shouldn't be able even to want to speak if I have an idea. *You* try and see.'

'Would you like us to begin with our usual procedure? We are in the habit of assuming a "form" in relation to each group of particular objects to which we apply the same name. Or do you not understand?'

'I understand.'

'Let us posit then any of the sets of many things you like. For instance, there are many beds and many tables.'

'Yes.'

'But there are only two forms of these articles, one of bed and one of table.'

'Yes.'

'Now we are in the habit of saying that the manufacturer of these two articles looks to the form and so makes either the beds or the tables we use and similarly with everything else. None of the manufacturers makes the form itself, surely?'

'Of course not.'

'Now see what you call the manufacturer I'm going to describe.'

'What manufacturer?'

'The one who makes all the things that each of the workmen makes.'

'That's a very marvellous person.'

'You'll say that even more in a moment. For this same workman is capable of making not only articles of furniture but everything that grows out of the earth and every animal, including himself, and indeed earth and heaven and gods and everything in heaven and in Hades beneath the earth. He makes it all.'

'That's a very clever professional you're talking about.'

'Don't you believe me? Tell me now, do you think that there can't be such a manufacturer, or that there might be a maker of all these things in some way? Don't you realize that you might yourself be able to make all these things in a way?'

'What way?'

'Not a difficult one, but contrived in many ways and quickly— quickest of all, perhaps, if you will pick up a mirror and carry it round. You'll soon create the sun and the objects in the sky, and the earth, and yourself and all the other animals and articles and plants and everything we were talking about.'

'Yes, but appearances, not the real things.'

'Well said, and to the point. The painter also is a craftsman of this sort, isn't he?'

'Yes, of course.'

'But you will say that what he makes isn't real, though in a way the painter also makes a bed?'

'Yes, the appearance of a bed.'

'But what about the bed-maker? Didn't you say just now that he doesn't make the form, which we call "what a bed is", but an individual bed?'

'I did.'

'So, if he doesn't make what is, he doesn't make the real thing, but something resembling it but distinct from it. And it might not be right if one said that the work of the bed-maker or any other workman was completely the real thing?'

'Well, no, at least in the view of people who are familiar with this sort of argument.'

'So let us not be surprised if this too is a dim object compared with reality.'

'Indeed not.'

'Would you like us then, using these examples, to investigate this imitator, and see who he is?'

'If you like.'

'Well then, there are these three beds: one in nature, which we might say god makes—or is there someone else?'

'No, there isn't.'

'And one which the carpenter makes.'

'Yes.'

'And one which the painter makes.'

'Let us say so.'

'Painter, bed-maker, god—these three preside over three sorts of beds.'

'Yes.'

'Now god—whether he so chose, or whether there was some necessity not to make more than one bed in nature—made just this one, which is what a bed is; two or more such beds never were produced by god nor will they ever be.'

'How so?'

'Because, if he made just two, there would be one other the form of which both would possess, and this would be "what a bed is", not the two.'

'Right.'

'Well, god knew this, I imagine, and wanting to be the real maker of a real bed, not an individual maker of an individual bed, produced the one in nature.'

'Seems likely.'

'Then would you like us to call him its "nature-maker" or something like that?'

'That would be proper, seeing that he has made this and everything else in nature.'

'Then what about the carpenter? Is not he a manufacturer of a bed?'

'Yes.'

'Is the painter also a manufacturer and maker of such a thing?'

'Certainly not.'

'What would you say is his relationship to the bed?'

'I think the fairest thing would be to call him an imitator of that of which the others are manufacturers.'

'Very well. You call him an imitator in respect of the product third removed from nature?'

'That's right.'

'Then the tragic poet also, since he is an imitator, will be in the same position, third in order from king and truth, and so will all other imitators be.'

'It looks like it.'

'Then we have agreed about the imitator. Tell me now about the painter. Do you think he tries to imitate the object in nature 598 or the works of the manufacturers?'

'The works of the manufacturers.'

'As they are or as they seem? You have still got to settle this.'

'What do you mean?'

'This: if you look at a bed from the side or from the front or from any point, does it vary from itself or only appear different, and likewise with other objects?'

'It appears different, but isn't really so.'

'Now consider this point. Which is painting concerned with— to imitate the reality as it is or the appearance as it appears? Is it an imitation of appearance or of reality?'

'Of appearance.'

'The art of imitation therefore is far removed from the real, and, it seems, achieves all its results because it grasps only a small part of each object, and an image at that. The painter for example (we say) will paint us a cobbler, a carpenter or any craftsman, though he knows nothing of their arts: if he were a good painter, and painted a carpenter and displayed him at a distance, he might deceive children or foolish persons into thinking it really was a carpenter.'

'Doubtless.'

'But what we ought to have in mind about all things, my friend, is this. When someone tells us about somebody that he has met a man who knows all crafts, and understands better than anybody every single thing that any individual person knows, we must retort that the man is a fool, and must have met a conjurer and an imitator and been deceived by him into imagining him fantastically wise, because he himself can't make the distinction between knowledge and lack of knowledge or imitation.'

'Very true.'

'We must now consider tragedy and its leader, Homer, in the light of this, for we hear it said by some that tragedians know all arts, all human affairs where vice and virtue are involved, and all divine things too: for, they say, the good poet must compose with knowledge if he is to compose well on any subject. We must therefore consider whether these people have fallen in with a set of imitators who have deceived them and have failed to realize 599 that their works, which they see, are 'third removes' from the reality and are easy to make even if you don't know the truth. They are images, not realities. Or do you think there is something in what they say, and good poets really do know about the things which ordinary people think they describe as well?'

'We must certainly go into this.'

'Do you think then that if anyone could make *both* the objects of imitation *and* the image, he would let himself take image-construction seriously and make it the guiding principle in his life, as though it were the best thing he had?'

'No.'

'But if he was really knowledgeable about the things he imitates, he would take trouble over the real object rather than the imitation, and try to leave many beautiful objects behind as his memorial. He would rather be praised than compose the praises of others.'

'Surely: the honour and the advantage are not comparable.'

'There are things we need not ask Homer or any other poet about. We need not ask whether, supposing one of them was a doctor and not an imitator of medical language, anyone is said to

have been made healthy by a poet, old or new, as by Asclepius, or
whether any poet has left pupils in medicine, as Asclepius left
descendants. Nor need we ask such questions about the other
arts. We can let them be. But it's fair to ask about the grandest
and most splendid subjects that Homer tries to speak of—wars,
strategy, government, education. "Dear Homer," let us say, "if
you are not at third remove from truth in the matter of goodness,
an image-maker, an *imitator* as we defined it, but only at two
removes, and if you have been able to know what pursuits make
men better and worse in their private and public conduct—tell us
what city was better governed because of you, as Sparta was
because of Lycurgus, and many others, great and small, because
of others? What city claims you as a good lawgiver and its
benefactor? Italy and Sicily claim Charondas, we claim Solon.
Who claims you?" Will he be able to name anywhere?'

'I don't think so; at any rate nothing is said even by the
Homeridae.'*

'But is there record of any war in Homer's time which was well   600
conducted thanks to his generalship or advice?'*

'No.'

'Then are there many ingenious ideas for techniques or other
activities reported of Homer as being a clever man in some craft?
I am thinking of Thales of Miletus and Anacharsis the Scythian.'

'Nothing like that.'

'Well, if there is no public service, perhaps Homer is said to
have guided the education of some privately—people who
respected him for his company and handed down to posterity a
Homeric Way of Life, as Pythagoras was respected in this way
and his followers still speak of a Pythagorean life which
distinguishes them from the rest of the world.'

'Nothing like that is reported. Indeed Creophylus,* Homer's
friend, may prove even more ridiculous in his education than in
his name, if what we are told about Homer is true. Homer is said
to have been very much neglected by him in his lifetime.'

'So they say. But, Glaucon, do you think that if Homer had
really been able to educate men and make them better—being
capable of knowing about these things, not just imitating—he
would have failed to acquire many friends and earn their respect
and liking? Protagoras of Abdera, Prodicus of Ceos, and many

others are able to convince their contemporaries in private conversation that they will be incapable of managing house or city unless *they* take charge of their education. They earn such affection for this expertise that their friends almost carry them round on their shoulders. Now if Homer had been able to help men to acquire virtue, would his contemporaries have let him—and the same goes for Hesiod—wander round reciting poetry? Would they not have held on to him more eagerly than gold and forced him to stay at home with them? Failing that, wouldn't they have danced attendance wherever he went till they got enough education?'

'I think you're absolutely right, Socrates.'

'Shall we then put down all poets, from Homer onwards, as imitators of images of virtue and of all their other subjects, without any contact with the truth? As we were saying just now, the painter will make a semblance of a cobbler, though he knows 601 nothing about cobbling, and neither do his public—they judge only by colours and shapes.'

'Yes.'

'Similarly, we can say that the poet with his words and phrases lays on the colours of every art, though all he understands of it is how to imitate it in such a way that other people like himself, judging by the words, think it all very fine if someone discusses cobbling or strategy or anything in metre, rhythm, and harmony. These have by their very nature such immense fascination. I imagine you know what the content of poetry amounts to, stripped of the colours of music, just on its own. You must have seen it.'

'I have.'

'It's like a pretty but not beautiful face, isn't it, when youth has departed from it?'

'Exactly.'

'Come then, consider this point. The maker of the image, the imitator, on our view, knows nothing of the reality, but only the appearance.'

'Yes.'

'So let us not leave it half said, but get a complete view.'

'Speak on.'

'The painter, we say, will paint reins and bit?'

What is allowable censorship?

'Yes.'

'And the leather-worker and the smith will make them?'

'Of course.'

'Now does the painter understand what the reins and the bit should be like? Or is it not even the maker, the smith and the leather-worker, who knows this, but only the man who knows how to use them, the horseman?'

'Very true.'

'Then shall we say the same about everything?'

'What do you mean?'

'That there are three arts relating to each thing, one to use it, one to make it, one to imitate it.'

'Yes.'

'Now the excellence, beauty, and correctness of any article, animal, or action relates—doesn't it—solely to the use for which each was made or has come to exist?'

'Yes.'

'Therefore the user must inevitably be the most experienced, and must report to the maker what good or bad results the thing he uses shows in use: for example, the flute-player tells the flute-maker about the flutes that will serve him well in making music, and will instruct him what sort he is to make, and the maker will do his bidding.'

'Of course.'

'So he gives information about good and bad flutes out of knowledge, and the maker will make them because he believes him.'

'Yes.'

'So, in relation to the same article, the maker will have a correct belief of its goodness or badness, because he talks to the man who knows and is forced to listen to him, whereas the user 602 has knowledge.'

'Certainly.'

'Now will the imitator have knowledge, from use, of what he paints, whether it is good and right or not, or a right opinion from having necessarily talked to the person who knows and received instruction as to what he should paint?'

'Neither of these.'

'So the imitator will neither know nor have a right opinion about the goodness or badness of what he imitates.'

'It seems not.'

'The poetical imitator will be in a very fair position then as regards wisdom about the things he writes about!'

'Indeed he won't.'

'None the less, he will imitate, though he won't know in what way anything is good or bad. He will presumably imitate what seems to be good to the ignorant majority.'

'What else?'

'Then it seems to me we've pretty well agreed that the imitative person knows nothing of significance about what he imitates; imitation is a game and not serious; and practitioners of tragic poetry, in iambics and hexameters, are all of them imitative persons in the highest degree.'

'Yes, indeed.'

'So this imitation relates to something three removes from truth, does it?'

'Yes.'

'Now what element in human nature does it affect?'

'What do you mean?'

'Something like this. The same size appears different according to whether it is seen close at hand or at a distance.'

'Yes.'

'A thing may seem straight or crooked according to whether it is seen in or out of water. Similarly with the concave and convex, because of visual error connected with colours. This is evidently a sort of total mental confusion: and it's this natural experience that perspective drawing exploits with its magic, and conjuring tricks too, and many other such devices.'

'True.'

'Now the best aid in all this is measurement, counting and weighing. These prevent the *apparently* bigger or smaller, heavier or more numerous, from prevailing in our minds, and make the calculating, measuring, and weighing element do so.'

'Just so.'

'Now this will be the work of the ratiocinative part of our mind.'

'It will.'

'Now it often happens that when this faculty has measured and indicates that A is bigger or smaller than B, or equal to it, it nevertheless finds contrary *appearances* at the same time about the same object.'

'Yes.'

'Now we said that the same thing cannot make contrary judgements at the same time about the same object.'

'And that was surely right.'

'Then the element of the mind that judges against the measurements is not the same as that which judges with them.'

'No.'

'But that which relies on measurement and calculation will be the best element of the mind.'

'Of course.'

'So its opponent will be one of the inferior elements.'

'Necessarily.'

'This is the agreement I was aiming at when I said that painting, and imitative art generally, accomplishes work that is far removed from truth and addresses itself to an element in us that is far removed from wisdom, becoming this element's friend and close associate for no good or honest purpose.'

'Quite so.'

'So the art of imitation is an inferior thing, its associate is inferior, and its products are inferior.'

'So it seems.'

'Does this apply only to visual imitation or also to auditory imitation—what we call poetry?'

'Probably to this too.'

'Then let us not simply trust the probability on the evidence of painting, but consider what mental element it is that poetical imitation consorts with. Is it good or bad?'

'We must indeed consider that.'

'Let us set the question out like this. Imitation imitates men performing actions* either forced or voluntary, and believing that they are either successful or not in these actions, and feeling pain or pleasure as a result of it all. Is there anything else?'

'No.'

'Now is a man in a state of concord with himself in all these circumstances? Or does he dissent and quarrel within himself in his actions as he did visually when he had contrary judgements at the same time about the same things? But I recall that we need not agree this point now, because we agreed earlier quite adequately that our minds are full of contradictions of this kind.'

'Quite rightly, too.'

'Yes: but I think we must now go into the point which we omitted then.'

'What is that?'

'We said that a good man who has, for example, lost a son or something else to which he attaches great value, will bear the disaster more easily than others.'

'Yes'.

'Let us now consider whether he will feel no grief at all or, that being impossible, show moderation in his grief.'

'The second seems right.'

604 'Then tell me one thing more. Do you think he will resist and fight his grief more when he is seen by his peers, or when he is alone by himself in solitude?'

'When he's being seen, by a long way.'

'Yes: when he's alone, I imagine, he will allow himself to say many things he would be ashamed to be heard saying, and do many things he would not allow anyone to see him doing.'

'Yes.'

'Now the element that bids him resist is reason and law; that which pulls him towards the grief is the painful experience itself.'

'True.'

'And if there are contrary pulls in the man at the same time in regard to the same situation, we say that there must be two elements in him.'

'Of course.'

'One of which is ready to obey the law, wherever it gives guidance.'

'What do you mean?'

'The law says it is best to keep as quiet as possible in misfortune and not show distress. The good and the evil in such situations are not clear, nothing is gained for the future by indignation, no human affairs are worth great trouble, and, finally, grief prevents the arrival of what ought to be our most present help.'

'What do you mean by that?'

'Planning in relation to the event. We have to make the right move to respond to the throw of the dice, as it were, and do what reason dictates as best. If we fall down, we mustn't clap our hands to the hurt place and scream like babies, but accustom our mind to attend as quickly as it can to the healing and setting upright of the fallen and sick. Medicine must drown threnodies.'

'Certainly that is the right way to react to disasters.'

'So the best part of us wants to follow this reasoning.'

'Obviously.'

'And the element that encourages recollection of the trouble and lamentation, and is never sated with these, is irrational, inert, and associated with cowardice?'

'So we shall say.'

'Now the indignant element admits much varied imitation, while the quiet and sensible personality, always very much on the same level, is difficult to imitate—and difficult to detect if someone does try to imitate it, especially at a festival where miscellaneous multitudes throng into the theatre, for it's an imitation of an experience which is foreign to them.'

'Quite so.'   605

'So the imitative poet is obviously not made for this element in the mind—nor is his skill directed to please it, if he is to win popular renown—but for the indignant and variable personality, because it is easy to imitate.'

'Clearly.'

'So we can now properly take hold of him and place him as corresponding to the painter. He is like him in his inferiority with regard to truth, and also in his habitual association with an element of the mind which has the same characteristics, rather than with the best element. We should now be right not to admit him into a potentially well-governed city, because he rouses and feeds this part of the mind and by strengthening it destroys the rational part. It is like giving power to bad men in a city and handing it over to them, while ruining the better. The imitative poet, we shall say, produces a bad government in the individual mind, indulging the foolish element that cannot recognize greater and less but thinks the same thing one moment big, and the next little; he is an image-maker, far removed indeed from the truth.'

'Yes.'

'But we still haven't brought the greatest accusation against him. It is a terrible thought that he can ruin good men, apart from a very few.'

'But of course he can, if he does this.'

'Listen and think. When the best of us hear Homer or some other tragic poet imitating a hero in mourning, delivering a long speech of lamentation, singing, or beating his breast, you know how we feel pleasure and give ourselves up to it, how we follow in sympathy and praise the excellence of the poet who does this to us most effectively.'

'Of course I know.'

'But when we have some private bereavement, you notice how we pride ourselves on the opposite reaction—on keeping quiet and sticking it out—because this is a man's reaction, and the other, which we were praising just now, a woman's.'

'I notice that.'

606   'Is this approval proper? Is it right not to be disgusted, but to feel pleasure and give praise when you see a man who you would be ashamed to be yourself?'

'Well, it's not reasonable.'

'No, especially if you look at it like this.'

'Like what?'

'The element which is forcibly restrained in our own misfortunes, starved of tears and the satisfaction of lamentation, though it naturally desires this, is the very element which is satisfied and given pleasure by the poets. In these circumstances, our best element, not being adequately trained by reason or habituation, relaxes its watch over this element of lamentation, because the sorrows it sees are others' sorrows and there seems no disgrace in praising and pitying a man who claims to be virtuous and is mourning out of season; indeed, the pleasure seems a positive gain, and we can't bear to reject the whole poem and so be deprived of it. Not many people can see that the consequences of others' experience invade one's own, because it is difficult to restrain pity in one's own misfortunes when it has grown strong on others'.'

'Very true.'

'Does not the same apply to the ridiculous? Suppose you enjoy in a comedy or a private conversation jokes you would be ashamed to make yourself, instead of disliking them as morally bad—aren't you doing the same thing as with the expressions of pity? You are releasing the element in you that likes jokes, and that you used to restrain by reason because you were afraid of a reputation for buffoonery. Without realizing it, you have made a big thing of it by your frequent indulgence in private conversation, with the result that you've become a comedian.'

'Quite so.'

'Poetical imitation in fact produces the same effect in regard to sex and anger and all the desires and pleasures and pains of the mind—and these, in our view, accompany every action. It waters them and nourishes them, when they ought to be dried up. It makes them our rulers, when they ought to be under control so that we can be better and happier people rather than worse and more miserable.'

'I cannot but agree.'

'So when you find admirers of Homer saying that he educated Greece and that for human management and education one ought to take him up and learn his lesson and direct one's whole life on his principles, you must be kind and polite to them—they are as good as they are able to be—and concede that Homer is 607 the foremost and most poetical of the tragic poets; but you must be clear in your mind that the only poetry admissible in our city is hymns to the gods and encomia to good men. If you accept the "sweetened Muse" in lyric or epic, pleasure and pain will be enthroned in your city instead of law and the principle which the community accepts as best in any given situation.'

'True.'

'Well, these were the points that I wanted to recall to complete our justification for wishing to banish poetry from the city, such being its nature. The argument forced us. But let us say to her, lest she damn us as coarse and philistine, that there is an old quarrel between poetry and philosophy. I could quote a lot of passages for that: "the yapping bitch that barks at her master",* "a great man amid the vanities of fools", "the rabble of know-all heads", "thin thinkers starve", and so on. However, let us make it clear that if poetry for pleasure and imitation have any arguments to advance in favour of their presence in a well-governed city, we should be glad to welcome them back. We are conscious of their charms for us. But it would be wrong to betray what we believe to be the truth. Doesn't poetry charm you, especially when you see her in Homer?'

'Indeed she does.'

'So she deserves to return from exile, if she can make her defence in lyric or other metre?'

'Yes.'

'And we might also allow her defenders, who are lovers of poetry but not themselves poetical, to make a prose speech on her behalf, to show that she is not only pleasing but useful for government and human life; and we shall be glad to listen. After all, it will be our gain if she turns out useful as well as pleasing.'

'Certainly it will.'

ARISTOTLE: *POETICS*

CHAPTER I

pleasure

THE PRELIMINARIES TO THE DEFINITION OF TRAGEDY

Contents

The subject I wish us to discuss is poetry itself, its species with 1447ᵃ
their respective capabilities, the correct way of constructing plots 1
so that the work turns out well, the number and nature of the
constituent elements [of each species], and anything else in the
same field of inquiry.

SECTION A. THE DIVISION *PER GENUS ET DIFFERENTIAM*

1. *The genus we are here concerned with stated**

To follow the natural order and take first things first, epic and
tragic poetry, comedy and dithyrambic, and most music for the
flute or lyre are all, generally considered, varieties of *mimēsis*,
differing from each other in three respects, the media, the
objects, and the mode of *mimēsis*. ['Media' needs explaining]: in
some cases where people, whether by technical rules or practised
facility, produce various *mimēseis* by portraying things, the media
are colours and shapes, while in others the medium is the voice;*
similarly in the arts in question, taken collectively, the media of
mimēsis are rhythm, speech, and harmony, either separately or in
combination.

2. *The genus divided*

(*a*) ACCORDING TO DIFFERENCES OF MEDIA

(i) *Those which do not use speech*

For example, harmony and rhythm are the media of instrumental
music, rhythm alone without harmony the medium of dancing, as
dancers represent characters, passions, and actions by rhythmic
movement and postures.

(ii) *Those which do use speech (i.e. the poetic kinds)**

The art that uses only speech by itself or verse [that is, rhythmical speech], the verses being homogeneous or of different kinds, has as yet no name,* for we have no common term to apply to the [prose] mimes of Sophron and Xenarchus and to the Socratic dialogues, nor any common term for *mimēseis* produced in verse, whether iambic trimeters or elegiacs or some other such metre. True, people do attach the making [that is the root of the word *poiētēs*] to the name of a metre and speak of elegiac-makers and hexameter-makers; they think, no doubt, that 'makers' is applied to poets not because they make *mimēseis* but as a general term meaning 'verse-makers', since they call 'poets' or 'makers' even those who publish a medical or scientific theory in verse. But [this is open to two objections]: (1) as Homer and Empedocles have nothing in common except their metre, the latter had better be called a scientific writer, not a poet, if we are to use 'poet' of the former; (2) similarly, if we suppose a man to make his *mimēsis* in a medley of all metres, as Chaeremon in fact did in the *Centaur*, a recitation-piece in all the various metres, we still have to call him a poet, a 'maker'.*

So much for the simpler kinds. Some use all the media mentioned, rhythm, song, and verse:* these are dithyrambic and nomic poetry, tragedy and comedy. But the two former use them all simultaneously, while the latter use different media in different parts. So much for the differentiae derived from the media.

(b) ACCORDING TO DIFFERENCES OF OBJECTS

The objects of this *mimēsis* are people doing things,* and these people [as represented] must necessarily be either good or bad, this being, generally speaking, the only line of divergence between characters, since differences of character just are differences in goodness and badness, or else they must be better than are found in the world or worse or just the same, as they are represented by the painters, Polygnotus portraying them as better, Pauson as worse, and Dionysius as they are;* clearly therefore each of the varieties of *mimēsis* in question will exhibit these differences, and one will be distinguishable from another in virtue of presenting things as different in this way.

These dissimilarities can in fact be found in dancing and instrumental music, and in the arts using speech and unaccompanied verse: Homer for instance represents people as better and Cleophon as they are, while Hegemon of Thasos, the inventor of parodies, and Nicochares, the author of the *Deiliad*, represent them as worse; the same is true of dithyrambs and nomes, where the *mimēsis* can differ as . . .,* and as that of the Cyclopes does in Timotheus and Philoxenus; this is also the differentia that marks off tragedy from comedy, since the latter aims to represent people as worse, the former as better, than the men of the present day.

(c) ACCORDING TO DIFFERENCES OF MODE

There is still a third difference, the mode in which one represents each of these objects. For one can represent the same objects in the same media

  (i) sometimes in narration and sometimes becoming someone else, as Homer does, or

 (ii) speaking in one's own person without change, or

(iii) with all the people engaged in the *mimēsis* actually doing things.*

These three then, media, objects, and mode, are, as I said at the beginning, the differentiae of poetic *mimēsis*. So, if we use one of them [to separate poets into classes], Sophocles will be in the same class as Homer, since both represent people as good, and if we use another, he will be in the same class as Aristophanes, since they both represent people as actively doing things.

Digression on the etymological fancies of the Dorians

Some people say that this verb *drān*, 'to do', is why plays are called dramas, because such poets represent people as doing things; and this is the ground on which the Dorians claim the invention of both tragedy and comedy. Comedy is claimed by the Megarians, both by those of mainland Greece, who say it arose when their democracy was established,* and by those of [Megara Hyblaea in] Sicily, the home of Epicharmus, who lived well before Chionides and Magnes.* Tragedy is claimed by some of the Peloponnesians. In each case they found their claim on etymology: they say that while they call outlying villages *kōmai*, the Athenians call them *dēmoi*, and they take 'comedy' to be derived not from *kōmazein*, 'to revel', but from the fact that the comic actors wandered among the villages because driven in 1448ᵇ contempt from the city; and they say that they use the word *drān* of doing, while the Athenians say *prattein*.

Conclusion

So much for the number and nature of the differentiae of poetic *mimēsis*.

SECTION B. THE PROOF THAT THE KINDS WE ARE INTERESTED IN DEFINING ARE EACH A COMPLETELY DEVELOPED AND A SINGLE SPECIES

1. *The origins of poetry*

4 Poetry, I believe, has two over-all causes, both of them natural:

(a) *Mimēsis* is innate in human beings from childhood—indeed we differ from the other animals in being most given to *mimēsis* and in making our first steps in learning through it—and pleasure in instances of *mimēsis* is equally general. This we can see from the facts: we enjoy looking at the most exact portrayals of things we do not like to see in real life, the lowest animals, for instance, or corpses. This is because not only philosophers, but all men, enjoy getting to understand something, though it is true that most people feel this pleasure only to a slight degree; therefore they like to see these pictures, because in looking at them they come to understand something and can infer what each thing is, can say, for instance, 'This man in the picture is so-and-so'. If you happen not to have seen the original, the picture will not produce its pleasure *qua* instance of *mimēsis*, but because of its technical finish or colour or for some such other reason.

(b) As well as *mimēsis*, harmony and rhythm are natural to us, and verses are obviously definite sections of rhythm.

action is dependent on char.

2. *The development of pre-dramatic poetry**

These two were gradually developed by those who had most natural gift for them. Poetry, arising from their improvisations, split up according to the authors' divergent characters: the more dignified represented noble actions and those of noble men, the less serious those of low-class people; the one group produced at first invectives, the others songs praising gods and men. We cannot name any author of a poem of the former kind before Homer's time, though there were probably many of them, but from Homer on we do find such poems—his own *Margites*, for instance, and others of the kind. These introduced the metre that suited them, still called 'iambic' (from *iambizein*, 'to lampoon'), because it was the metre of their lampoons on each other. So some of the ancients produced heroic [i.e. hexameter] verse and the others iambics.

As well as being the most creative poet of high actions,* his *mimēseis* in this kind being the only ones that are not only well done but essentially dramatic, Homer also first adumbrated the form of comedy by dramatizing the ridiculous instead of producing invectives; his *Margites* bears the same relation to comedy as the *Iliad* and *Odyssey* do to tragedy. 1449^a

On the subsequent appearance of tragedy and comedy, those whose natural bent made lampooners of them turned to comedy, while those naturally inclined to epic became tragedians, because the new forms were more ample and more highly esteemed than the old.

3. *The development of tragedy*

To inquire whether even tragedy [as distinct from epic] is sufficiently elaborated in its qualitative elements, judging it in itself and in its relation to the audience, is another story. At any rate, after originating in the improvisations of the leaders of the dithyramb, as comedy did in those of the leaders of the phallic songs still customary in many Greek cities, tragedy gradually grew to maturity, as people developed the capacities they kept discovering in it, and after many changes it stopped altering, since it had attained its full growth. The main changes were:

(i) in the number of actors, raised from one to two by Aeschylus, who made the choral part less important and gave speech the leading role; Sophocles added a third—and also scene-painting;

(ii) in amplitude: as tragedy developed from the satyr-style, its plots were at first slight and its expression comical, and it was a long time before it acquired dignity;

(iii) in metre: the iambic trimeter replaced the trochaic tetrameter, which had been used before as suitable for a satyr-style poetry, that is, for productions involving more dancing; when verbal expression came to the fore, however, nature herself found the right metre, the iambic being the most speakable of all metres; this we can see from the fact that it is the one we most often produce accidentally in conversation, where hexameters are rare and only occur when we depart from conversational tone;

(iv) in the increased number of episodes.

There is no need to say more of this or of the other developments that gave it beauty; it would take too long to go through them in detail.

4. *The development of comedy*

5   Comedy is, as I said, a *mimēsis* of people worse than are found in the world—'worse' in the particular sense of 'uglier', as the ridiculous is a species of ugliness; for what we find funny is a blunder that does no serious damage or an ugliness that does not imply pain, the funny face, for instance, being one that is ugly and distorted, but not with pain. While the changes and the authors of the changes in tragedy are known, the development of 1449[b] comedy is obscure because it was not at first taken seriously; the chorus, for instance, were for a long time volunteers, and not provided officially by the archon. The form was already partly fixed before the first recorded comic poets, and so we do not know who introduced masks, prologues, numerous actors, and so on; the making of plots, however, certainly came first from Sicily, Crates being the first Athenian to drop the lampoon form and construct generalized stories or plots.

SECTION C. APOLOGY FOR POSTPONING THE
TREATMENT OF EPIC, IN DEFIANCE OF CHRONOLOGY

Epic, in so far as it is a sizeable *mimēsis* in verse of noble
personages, goes along with tragedy, but differs from it in using
metre alone [without music] and in being in narrative form; it
also differs in length, tragedy attempting so far as possible to
keep to the limit of one revolution of the sun or not much more
or less, while epic is unfixed in time. This differentiates them
now, but at first tragic practice was the same as epic. Of their
elements some are the same, some peculiar to tragedy, so that
any judge of excellence in tragedy can judge of epic too, since
tragedy has everything that epic has, while epic lacks some of
tragedy's elements. I shall deal later with the art of *mimēsis* in   6
hexameters and with comedy; here I want to talk about tragedy,
picking up the definition of its essential nature that results from
what I have said.

CHAPTER II

THE NATURE OF TRAGEDY

SECTION A. THE NATURE OF TRAGEDY ACCORDING TO
THE CATEGORY OF SUBSTANCE

Well then, a tragedy is a *mimēsis* of a high, complete action
('complete' in the sense that implies amplitude), in speech
pleasurably enhanced, the different kinds [of enhancement]
occurring in separate sections, in dramatic, not narrative form,
effecting through pity and fear the *catharsis* of such emotions. By
'speech pleasurably enhanced' I mean that involving rhythm and
harmony or song, by 'the different kinds separately' that some
parts are in verse alone and others in song.

SECTION B. THE NATURE OF TRAGEDY ACCORDING TO
THE CATEGORY OF QUALITY

1. *The deduction of the qualitative elements of tragedy*

One can deduce as necessary elements of tragedy (*a*) [from the
mode] the designing of the spectacle, since the *mimēsis* is
produced by people doing things; (*b*) [from the media] song-
writing and verbal expression, the media of tragic *mimēsis*; by
'verbal expression' I mean the composition of the verse-parts,*
while the meaning of 'song-writing' is obvious to anybody.
[Others can be inferred from (*c*) the objects of the *mimēsis*:] A
tragedy is a *mimēsis* of an action; action implies people engaged in
it; these people must have some definite moral and intellectual
qualities, since it is through a man's qualities that we characterize
1450ᵃ his actions, and it is of course with reference to their actions that
men are said to succeed or fail. We therefore have (i) the *mimēsis*
of the action, the plot, by which I mean the ordering of the
particular actions; (ii) [the *mimēsis* of] the moral characters
of the personages, namely that [in the play] which makes us say
that the agents have certain moral qualities; (iii) [the *mimēsis* of]
their intellect, namely those parts [of the play] in which they
demonstrate something in speech or deliver themselves of some
general maxim.

So tragedy as a whole will necessarily have six elements, the
possession of which makes tragedy qualitatively distinct [from
other literary kinds]: they are plot, the *mimēsis* of character,
verbal expression, the *mimēsis* of intellect, spectacle, and song-
writing. The media of *mimēsis* are two, the mode one, the objects
three, and there are no others. Not a few tragedians do in fact use
these as qualitative elements; indeed virtually every play has
spectacle, the *mimēsis* of character, plot, verbal expression, song,
and the *mimēsis* of intellect.

2. *The qualitative elements ranged in order of importance*

(*a*) THE ARGUMENTS FOR THE PRE-EMINENCE OF PLOT

The most important of these elements is the arrangement of the
particular actions [as the following arguments show]:

(*a*) A tragedy is [by definition] a *mimēsis* not of people but of their actions and life. Both success and ill success are success and ill success in action—in other words the end and aim of human life* is doing something, not just being a certain sort of person; and though we consider people's characters in deciding what sort of persons they are, we call them successful or unsuccessful only with reference to their actions. So far therefore from the persons in a play acting as they do in order to represent their characters, the *mimēsis* of their characters is only included along with and because of their actions. So the particular actions, the plot, are what the rest of the tragedy is there for,* and what the rest is there for is the most important.

(*b*) [By definition] a work could not be a tragedy if there were no action. But there could be a tragedy without *mimēsis* of character, and the tragedies of most of the moderns are in fact deficient in it; the same is true of many other poets, and of painters for that matter, of Zeuxis, for instance, in comparison with Polygnotus: the latter is good at depicting character, while Zeuxis' painting has no *mimēsis* of character to speak of.

Gk painter put on pedestal as great.

(*c*) If you put down one after another speeches that depicted character, finely expressed and brilliant in the *mimēsis* of intellect, that would not do the job that, by definition, tragedy does do, while a tragedy with a plot, that is, with an ordered series of particular actions, though deficient in these other points, would do its job much better.

(*d*) The most attractive things in tragedy, *peripeteiai* and recognition scenes, are parts of the plot.

(*e*) Novices in poetry attain perfection in verbal expression and in the *mimēsis* of character much earlier than in the ordering of the particular actions; this is also true of almost all early poets.

(*b*) THE STATEMENT OF THE ORDER

The plot therefore is the principle, or one might say the principle of life,* in tragedy, while the *mimēsis* of character comes second in importance, a relation similar to one we find in painting, where the most beautiful colours, if smeared on at random, would give less pleasure than an uncoloured outline that was a picture of something. A tragedy, I repeat, is a *mimēsis* of an

1450^b

action, and it is only because of the action that it is a *mimēsis* of
the people engaged in it. Third comes the *mimēsis* of their
intellect, by which I mean their ability to say what the situation
admits and requires; to do this in speeches is the job of political
sense and rhetoric, since the older poets made their people speak
as the former directs, while the moderns make them observe the
rules of rhetoric. Of these two, the *mimēsis* of character is that [in
the play] which makes plain the nature of the moral choices the
personages make, so that those speeches in which there is
absolutely nothing that the speaker chooses and avoids involve no
mimēsis of character. By '*mimēsis* of intellect'* I mean those
passages in which they prove that something is or is not the case
or deliver themselves of some general statement. Fourth comes
the expression of the spoken parts, by which I mean, as I said
before, the expression of thought in words; the meaning is the
same whether verse or prose is in question. Of the others, which
are there to give pleasure, song-writing is the most important,
while spectacle, though attractive, has least to do with art, with
the art of poetry, that is; for a work is potentially a tragedy* even
without public performance and players, and the art of the stage-
designer contributes more to the perfection of spectacle than the
poet's does.

3. *Closer analysis of plot**

(*a*) THE ESSENTIAL CHARACTERISTICS OF A PLOT,
    WITH REFERENCE TO ITS DEFINITION AS THE
    MIMĒSIS OF A WHOLE ACTION*

(i) *The first implication of wholeness: order*

7 Now that these definitions are out of the way, I want to consider
what the arrangement of the particular actions should be like,
since that is the prime and most important element of tragedy.

Now, we have settled that a tragedy is a *mimēsis* of a complete,
that is, of a whole action, 'whole' here implying some amplitude
(there can be a whole without amplitude).

By 'whole' I mean 'with a beginning, a middle, and an end'. By
'beginning' [in this context] I mean 'that which is not necessarily
the consequent of something else, but has some state or
happening naturally consequent on it', by 'end' 'a state that is the

necessary or usual consequent of something else, but has itself no such consequent', by 'middle' 'that which is consequent and has consequents'. Well-ordered plots, then, will exhibit these characteristics, and will not begin or end just anywhere.

(ii) *The second implication of wholeness: amplitude*

It is not enough for beauty that a thing, whether an animal or anything else composed of parts, should have those parts well-ordered; since beauty consists in amplitude as well as in order, the thing must also have amplitude—and not just any amplitude. Though a very small creature could not be beautiful, since our view loses all distinctness when it comes near to taking no perceptible time, an enormously ample one could not be beautiful either, since our view of it is not simultaneous, so that 1451^a we lose the sense of its unity and wholeness as we look it over; imagine, for instance, an animal a thousand miles long. Animate and inanimate bodies, then, must have amplitude, but no more than can be taken in at one view; and similarly a plot must have extension, but no more than can be easily remembered. What is, for the poetic art, the limit of this extension? Certainly not that imposed by the contests and by perception—if a hundred plays had to be performed during the festival, they would time the performances by the hour glass, †as they say once on another occasion. . .†* As the limit imposed by the actual nature of the thing, one may suggest 'the ampler the better, provided it remains clear as a whole', or, to give a rough specification, 'sufficient amplitude to allow a probable or necessary succession of particular actions to produce a change from bad to good or from good to bad fortune'.

(iii) *The third implication of wholeness: unity*

Unity of plot is not, as some think, achieved by writing about 8 one man; for just as the one substance admits innumerable incidental properties, which do not, some of them, make it a such-and-such,* so one man's actions are numerous and do not make up any single action. That is why I think the poets mistaken who have produced *Heracleids* or *Theseids* or other poems of the kind, in the belief that the plot would be one just because Heracles was one. Homer especially shows his superiority in taking a right view here—whether by art or nature: in writing a poem on Odysseus he did not introduce everything that was incidentally true of him, being wounded on Parnassus, for instance, or pretending to be mad at the mustering of the fleet, neither of which necessarily or probably implied the other at all; instead he composed the *Odyssey* about an action that is one in the sense I mean, and the same is true of the *Iliad*. In the other mimetic arts a *mimēsis* is one if it is a *mimēsis* of one object; and in the same way a plot, being a *mimēsis* of an action, should be a *mimēsis* of one action and that a whole one, with the different sections so arranged that the whole is disturbed by the transposition and destroyed by the removal of any one of them; for if it makes no visible difference whether a thing is there or not, that thing is no part of the whole.

(iv) *The fourth implication of wholeness: probable and necessary connection*

9   What I have said also makes plain that the poet's job is saying not what did happen but the sort of thing that would happen, that is, what can happen in a strictly probable or necessary sequence. 1451^b The difference between the historian and the poet is not merely that one writes verse and the other prose—one could turn Herodotus' work into verse and it would be just as much history as before; the essential difference is that the one tells us what happened and the other the sort of thing that would happen. That is why poetry is at once more like philosophy and more worth while than history, since poetry tends to make general statements, while those of history are particular. A 'general statement' means [in this context] one that tells us what sort of man would, probably or necessarily, say or do what sort of thing, and this is what poetry aims at,* though it attaches proper names; a particular statement on the other hand tells us what Alcibiades, for instance, did or what happened to him.

That poetry does aim at generality has long been obvious in the case of comedy, where the poets make up the plot from a series of probable happenings and then give the persons any names they like, instead of writing about particular people as the lampooners did. In tragedy, however, they still stick to the actual names; this is because it is what is possible that arouses conviction, and while we do not without more ado believe that what never happened is possible, what did happen is clearly possible, since it would not have happened if it were not. Though as a matter of fact, even in some tragedies most names are invented and only one or two well known: in Agathon's *Antheus*, for instance, the names as well as the events are made up, and yet it gives just as much pleasure. So one need not try to stick at any cost to the traditional stories, which are the subject of tragedies; indeed the attempt would be absurd, since even what is well known is well known only to a few, but gives general pleasure for all that.

It is obvious from all this that the poet should be considered a maker of plots, not of verses, since he is a poet *qua* maker of *mimēsis* and the objects of his *mimēsis* are actions. Even if it is incidentally true that the plot he makes actually happened, that does not mean he is not its maker; for there is no reason why some things that actually happen should not be the sort of thing that would probably happen, and it is in virtue of that aspect of them that he is their maker.

(v) *Plots that fail to exhibit the essential characteristics*

Of defective* plots or actions the worst are the episodic, those, I mean, in which the succession of the episodes is neither probable nor necessary; bad poets make these on their own account, good ones because of the judges; for in aiming at success in the competition and stretching the plot more than it can bear they often have to distort the natural order. 1452ᵃ

(*b*) A FIFTH REQUIREMENT, SUGGESTED BY THE MENTION OF PITY AND FEAR IN THE DEFINITION: SURPRISE

Tragedy is a *mimēsis* not only of a complete action, but also of things arousing pity and fear, emotions most likely to be stirred when things happen unexpectedly but because of each other (this arouses more surprise than mere chance events, since even chance events seem more marvellous when they look as if they were meant to happen—take the case of the statue of Mitys in Argos killing Mitys' murderer by falling on him as he looked at it;

for we do not think that things like this are merely random); so such plots* will necessarily be the best.

(*c*) THE SPECIES OF PLOT

10   Some plots are simple, some complex, since the actions of which the plots are *mimēseis* fall naturally into the same two classes. By 'simple action' I mean one that is continuous in the sense defined* and is a unity and where the change of fortune takes place without *peripeteia* or recognition, by 'complex' one where the change of fortune is accompanied by *peripeteia* or recognition or both. The *peripeteia* and recognition should arise just from the arrangement of the plot, so that it is necessary or probable that they should follow what went before; for there is a great difference between happening next and happening as a result.

(*d*) THE ELEMENTS OF PLOT

(i) *Peripeteia*

11   A *peripeteia* occurs when the course of events takes a turn to the opposite in the way described,* the change being also probable or necessary in the way I said. For example, in the *Oedipus*, when the man came and it seemed that he would comfort* Oedipus and free him from his fear about his mother, by revealing who he was he in fact did the opposite. Again in the *Lynceus*,* Lynceus was being led off and it seemed that he would be put to death and that Danaus who was with him would kill him, but the earlier actions produced Danaus' death and Lynceus' release.

(ii) *Recognition*

Recognition is, as its name indicates, a change from ignorance to knowledge, tending either to affection or to enmity; it determines in the direction of good or ill fortune the fates of the people involved. The best sort of recognition is that accompanied by *peripeteia*, like that in the *Oedipus*. There are of course other kinds of recognition. For a recognition of the sort described can be a recognition of inanimate objects, indeed of quite indifferent ones, and one can also recognize whether someone has committed an act or not. But the one mentioned has most to do

with the plot, that is, most to do with the action; for a recognition
accompanied by *peripeteia* in this way will involve either pity or 1452^b
fear, and tragedy is by definition a *mimēsis* of actions that rouse
these emotions; it is moreover such recognitions that lead to good
or bad fortune.

Since recognition involves more than one person, in some
cases only one person will recognize the other, when it is clear
who the former is, and sometimes each has to recognize the
other: Orestes, for example, recognized Iphigenia from her
sending the letter, but a second recognition was necessary for her
to recognize him.

(iii) *Pathos*

These then are two elements of the plot, and a third is *pathos*. I
have dealt with the first two, *peripeteia* and recognition. A *pathos* is
an act involving destruction or pain, for example deaths on stage
and physical agonies and woundings and so on.

So much for the parts of tragedy that one ought to use as 12
qualitative elements.

SECTION C. THE NATURE OF TRAGEDY ACCORDING TO THE CATEGORY OF QUANTITY

Now for the category of quantity and the quantitative divisions of
a tragedy: they are prologue, episode, *exodos*, choral part, the last
being divided into *parodos* and *stasimon*; the last two are common
to all plays, while some have as well songs from the actors and
kommoi.

The prologue is the complete section of a tragedy before the
entrance of the chorus, an episode the complete section of a
tragedy between complete choral odes, the *exodos* a complete
section of a tragedy not followed by a choral ode. Of the choral
part, the *parodos* is the first complete utterance of the chorus, a
stasimon a choral song not using the anapaestic dimeter or
trochaic tetrameter,* a *kommos* a lament shared by the chorus and
the actors.

Having dealt beforehand with the parts of tragedy that one
ought to use as quantitative elements, I have now dealt with the
category of quantity and the quantitative divisions of a tragedy.

Chapter III

Excellence in Tragedy

SECTION A. WITH RESPECT TO PLOT

13 What ought one to aim at and beware of in composing plots? And
what is the source of the tragic effect? These are the questions
that naturally follow from what I have now dealt with.

1. *Things to aim at and beware of*

Well, the arrangement of tragedy at its best should be complex,
not simple, and it should also present a *mimēsis* of things that
arouse fear and pity, as this is what is peculiar to the tragic
mimēsis.

   So it is clear that one should not show virtuous men passing
from good to bad fortune, since this does not arouse fear or pity,
but only a sense of outrage. Nor should one show bad men
passing from bad to good fortune, as this is less tragic than
1453ᵃ anything, since it has none of the necessary requirements; it
neither satisfies our human feeling nor arouses pity and fear. Nor
should one show a quite wicked man passing from good to bad
fortune; it is true that such an arrangement would satisfy our
human feeling, but it would not arouse pity or fear, since the one
is felt for someone who comes to grief without deserving it, and
the other for someone like us (pity, that is, for the man who does
not deserve his fate, and fear for someone like us); so this event
will not arouse pity or fear. So we have left the man between
these. He is one who is not pre-eminent in moral virtue, who
passes to bad fortune not through vice or wickedness, but
because of some piece of ignorance, and who is of high repute
and great good fortune, like Oedipus and Thyestes and the
splendid men of such families.*

   So the good plot must have a single line of development, not a
double one as some people say; that line should go from good
fortune to bad and not the other way round; the change should
be produced not through wickedness, but through some large-
scale piece of ignorance; the person ignorant should be the sort

of man I have described—certainly not a worse man, though perhaps a better one.

This is borne out by the facts: at first the poets recounted any story that came to hand, but nowadays the best tragedies are about a few families only, for example, Alcmaeon, Oedipus, Orestes, Meleager, Thyestes, Telephus, and others whose lot it was to suffer or commit fearful acts.

Well then, the best tragedy, judged from the standpoint of the tragic art, comes from this sort of arrangement. That is why those who censure Euripides for doing this in his tragedies and making many of them end with disaster are making just the same mistake.* For this is correct in the way I said. The greatest proof of this is that on the stage and in the contests such plays are felt to be the most properly tragic, if they are well managed, and Euripides, even if he is a bad manager in the other points, is at any rate the most tragic* of the poets.

Second comes the sort of arrangement that some people say is the best: this is the one that has a double arrangement of the action like the *Odyssey*, and ends with opposite fortunes for the good and bad people. It is thought to be the best because of the weakness of the audiences; for the poets follow the lead of the spectators and make plays to their specifications. But this is not the pleasure proper to tragedy, but rather belongs to comedy; for in comedy those who are most bitter enemies throughout the plot, as it might be Orestes and Aegisthus, are reconciled at the end and go off and nobody is killed by anybody.

2. *The source of the tragic effect*

Now though pity and fear can be elicited by the spectacle, they can also be elicited just by the arrangement of the particular actions [that make up the plot], and this is a prior consideration and the sign of a better poet. For the plot ought to be so composed that even without seeing the action, a man who just hears what is going on shudders and feels pity because of what happens; this one would feel on hearing the plot of the *Oedipus*, for instance. But to produce this effect via the spectacle has less to do with the art of tragedy and needs external aids. To go further and use the spectacle to produce something that is merely

1453^b
14

monstrous, instead of something that rouses fear, is to depart entirely from tragedy. For one should look to tragedy for its own pleasure, not just any pleasure; and since the poet's job is to produce the pleasure springing from pity and fear via *mimēsis*, this clearly ought to be present in the elements of the action.

What sort of events, then, do seem apt to rouse fear, or [rather] pity? This is my next subject. In such actions, people must do something to those closely connected with them, or to enemies, or to people to whom they are indifferent. Now, if it is a case of two enemies, this arouses no particular pity, whether the one damages the other or only intends to; or at least, pity is felt only at the *pathos* considered in itself. The same is true in the case when people are indifferent to each other. The cases we must look for are those where the *pathos* involves people closely connected, for instance where brother kills brother, son father, mother son, or son mother—or if not kills, then means to kill, or does some other act of the kind.

Well, one cannot interfere with the traditional stories, cannot, for instance, say that Clytaemestra was not killed by Orestes or Eriphyle by Alcmaeon; what one should do is invent for oneself and use the traditional material well. Let me explain more clearly what I mean by 'well'. One can make the act be committed as the ancient poets did, that is, with the agents knowing and aware [whom they are damaging]; even Euripides has the example of Medea killing her children with full knowledge. [And they can have knowledge and not act]. Or they can commit the deed that rouses terror without knowing to whom they are doing it, and later recognize the connection, like Sophocles' Oedipus; this indeed happens outside the play, but we have examples in the tragedy itself, for example, Astydamas' *Alcmaeon* and Telegonus in the *Wounded Odysseus*. Again, apart from these one might through ignorance intend to do something irreparable, and then recognize the victim-to-be before doing it. These are the only possible ways, as they must either do it or not, and in knowledge or ignorance.

The worst of these is to have the knowledge and the intention and then not do it; for this is both morally outraging and
1454ª untragic—'untragic' because it involves no *pathos*. That is why nobody does behave in this way except very rarely, as Haemon,

for example, means to kill Creon in the *Antigone*. The second worst is doing it: the better form of this is when the character does it in ignorance, and recognizes his victim afterwards; for this involves no feeling of outrage and the recognition produces lively surprise. But the best is the last, for example, the case in the *Cresphontes* where Merope means to kill her son and does not, but recognizes him instead, and the case involving brother and sister in the *Iphigenia in Tauris*; again in the *Helle* the son recognized his mother when on the point of giving her up.*

As I said before, this is why tragedies are about very few families. As it was not art but chance that led the poets in their search to the discovery of how to produce this effect in their plots, they have to go to the families in which such *pathē* occurred.

So much for the arrangement of the particular acts and the qualities required of plots.

SECTION B. WITH RESPECT TO CHARACTER

In the representation of character, there are four things that one ought to aim at:

(*a*) First and foremost, the characters represented should be morally good. The speech or action will involve *mimēsis* of character if it makes plain, as said before, the nature of the person's moral choice, and the character represented will be good if the choice is good. This is possible in each class: for example, a woman is good and so is a slave, though the one is perhaps inferior, and the other generally speaking low-grade.

(*b*) The characters represented should be suitable: for example, the character represented is brave, but it is not suitable for a woman to be brave or clever in this way.*

(*c*) They should be life-like; this is different from the character's being good and suitable in the way I used 'suitable'.

(*d*) They should be consistent: for even if the subject of the *mimēsis* is an inconsistent person, and that is the characteristic posited of him, still he ought to be consistently inconsistent.

An example of unnecessary badness of character is Menelaus in the *Orestes*,* of the unsuitable or inappropriate Odysseus' lament in the *Scylla* and Melanippe's speech, of the inconsistent

Iphigenia in the *Iphigenia at Aulis*, as the girl who pleads for her life is quite different from the later one.

In the representation of character as well as in the chain of actions one ought always to look for the necessary or probable, so that it is necessary or probable that a person like this speaks or acts as he does, and necessary or probable that this happens after that. Clearly then, the dénouements of plots ought to arise just from the *mimēsis* of character,* and not from a contrivance, a *deus ex machina*, as in the *Medea* and in the events in the *Iliad* about the setting off. The contrivance should be used instead for things outside the play, either all that happened beforehand that a human being could not know, or all that happens later and needs foretelling and reporting; for we attribute omniscience to the gods. In the particular actions themselves there should be nothing irrational, and if there is it should be outside the tragedy,* like that of Sophocles' *Oedipus*.

1454^b

Since a tragedy is a *mimēsis* of people better than are found in the world, one ought to do the same as the good figure-painters; for they too give us the individual form, but though they make people lifelike they represent them as more beautiful than they are. Similarly the poet too in representing people as irascible and lazy and morally deficient in other ways like that, ought nevertheless to make them good, as Homer makes Achilles both good and an example of harsh self-will.

One must watch out for all these points, and also for the errors against the perceptions necessarily attending on the poetic art; for in these perceptions too one can often go wrong. But I have said enough about them in my published works.

DIGRESSION ON VARIOUS TOPICS OF INTEREST TO THE PRACTISING PLAYWRIGHT*

1. *Recognition*

16 I gave before the genus definition of recognition. Now for its species:

(a) The first and least artistic (and the one most used because people can think of nothing better) is recognition by visible signs. These signs may be birthmarks, like 'the spear the earth-born bear' or stars like those Carcinus supposed in his *Thyestes*, or acquired after birth; there are two kinds of the latter, bodily ones like scars, or external ones, like necklaces and the recognition by means of the cradle in Sophocles' *Tyro*. Even such signs can be well or badly handled: for example, Odysseus' scar leads to his being recognized in one way by his nurse and in another by the swineherds; recognitions like the latter, which are just meant to convince [the other characters in the poem], are less artistic, and so are all others similarly contrived; those that spring from a *peripeteia*, like that in the Bath episode,* are better.

(*b*) The next are those manufactured by the poet: this makes them inartistic. An example is Orestes' making himself known in the *Iphigenia in Tauris*; for she herself was recognized by means of her letter, but Orestes says without more ado what the poet wants him to say, not what the plot demands. So this is quite near the previous fault, since it would have been possible for him to bring some tokens too. There is also the 'voice of the shuttle'* in Sophocles' *Tereus*.

(*c*) The third is by means of memory, that is, when one's awareness is roused by seeing something: for example, in Dicaeogenes' *Cyprians*, he sees the picture and bursts into tears, and in the story of Alcinous Odysseus is reminded by listening to the harpist, and weeps; this leads to the recognition in each case.

(*d*) The fourth is recognition on the basis of reasoning: in the *Choephoroe*, for instance, we have the argument 'Somebody like me has come; nobody but Orestes is like me; so Orestes has come'.* Another example is the way the sophist Polyidus dealt with Iphigenia; it was natural, he thought, for Orestes to argue that his sister had been sacrificed and now it was his turn to be sacrificed. Another is in Theodectes' *Tydeus* to the effect that in coming to find his son he was losing his own life. Again, in the *Sons of Phineus*, when the women saw the place they inferred that they were destined to die there, since that was where they had been exposed.

There is also a composite kind involving a false inference on the part of the other character. An example of this is in *Odysseus the False Messenger*. For that Odysseus and only he can string the bow is something manufactured by the poet, and there is a hypothesis 'If he said that he would know the bow that he has not seen',* but to construct the plot so that it looks as if he will recognize him through this [false inference] is [the case of] paralogism [being described].*

(e) The best kind of all is that which arises from the actions alone, with the surprise developing through a series of likelihoods; examples are that in Sophocles' *Oedipus* and Euripides' *Iphigenia in Tauris*; for it was likely that she would want to send a letter. Only such recognitions are really free from manufactured signs and necklaces. The next best are those that come from reasoning.

2. *Poetic imagination*

17   In composing plots and working them out so far as verbal expression goes, the poet should, more than anything else, put things before his eyes, as he then sees the events most vividly as if he were actually present, and can therefore find what is appropriate and be aware of the opposite. The censure on Carcinus is an indication of this: that was a matter of Amphiaraus' coming from the temple, which would have escaped notice if it had not been seen, but fell flat on the stage, because the audience made a fuss about it. So far as possible one should also work it out with the appropriate gestures. For given the same natural endowment, people who actually feel passion are the most convincing; that is, the person who most realistically expresses distress is the person in distress and the same is true of a person in a temper. That is why poetry is the work of a genius rather than of a madman; for the genius is by nature adaptable, while the madman is degenerate.*

1455ᵇ   Whether the argument of a play is pre-existent or whether one is inventing it oneself, one should set it out in general terms, and only then make it into episodes and extend it. By 'setting it out in general terms' I mean, to take the case of the *Iphigenia in Tauris*: [before the action proper begins] a girl was sacrificed and disappeared without the sacrificers knowing what had happened to her, and she was settled in another country where there was a law that one sacrificed strangers to the goddess; she was installed as priestess of this rite; [then in the action proper] it came about later that the priestess's brother arrived (that he came because of an oracle and his purpose in coming are things outside the action); anyway he came and was captured and when on the point of being sacrificed disclosed himself, either as in Euripides' poem or as in Polyidus, saying, that is, as was natural, that it turned out that he was destined to be sacrificed as well as his sister; and this recognition produced his rescue. After this one should come to adding the names and making the episodes. Take care that the episodes are relevant; for example, in the case of Orestes in the *Iphigenia* such episodes are the fit of madness that led to his capture, and his escape through being purified.

In plays episodes are brief, but epic uses them to increase its length. The *Odyssey*, for instance, has a very brief argument: [as preliminary to the action] a man is away from home for many years and jealously watched by Poseidon and has lost his followers; moreover at home his affairs are such that his property is being wasted by suitors and plots laid against his son; [and in the action proper] he comes home in dire distress and after disclosing himself makes an attack and destroys his enemies without being killed himself. This is what is proper to the action; the rest of the poem is episodes.

3. *Complication and dénouement* (desis *and* lusis)

Part of every tragedy is the complication, part the dénouement: 18 the preliminaries and often some of the action proper are the complication, the rest the dénouement. By 'complication' I mean the section from the beginning to the last point before he begins to change to good or bad fortune, by 'dénouement' the part from the beginning of the change to the end; for example, in Theodectes' *Lynceus* the complication is made up of the preliminaries, the kidnapping of the child and their being found out, the dénouement is everything from the capital charge to the end.

4. *The species of tragedy*

Tragedy has four species, the complicated, whose entire nature depends on *peripeteia* and recognition, the tragedy of *pathos*, for example those about Aias and Ixion, the tragedy of character, for example the *Phthiotides* and the *Peleus*, while the fourth is 1456ᵃ spectacle, like the *Phorcides* and *Prometheus* and any set in hell.

Preferably, of course, one should try to have all four, but if not, to have the most important and as many as may be, especially given the way people criticize poets nowadays; for since there have been poets good in each kind, they demand that a poet should all by himself surpass the peculiar excellence of each of them. It is fair too to say that tragedies are the same or different principally on the basis of their plots, that is, when they have the same complication and dénouement. Many can manage the first but not the second, but one should always be master of both.

5. *The selection of tragic material*

One ought to remember what I have often said and not make an epic body of material into a tragedy (by 'epic' I mean one containing many stories), as if, for instance, one were to compose a play on the whole story of the *Iliad*. For in epic because of its length the parts can have a size that suits them, whereas in plays things turn out quite contrary to what one expected. We can find a proof of this in the poets who have dealt with the whole of the sack of Troy and not with a part of it as Euripides did, or with the story of Niobe and not in the way Aeschylus did; such poets are either hissed off the stage or do badly in the contest—even Agathon was hissed off just for this reason.

6. *The element of surprise*

In *peripeteiai* and also in simple plots poets aim at the effects they want by means of surprise, as surprise is tragic and satisfies our human feeling. This happens when a clever scoundrel is deceived, like Sisyphus, and a courageous wrongdoer worsted. For this is not only surprising but likely in the way described by Agathon, when he said it is likely that many things should happen contrary to likelihood.

7. *The treatment of the chorus*

One should regard the chorus too as one of the actors, and as a part of the whole and taking part in the action; that is, one should follow Sophocles' practice rather than Euripides'. In poets apart from these,* the songs have no more to do with the plot than with some quite other tragedy; this is why they [nowadays] sing interpolated songs (the first who began this practice was Agathon). But it is absurd, for there is no difference between singing interpolated songs and transferring a speech or a whole episode from one play to another.

SECTION C. WITH RESPECT TO THE *MIMĒSIS* OF INTELLECT

As I have dealt with the other qualitative elements,* I now have to talk about the representation of intellect and about verbal expression. The representation of intellect we may take to be covered by the *Rhetoric*; for it does belong rather to that inquiry. What is involved in the representation of intellect is every effect to be produced by speech. Its sections are proof and disproof, rousing emotion (pity, fear, anger, and so on), making a thing look important or unimportant.* Clearly in the plot too one ought to proceed from just these same main heads, when one needs to produce an effect of pity or fear, likelihood or importance. There is some difference, though; in the action these should be obvious without one's being told, whereas the other effects should be produced in words by the person using them and should result from his words, as the speaker would be quite unnecessary if the desired result were obvious without his saying anything.

19

1456^b

SECTION D. WITH RESPECT TO VERBAL EXPRESSION

1. *Exclusion of subjects that fall under delivery*

So far as verbal expression goes, one branch of inquiry is that into the forms of speech. Knowledge of this really falls under the study of delivery and is the province of the expert in that subject. I mean such questions as 'What is a command, a wish, a statement, a threat, a question, an answer?' and so on. A poet's knowledge or ignorance in this sphere does not leave him open to any critical censure worth bothering about. For anyone would think pretty trivial the fault censured by Protagoras, when he says: 'Homer thinks he is beginning with a prayer and in fact uses a command, when he says, "Sing of the wrath, goddess", since to tell somebody to do something or not is a command.' So let us leave that alone, since it belongs to another field and not to poetry.

2. *The grammatical basis of the discussion*

20 Verbal expression as a whole has the following parts: element, syllable, linking word, articulatory word, noun, verb, termination, statement.

An element is an indivisible sound, not any sound, but that capable of producing intelligible utterance; for some animals produce indivisible sounds, which I do not, however, call elements. This class has three subdivisions, sounded, half-sounded, and soundless.* A sounded element is that which has an audible sound without any contact occurring. A half-sounded element is one that produces an audible sound when contact does occur: such are *s* and *r*. A soundless element is one where contact occurs without the element itself having any audible sound, though it is audible when combined with elements that have audible sound: such are *g* and *d*. The elements in these three classes can be further classified, according to the shape of the mouth, the place of contact, rough or smooth breathing, length or shortness of quantity, and accent, acute, grave, or intermediate. One can investigate the subject further in works on metric.

A syllable is a composite non-significant sound made up of a voiceless element and one with voice: *gr*, for example, is a syllable by itself without *a*, and also if *a* is added to make *gra*. But the investigation of this too is a matter of metric.

1457ᵃ A linking word is (*a*) a non-significant sound which neither prevents nor produces the formation from a number of sounds of one significant utterance; it ought not to stand alone at the beginning of a statement: examples are *men*, *toi*, *dē*, *de* [the linking particles]; (*b*) a non-significant sound that naturally produces from a plurality of sounds that nevertheless signify one thing a single significant utterance: examples are *amphi*, *peri*, and the rest [of the prepositions].

An articulatory word (*arthron*) is a non-significant sound that indicates the beginning or end or dividing point of a statement; it is naturally put at either end (?) of a statement or in the middle.

A noun is a composite significant sound with no temporality, and made up of parts not in themselves significant. For in compound words we do not take the parts to be significant in themselves; in *Theodorus*, for example, the *dōron* has no significance.

A verb is a composite significant sound with temporality, and, like a noun, is made up of parts not in themselves significant; by 'with temporality' I mean that, while 'man' and 'white' do not signify when, 'walks' and 'walked' do signify present and past time respectively.

Termination is the part of a noun or verb that signifies case and number and also the part concerned with delivery, for example, question and command: 'Did he walk?' and 'Walk' show terminations of the verb under the sections of this class.

A statement is a composite significant sound whose separate parts are themselves significant; I give this definition because not every statement is made up of nouns and verbs—the definition of man, for instance; one can, that is, have a statement with no verb, but it will always have a significant part. A statement is one statement in two senses: (*a*) as signifying one thing, (*b*) by being composed of a plurality of statements: the *Iliad*, for example, is one as being composite, and the definition of man as signifying one thing.

3. *Different ways of classifying nouns**

The species of nouns are: (*a*) simple: by this I mean 'not 21 composed of significant parts', for example, 'earth'; (*b*) double: this has two varieties: (i) composed of a significant element and a non-significant element [e.g. prepositional compounds]; one must qualify this by saying that they are not significant and non-significant in the word; (ii) composed of significant elements; (*c*) possible species are also triple, quadruple, and indeed multiple, like most aggrandized words, 'Hermocaicoxanthus'. . . 1457^{b}

Nouns may also be divided into standard terms, dialect terms, metaphorical terms, decorative terms,* neologisms, lengthened words, shortened words, altered words.

By 'standard term' I mean that used by any society.

By 'dialect term' I mean one used by another people. The same word can obviously be both a standard term and a dialect term, though not in the same society: *sigunon* is a standard term in Cyprus, a dialect term in Athens.

A 'metaphorical term' involves the transferred use of a term that properly belongs to something else; the transference can be from genus to species, from species to genus, from species to species, or analogical. By 'from genus to species' I mean, for example, 'Here my ship is still',* as lying at anchor is a species of being still. By 'from species to genus', 'Odysseus conferred ten thousand benefits',* as 'ten thousand' is a specific example of plurality and he uses this instead of 'many'. By 'species to species', 'drawing the life with the bronze' and 'cutting off [the water] with the unwearying bronze';* in these examples 'drawing' is used for 'cutting off' and 'cutting off' for 'drawing', and both are species of the genus 'removing'. By 'analogical' I mean where the second term is related to the first as the fourth is to the third; for then the poet will use the fourth to mean the second and vice versa. And sometimes they add the term relative to the one replaced: I mean, for example, the cup is related to Dionysus as the shield is to Ares; so the poet will call the cup 'Dionysus' shield' and the shield 'Ares' cup';* again old age is to life what evening is to day, and so he will call evening 'the old age of the day' or use Empedocles' phrase, and call old age 'the evening of life' or 'the sunset of life'.* Sometimes one of the four related terms has no word to express it, but it can be expressed through a comparison; for example, scattering seed is called 'sowing', but there is no term for the scattering of light by the sun; but as this is related to the sun as sowing is to the scatterer of seed, we have the expression 'sowing the god-created flame'.* There is yet another form of analogical metaphor: this is the use of the transferred term coupled with the denial of one of its implications, for example, calling the shield 'the wineless cup' instead of 'Ares' cup'.

Neologisms are terms not in use at all, but invented by the poet himself; some are thought to be of this kind, for example, *ernuges* for 'horns' and *arētēr** for 'priest.'

1458ᵃ   A 'lengthened word'* is one using a longer vowel than is usual,

or an extra syllable: an example of the former is *polēos* for *polēōs*,
and of the second *Pēlēïadō* for *Pēleidou*.

A 'shortened word' is one where something is removed from it,
for example, *krī* for *krithē*, *dō* for *dōma*, and *ops* for *opsis*. . .

An 'altered word' is one where part of the ordinary term is left,
and something made up is added, like *dexiteron* for *dexion*. . .*

4. *Excellence in poetic style*

[In poetry] verbal expression is good if it is clear without being   22
mean. The clearest is of course that made up of standard words,
but it is mean: an example is the poetry of Cleophon and
Sthenelus. The style that uses strange expressions is solemn and
out of the ordinary; by 'strange expressions' I mean dialect terms,
metaphor, lengthening, and everything over and above standard
words. But if anyone made an entire poem like this, it would
be either a riddle or gibberish, a riddle if it were entirely
metaphorical, gibberish if all composed of dialect terms. For it is
the nature of a riddle that one states facts by linking impossibilities
together (of course, one cannot do this by putting the actual
words for things together, but one can if one uses metaphor), for
example 'I saw a man welding bronze on a man with fire' and so
on. And a poem wholly made up of dialect terms is gibberish. So
there ought to be a sort of admixture of these, as the one element
will prevent the style from being ordinary and mean, that is,
dialect, metaphor, decorative terms, and the other species I
mentioned, while standard terms will make it clear.

Quite a large contribution to a style both clear and out of the   1458ᵇ
ordinary is made by lengthenings, shortenings, and alterations of
words. For because it is other than standard, being unusual, it
will produce an effect of being out of the ordinary; at the same
time, it will be clear because of its element of the usual. So there
is something incorrect in the censure of those who blame this
sort of style and mock at Homer, in the way the elder Euclides
did, when he said it was easy to be a poet if one were allowed to
lengthen things as much as one liked. . .* Of course it is absurd
to be found obviously using this sort of thing; but all the kinds
demand a due measure, as one could also use metaphors and
dialect words and so on in an inappropriate and deliberately

ridiculous way and produce the same result. If one wants to see how important it is to use them suitably one should take epic verses and put ordinary words into them. In all cases, dialect, metaphor, and so on, if one substituted the standard word, one would easily see the truth of what I am saying. For example, Aeschylus and Euripides produced the same iambic line, with the change of a single word, as Euripides put a dialect term for the standard word, and so produced a beautiful line instead of an unimpressive one; for Aeschylus in his *Philoctetes* said 'The canker that eats the flesh of my foot', while Euripides substituted *thoinātai* for [the standard verb] *esthiei*. Again, take the line 'being little (*oligos*) and no worth (*outidanos*) and hideous (*aeikēs*)' and substitute the standard words *mikros*, *asthenikos*, *aeidēs*;* and for 'putting down a poor (*aeikelion*) chair and little (*oligēn*) table' put *mochthēron* (poor) and *mikran* (little);* and for *ēïones boöösin* ('the shores shout')* put *ēïones krazousin*.

1459ᵃ Ariphrades mocked the tragedians as well for using expressions that nobody would use in conversation*. . . Wrongly, for all such expressions, because not standard, produce a stylistic effect of being out of the ordinary; but Ariphrades did not know that.

It is extremely important to use in the proper place each of the kinds I have mentioned, but by far the most important is to be good at metaphor. For this is the only one that cannot be learnt from anyone else, and it is a sign of natural genius, as to be good at metaphor is to perceive resemblances. Of nouns, compounds best suit dithyrambs, dialect words hexameter verse, and metaphors iambic verse.* Though in hexameters all the kinds are useful, in iambics, because they most closely represent actual speech, the most suitable are those that one would also use in prose speeches, that is, standard words, metaphors, and decorative terms.

So much for tragedy and *mimēsis* via action.

Chapter IV

Epic

Section A. The Similarities Between Epic and Tragedy

1. *The need for unity*

Now for the narrative art that uses verse as its medium of *mimēsis*. 23
Clearly one should compose the plots here to be dramatic, just as
in the case of tragedies, that is, about one whole or complete
action with a beginning, middle parts,* and end, so that it
produces its proper pleasure like a single whole living creature.
Its plots should not be like histories; for in histories it is necessary
to give a report of a single period, not of a unified action, that is,
one must say whatever was the case in that period about one man
or more; and each of these things may have a quite casual
interrelation. For just as, if one thinks of the same time, we have
the battle of Salamis and the battle of Himera against the
Carthaginians not directed to achieve any identical purpose, so in
consecutive times one thing sometimes happens after another
without any common purpose being achieved by them. Most epic
poets do make plots like histories. So in this respect too Homer is
marvellous in the way already described, in that he did not
undertake to make a whole poem of the war either,* even though
it had a beginning and an end. For the plot would have been too
large and not easy to see as a whole, or if it had been kept to a
moderate length it would have been tangled because of the
variety of events. As it is he takes one part and uses many others
as episodes, for example, the catalogue of the ships and the other
episodes with which he breaks the uniformity of his poem. But
the rest make a poem about one man or one period of time, like
the poet of the *Cypria* or the *Little Iliad*. That is why the *Iliad* and 1459b
Odyssey have matter only for one tragedy or only for two, whereas
there is matter for many in the *Cypria*, and in the *Little Iliad* for
more than eight, for example, *The Adjudgement of the Arms*,
Philoctetes, *Neoptolemus*, *Eurypylus*, *Odysseus as a Beggar*, *The
Laconian Women*, *The Sack of Troy*, *The Departure*, plus the *Sinon*
and the *Trojan Women*.

2. *The species of epic*

24   Moreover, epic must have the same species as tragedy,* that is, must be simple or complex, a story of character or one of *pathos*. ⟦And the elements are the same except for music and spectacle.⟧ And it needs *peripeteiai* and recognitions and *pathē*. ⟦Moreover its *mimēsis* of intellect and its verbal expression should be good.⟧ All of these Homer was the first to use and his use of them is exemplary. For in the case of each of the poems, the composition of the *Iliad* is simple and full of *pathos*, that of the *Odyssey* complex, as there are recognitions throughout, and full of character. ⟦And in addition he is pre-eminent in his verbal expression and *mimēsis* of intellect.⟧*

SECTION B. THE DIFFERENCES BETWEEN EPIC AND TRAGEDY

Epic differs from tragedy in the length of its plot and in its metre.

1. *Length*

The above mentioned limit of length is an adequate guide:* that is, one should be able to get a synoptic view of the beginning and the end. This will be the case if the poems are shorter than those of the ancients,* and about as long as the number of tragedies offered at one sitting.

Epic has a peculiar characteristic in that its size can be considerably further extended; for though in tragedy it is impossible to represent many parts as at the moment of their occurrence, since one can only represent the part on the stage and involving the actors, in epic, because it is narrative, one can tell of many things as at the moment of their accomplishment, and these if they are relevant make the poem more impressive. So it has this advantage in the direction of grandeur and variety for the hearer and in being constructed with dissimilar episodes. For it is similarity and the satiety it soon produces that make tragedies fail.

2. *Metre*

The heroic verse was found suitable from experience. For if anyone were to make a narrative *mimēsis* in any other metre or in

many metres, it would be obviously unsuitable, as the heroic
metre is the steadiest and most weighty of all (which is why it is
most ready to admit dialect terms and metaphors); for the
narrative *mimēsis* has itself a sort of abundance in comparison
with the others. The iambic trimeter and trochaic tetrameter are
metres of movement, one of the dance, the other of action. It   1460ª
would be even stranger if one mixed them like Chaeremon. That
is why no one has composed a long composition except in heroic
verse; instead, nature herself teaches people to choose the metre
appropriate to the composition in the way I said.

SECTION C. THE SPECIAL MERITS OF HOMER

Homer especially deserves praise as the only epic poet to realize
what the epic poet should do in his own person, that is, say as
little as possible, since it is not in virtue of speaking in his own
person that he is a maker of *mimēsis*. Other poets are personally
engaged throughout, and only rarely use *mimēsis*; but Homer
after a brief preface at once brings on a man or woman or other
characterized person, none of them characterless, but all full of
character.*

Though one ought of course to aim at surprise in tragedy too,
epic is more tolerant of the prime source of surprise, the
irrational, because one is not looking at the person doing the
action. For the account of the pursuit of Hector would seem
ludicrous on the stage, with the Greeks standing still and not
pursuing him, and Achilles refusing their help; but in epic one
does not notice it. And surprise gives pleasure, as we can see
from the fact that we all make additions when telling a story, and
take it that we are giving pleasure. Now it was Homer who taught
other poets the proper way to tell lies, that is, by using
paralogism. For people think that if, whenever one thing is true
or happens, another thing is true or happens, then if the second
is true, the first is true or happens; but this is not so. That is why,
if the first is false, but if it were true something else must be true
or happen, one should add the second; for because we know that
the second is true, our soul falsely infers that the first is also true.
The thing in the Bath scene* is an example of this.

One ought to prefer likely impossibilities to unconvincing possibilities and not compose one's argument of irrational parts. Preferably there should be no irrationality at all, and if there is it should be outside the plot; the *Oedipus*, for example, has this sort of irrationality* in his not knowing how Laius died. It should not be inside the plot like the messengers from the Pythian games in the *Electra* or the man who went speechless from Tegea to Mysia in the *Mysians*. So it is absurd to say that otherwise the plot would have been ruined, as one should not compose them to be like this in the first place. If one does put in an irrationality and it is apparent that it could be dealt with more rationally, it is absurd as well. For it is clear that even the irrationalities in the *Odyssey* 1460ᵇ about his being put ashore on Ithaca would have been intolerable if produced by a bad poet; but as it is Homer completely disguises the flavour of absurdity by his other excellences. It is in the parts that involve no action and no *mimēsis* of character or intellect that one should be most elaborate in verbal expression; when character and intellect are being represented too brilliant a style often conceals them.

SECTION D. CRITICISMS OF HOMER AND HOW TO ANSWER THEM*

1. *The bases of the answers*

25 The next subject is questions about what is said and the answers to them. How many species do they fall under and what are the species? If we look at the matter as follows the answer will be clear.

(*a*) Since the poet produces *mimēsis*, just like a painter or other visual artist, the object of his *mimēsis* must always be one of three things, that is, what was or is, what is commonly said and thought to be the case, and what should be the case.

(*b*) The narration of these involves verbal expression, including the use of dialect terms and metaphor and many abnormal elements of expression, as these are licences we allow to poets.

(*c*) Further, correctness in poetry is not the same thing as correctness in morals, nor yet is it the same as correctness in any other art. Faults that are relevant to the art of poetry itself are of two kinds, one involving its essential nature, and the other incidental. If the poet is incapable of representing what he set out to represent, this is an error involving the essential nature of poetry. If the error arises through the poet's setting out to represent something incorrectly, for example, representing a horse with both its right legs forward, and this is the reason why we find in the poem either a mistake with reference to any particular art (for example, medicine or some other art) or, more generally, any other impossibility, this does not involve the essential nature of poetry.

So one should use these principles in examining and answering the questions raised.

2. *The twelve sorts of answer*

(*a*) ANSWERS DERIVED FROM BASIS (*c*)

Let us take first of all the errors that involve the art of poetry itself:

1. If the poem contains [,for instance,] an impossibility,* that is a fault; but it is all right if the poem thereby achieves what it aims at (what it aims at I have already discussed), that is, if in this way the surprise produced either by that particular passage or by another is more striking. An example is the pursuit of Hector. However, if it was possible for the aim to be attained either more or no less without any error in the art [essentially] concerned, it is not all right; for, if possible, there should be no error at all.

2. Secondarily, one should consider whether the error involves the essential nature of poetry or something incidental, as it is a lesser fault not to know that a hind has no antlers than to paint it in a way that is not adequate to *mimēsis*.

(*b*) ANSWERS DERIVED FROM BASIS (*a*)*

3. In answer to the charge of not being true, one can say, 'But perhaps it is as it should be': Sophocles, for example, said that he represented people as they should be, and Euripides as they are; this is the answer.

4. If it is neither true nor as it should be, one can reply, 'But it is what people say'. An example of this is the treatment of the gods: for this, perhaps, is neither a better thing to say nor a true

1461ª one, but instead the facts are perhaps as Xenophanes saw them; but anyhow that is what people say.

5. Again, if the reply that it is better is not open, the answer can be, 'It used to be so'; an example here is the remark about weapons, 'Their spears stood upright on their butt-ends'; that was the custom then, as it still is among the Illyrians.

6. Then there is the question whether someone's statement or action is good or not. Here one should not look just at what is said or done in considering whether it is good or bad, but should also take into account the person who says or does it, asking to whom he said or did it, when, with what, and for what motive. Was it, for instance, to produce a greater good or avert a greater evil?

(c) ANSWERS DERIVED FROM BASIS (b)*

Some objections should be answered by considering the expressions used:

7. A dialect word may be involved: for example, in 'First it attacked the mules', it may be that *ourēas* means 'sentinels', not 'mules'; and in the case of Dolon 'whose form (*eidos*) was not good', he means he had an ugly face, not a distorted body, since the Cretans use *eueidēs* to mean 'having a handsome face'; again, in 'make the mixture *zōroteron*', this word means, not 'stronger' with the implication that they were wine-bibbers, but 'faster'.

8. Some expressions are metaphorical. For example, in 'The rest of gods and men slept the night long', where he says at the same time 'when he looked toward the plain of Troy, he marvelled at the din of flutes and pipes', 'all' is used metaphorically for 'many', as totality is a species of plurality. Similarly 'The pole star alone has no contact with the Ocean' is also metaphorical; for 'alone' is put for 'best known'.

9. The answer may be to change the accents and breathing: such a solution was given by Hippias of Thasos in suggesting the imperatival infinitive *didómen* for *dídomen* in 'and *we grant* him the achievement of glory', and the negative *ou* for the partitive *hou* in '*part of it* is rotted by the rain'.

10. Some may be answered by a change of punctuation, for example, Empedocles 'at once things became mortal which had been used to be immortal, and things unmixed formerly mixed'.

11. Another reply is that the expression is ambiguous, for example, in 'more of the night was past than two thirds; the third was left'; here *pleō*, 'more', is ambiguous [and may mean 'full'].

12. Some things are a matter of usage. We call wine and water 'wine', and by analogy with this Homer says 'greaves of new-forged tin'. And we call iron-workers 'bronze-smiths', and on the analogy of this Ganymede is said to pour wine for Zeus, though gods do not drink wine; this could also be explained as an analogical metaphor.

3. *Summary*

In fact, whenever a word is thought to signify something involving a contradiction, we ought to consider how many meanings the word might have in the phrase in question; for example, in 'by it the bronze spear was stayed', in how many senses is it possible to take 'was stayed by it', and is it by taking it in this sense or in that sense that one would be going most contrary to the practice described by Glaucon, when he said that 1461^{b} some people make irrational assumptions about a thing and, having passed this vote of censure all by themselves, make an inference from it and blame the poet as if he had said what they think he did, if what he says contradicts what they imagine. This has happened in the argument about Icarius. They think he was a Spartan and therefore say it is absurd that Telemachus did not meet him when he went to Sparta. But the facts may be as stated by the Cephallenians; they say that Odysseus took his wife from among them and that his father-in-law was Icadius, not Icarius; so probably the criticism rests on a mistake.

Generally speaking, one should answer a charge that a thing is impossible by a reference to the demands of poetry (1), or to the fact that it is better so (3) or commonly thought to be so (4). By 'the demands of poetry' I mean that a convincing impossibility is preferable to something unconvincing, however possible; again it is perhaps impossible for people to be as beautiful as Zeuxis painted them, but it is better so, as the ideal should surpass reality.

A charge of irrationality should be dealt with by reference to what is commonly said (4). That is one answer. Another is that on some occasions it is not irrational, as it is likely that things happen even contrary to likelihood.

A charge of self-contradiction one should consider on the same basis as refutations in argument, asking, that is, whether it is itself the same, and related to the same thing, and used in the same sense, so that it is the poet himself who is contradicting either what he himself says or what a sensible man assumes.

A charge of irrationality or of representing wickedness is justified if there is no necessity for the irrationality or moral wickedness and no use is made of it. An example of the former is Euripides' treatment of Aegeus [in the *Medea*], of the latter his treatment of Menelaus in the *Orestes*.

Well then, people produce censures under five heads, claiming that things are impossible, irrational, morally dangerous, self-contradictory, or contrary to technical correctness.* The answers to them are on the basis of the points enumerated: they are twelve in number.

SECTION E. EPIC AND TRAGEDY

26 Which is better, the epic or the tragic *mimēsis*? This is a question one might raise.

1. *The statement of the opponents of tragedy**

Now if whichever is less vulgar is superior, and the less vulgar in any area is what is directed towards a superior audience, it is quite obvious that the one prepared to represent just anything is vulgar. For on the assumption that the audience will not grasp what is meant unless the performer underlines it, they go in for a variety of movements, like bad flute-players rolling about if they have to represent a discus, or dragging the chorus-leader up and down when they play Scylla. Now this is what tragedy is like, resembling in this the later actors, as their predecessors thought of them. For Mynniscus called Callippides an ape, meaning that 1462ª he went too far, and people thought the same about Pindarus; their relation to their own predecessors is the same as that of tragedy as a whole to epic. Epic, they say, is directed to a cultivated audience which does not need gesture, tragedy to a low-class one; so if it is vulgar, it must obviously be worse.

2. *The arguments for tragedy*

We may say first and foremost that this charge is directed against
the art of the performer, not that of the poet, since one can be
over-elaborate and over-emphatic in reciting epic as well, like
Sosistratus, and in a singing contest, like Mnasitheus of Opus.
Moreover not all movement is disreputable, given that not all
dancing is disreputable either, but only the movement of low-
class people; this censure was made against Callippides and
others, on the ground that they represent women of no repute.
Again, tragedy produces its effect even without movement, just as
epic does; for a reading makes its nature quite clear. So if it is
superior in all other respects, this charge will not necessarily lie.

Again, tragedy has everything that epic has (it can even use its
metre), and moreover has a considerable addition in the music
and the spectacle, which produce pleasure in a most vividly
perceptible way.

Moreover, it has vividness when read as well as when
performed.

Again, it takes less space to attain the end of its *mimēsis*; this is   1462^b
an advantage because what comes thick and fast gives more
pleasure than something diluted by a large admixture of time—
think, for instance, of the effect if someone put Sophocles'
Oedipus into as many lines as the *Iliad*.

Again, the *mimēsis* of the epic poets is less unified, as we can
see from the fact that any epic *mimēsis* provides matter for several
tragedies. The result of this is that if they do make a single plot, it
either appears curtailed, when it is only briefly indicated, or
follows the lead of its lengthy metre and becomes dilute; I mean
here the poem made up of several actions, in the way in which the
Iliad has many such parts and also the *Odyssey*, and these parts
have extension in themselves (and yet these two poems are as
admirably composed as can be and are, so far as possible, the
mimēsis of a single action).

If tragedy is superior in all these respects and also in artistic
effectiveness (for these arts should produce not just any
pleasure, but the one we have discussed), it would obviously be
superior to epic as it is more successful in attaining what it aims
at.

So much for tragedy and epic, their nature, the number and differences of their qualitative elements and quantitative parts, the reasons for success and failure in them, and criticisms of them and how to answer them.

HORACE: *A LETTER TO AUGUSTUS*

You have much important business to conduct with no one to help you, defending Italy with arms, adorning her with virtue, chastening her with laws; and I should thwart the public interest, Caesar, if I occupied your time with a lengthy conversation. Romulus and father Liber,* Castor and Pollux, were all received into the temples of the gods after a life of tremendous deeds; but while they looked after the world and the human race, settling bitter wars, allotting land, founding cities, they lamented that their services were not matched by the popularity for which they hoped. The hero who crushed the dread Hydra, and quelled   10 familiar monsters in labours assigned by fate, likewise found that death is the only cure for unpopularity. The man who is felt by inferior talents to weigh on them arouses envy by his brilliance; once he is eclipsed, he will be loved. Yet it is while you are still with us that we bestow on you honours that come before the usual time; we set up altars that bind oaths by your divinity, and acknowledge that nothing comparable has arisen before or will arise again.

All the same, this people of yours, wise and correct in preferring you to all rulers, Roman or Greek, do not apply similar   20 standards to other things: they scorn and hate everything that is not removed from the world and safely dead. They so favour the ancients that they have a tradition that the Muses spoke, on the Alban Hill,* the Tables* forbidding misdoing that the decemvirs sanctioned, the royal treaties made on equal terms with Gabii and the unyielding Sabines, the books of the Pontiffs, and the aged volumes of the prophets. The oldest writings of the Greeks are the best; and if one weighs Roman writers in the same scale   30 there is not much to say. On that principle,* an olive could be argued to have no stone, a nut no shell. We have reached the peak: therefore we paint and play the lyre and wrestle better than the well-oiled Achaeans.*

But if passage of time improves poems as it does wine, I have a question: how many years will give value to a book? Should a writer dead for a hundred years be registered under the perfect old or the worthless new? Let us have a limit, to stop disputes:

40 'He is old and good who completes a century.' What then of
someone who died a month or a year later—where will *he* come?
Among the old poets, or those to be rejected alike by the present
and the future? 'Of course it will be right to place him among the
ancients, if he is a short month, or even a whole year, more
recent.' I follow up this concession, and gradually pluck the hairs
from the horse's tail, taking away one and then another until,
baffled by the Fallacy of the Diminishing Heap,* the searcher of
annals, the man who judges quality by age, the admirer of
nothing that Death has not sanctified, is brought to his knees.

50 Ennius is—so the critics say—wise, strong, a second Homer,
and doesn't much care how the expectations aroused by his
Pythagorean dreams turn out.* Naevius is on our shelves and in
our minds, almost undated. Such is the sanctity of every old
poem. When dispute arises who excels whom, Pacuvius carries
off.the reputation of being an erudite oldster, Accius a sublime
one. The Roman dress of Afranius' comedies, they say, fitted
Menander's back. Plautus hurries along after the manner of the
Sicilian Epicharmus. Caecilius excels in dignity, Terence in
60 technique. These are the poets Rome at the height of its power
learns by heart, these it packs the narrow theatre to see. These
are the poets it reckons up between the writer Livius (Andronicus)
and our own day.

Sometimes the majority gets things right, sometimes it gets
them wrong. If it admires and praises the old poets without
allowing anything to excel or compare with them, it is mistaken.
If it believes that they wrote some things over-archaically, a
certain amount harshly, a great deal casually—then it has taste: it
agrees with me—and Jupiter favours its judgement. I don't
inveigh against Livius' poems or suppose that they should be
70 consigned to destruction (I remember Orbilius beating them into
me when I was a boy). But I'm astonished they should be thought
polished, beautiful and nearly perfect. Perhaps a fine word
gleams out in them, or one or two verses more elegant than the
rest; but it's wrong that this should support and sell the whole
volume. I get annoyed to hear something criticized, not for being
grossly and disagreeably put together, but for being recent: to see
honour and glory sought for the ancients, not merely allowance
made. Should I dare to express a doubt whether it's right for the

comedies of Atta to walk the stage amidst the flowers and the 80
saffron, pretty well all respectable citizens shout that decency has
died, because I venture to find fault with pieces that grave
Aesopus and skilful Roscius played. Perhaps they think nothing
good unless *they* liked it; or perhaps they regard it as
embarrassing to follow the views of the young, and at their age to
acknowledge that what they learned before their beards grew
should be consigned to oblivion. Indeed, the encomiast of
Numa's Saliar Hymn,* who understands it no more than I,
though he would like to be thought the only person who follows
it—such a man is not really keen on the buried geniuses he
applauds, but merely likes attacking *our* handiwork. He is jealous;
he hates us and our products.

But if the Greeks had hated novelty as much as we, what 90
would exist now to be ranked as old? What would the public have
to read and thumb, man by man? When Greece first laid aside
her wars* and began to be frivolous, slipping into vice as fortune
smiled, she burned with favour now for athletes, now for horses,
loved craftsmen in marble or ivory or bronze, gazed long and
thoughtfully at paintings, enthused over flute-players and tragic
actors. Like a little girl playing around her nurse's feet, she soon 100
had had enough, and abandoned what she had sought so
greedily. What finds favour or disfavour that is not subject to
change? All this was the result of benign peace and favouring
winds.

At Rome it was for long usual, and agreeable, to get up early,
open the house up, tell one's client his rights, lend (with due
security) to respectable debtors, pass on to the young what one
heard from the old about the increasing of one's property and the
avoidance of damaging self-indulgence. Now the fickle people
has changed: it has only one enthusiasm to excite it—writing.
Boys and dignified fathers alike dine with leaves in their hair, and 110
dictate poetry. I swear I write no verse, but I'm a bigger liar than
a Parthian: I get up before dawn, to call for pen, paper, desk.

One who knows nothing about ships hesitates to steer them.
You don't venture to prescribe southernwood* to the sick unless
you've been to medical school—doctors look after their own
profession. Craftsmen ply crafts. But we all write poetry, taught
and untaught alike.

120 This is an aberration, a mild form of madness, but it has many advantages. Look at it this way. A poet's mentality will not readily prove avaricious. He likes verses—that's his one hobby. He smiles at loss, escaped slaves, fires. He won't plot frauds against his partner or his ward. He lives on pulse and black bread. He's an inefficient and lazy soldier—but he has his uses to the city, if you will grant that great affairs are helped by small. It is the poet who gives shape to the pliant, stuttering lips of the young boy; even at this early stage, he is diverting his ears from obscenity: soon he is forming his character with friendly precept, suppressing

130 cruelty and envy and anger. He relates good deeds, equips youth with familiar instances, consoles the poor and the sick. Where would chaste boys and virgin girls learn their prayers if the muse had not provided us with poets? The choir asks for help from the gods, feels the divine presence: winningly, with the prayers it is taught, it implores rain from heaven, turns away plagues, wards off fearful dangers, wins peace and a fruitful year. It is poetry that placates the gods of heaven and underworld.

Primitive farmers, brave men whom a little made rich, used to appease Earth with a pig, Silvanus with milk, their Genius* (who knows how short life is) with flowers and wine at feast-time,

140 when they had brought the crops in and were relaxing body and mind (it's the prospect of an end that makes the mind endure) in company with their loyal wives and the sons who shared their labours. In this manner, the licentious Fescennines* were discovered, that made verse dialogues the vehicle for rustic insult; this freedom, handed down through the years, gave agreeable sport, until the joking became savage, turned to open madness, and raced, menacing and unpunished, through decent

150 households. Those who were attacked had something to cry about—a tooth that drew blood. But even those unaffected began to worry about the situation in general. In fact a law and penalties were provided, forbidding anyone to be savaged in a malicious poem. Men were given the cudgel to fear, and so they changed their ways, and returned to innocent words and entertainment.

Greece, now captive, took captive its wild conqueror, and introduced the arts to rural Latium. The unprepossessing Saturnian* rhythm went out, and elegance drove off venom. All

the same, traces of the country long remained, and they are there 160
today. It was late in the day that the Roman applied his
intelligence to Greek literature; for it was in the lull after the
Punic Wars* that he began to inquire what use there might be in
Sophocles and Thespis and Aeschylus. He had a go himself too,
seeing whether he could make a decent translation, and wasn't
displeased with the result, thanks to a natural loftiness and bite.
The spirit was tragic enough, the innovations daring and
felicitous; but in his ignorance he feared erasure, and thought it
shameful.

Comedy is thought to involve less sweat, seeing that it takes its
material from daily life. But it is more burdensome in that it 170
receives less indulgence. See how badly Plautus maintains the
character of a youth in love, an economical father, a treacherous
pimp—what a Dossennus* he is with his greedy parasites,
shuffling in his loose slippers across the stage. The author only
wants money for his pocket—after that he doesn't care if the play
flops or keeps its footing.

If it was Fame that carried the playwright to the stage in her
airy chariot, he is deflated by an indifferent audience, encouraged
by an attentive one. So small and light a thing is it that can
overthrow or refresh a mind that is athirst for praise. Goodbye to 180
the stage if a prize denied sends me home thin, a prize won
makes me fat! And often, if a poet *is* brave, he is disconcerted and
put to flight by the fact that the majority (deficient, however, in
rank and virtue), stupid, illiterate, ready to fight it out with any of
their betters who differ from them, call for bears or boxers in the
middle of the play. That's what the plebs enjoys. In fact, even the
knights* have now transferred all their pleasure from the ear to
the shifting and empty delights of the eye. The curtain is up for
four hours or more while squadrons of horse and hordes of foot 190
pour over the stage. Once-glorious kings are dragged by, hands
pinioned; chariots, carriages, wagons, ships hurry on, carrying
looted ivory and models of captured Corinth.* If Democritus
were alive he'd laugh at the way the hybrid camelopard or the
white elephant keeps the crowds riveted; he'd watch the populace
more attentively than the actual spectacle, as being far more
worthy of his gaze. As for the writers, he's imagine they were
telling their tale to a deaf ass: no voice could make itself heard 200

above the clamour emitted by our theatres. You might think it was the moaning of the Apulian forests or the Tuscan sea—such is the noise as they watch the show, the *objets d'art* and the exotic wealth: when an actor is smeared over with that, he only needs to stand on the stage and hands start to clap. 'Has he said anything yet?' 'No, nothing.' 'What's so popular, then?' 'Wool turned violet by the purple of Tarentum.'

210   You mustn't suppose that I am being sparing in praise of things that I refuse to do because others do them well; the poet who tears my heart with imaginary griefs, provokes it, soothes it, fills it with unreal fears—such a poet I regard as capable of a tight-rope act. He is like a magician, who can transport me now to Thebes, now to Athens. But please spare a modicum of attention for those who devote themselves to a reader rather than put up with the haughty scorn of a spectator: if, that is, you want to fill your library (a gift worthy of Apollo)* and spur on the poets to seek green Helicon more diligently. We poets often do 220 ourselves damage (this is to take a sickle to my own vineyard) when we give you a book despite your being worried or tired; when we get hurt if a friend ventures to find fault with a single verse; when we come back unrequested to passages we've already recited; when we lament that our labour is lost and the fine craftsmanship unnoticed; when we hope that the day will come when you're nice enough to send for us the moment you hear we're composing and say to us: 'Write—and want for nothing.'

230   All the same, it's worth finding out what sort of priests should serve virtue well-tried at home and abroad—for it's not something to be handed over to an unworthy poet. The great king Alexander gave his favour to the notorious Choerilus, who repaid the royal gifts of gold pieces in verses ill-born and inelegant. Black ink when handled leaves a disagreeable blot; similarly writers often smear disgusting poems over fine deeds. All the same, this king who so dearly bought such absurd poetry (improvident man!) made an edict that he was to be painted by 240 none but Apelles, and that only Lysippus should cast statues to represent the martial features of Alexander. He had, then, an acute taste in the visual arts—but summon it to pronounce on books and poetry, and you'd swear he was a Boeotian,* born in a gross climate.

But your judgement of your favourite poets, Virgil and Varius, has not been disgraced by them, nor the gifts which they have received from you, so much to your credit. And for portraying the character and mind of famous men, the work of the poet is as satisfactory as the representation of their features in bronze statues. I wouldn't choose these conversation pieces that creep 250 along the ground in preference to writing history, telling of the lie of lands and the course of rivers, of mountain-top citadels and foreign kingdoms, of wars won over all the world under your auspices, of Janus, guardian of Peace, shut up behind his gates, of Rome a terror to Parthia now that you are emperor—if, that is, my abilities measured up to my desires. But your greatness will not tolerate a slight poem, and I am ashamed to try a theme that my strength won't stand. Attentiveness tends to be stupid and 260 annoy the object of its attentions, particularly when it uses verse and art to commend itself. What we admire and venerate is less likely to impress itself on our memory than the risible. I* don't care for attentions that annoy me. I don't ever want to be set up in wax, my face portrayed for the worse. I don't want to be celebrated in badly-turned verse: I'd only blush when I got such a coarse gift; and along with the writer, laid out in an open book-case, I'd be removed to the quarter where they sell perfumes and scent and pepper and everything else that gets wrapped up in 270 worthless literature.

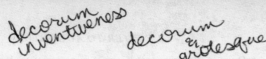

how far take

decorum inventiveness

decorum & grotesque

HORACE: *THE ART OF POETRY*

nature & nurture

untruth doesn't occur in nature?

Imagine a painter who wanted to combine a horse's neck with a human head, and then clothe a miscellaneous collection of limbs with various kinds of feathers, so that what started out at the top as a beautiful woman ended in a hideously ugly fish. If you were invited, as friends, to the private view, could you help laughing? Let me tell you, my Piso friends*, a book whose different features are made up at random like a sick man's dreams, with no unified form to have a head or a tail, is exactly like that picture.

10   'Painters and poets have always enjoyed recognized rights to venture on what they will.' Yes, we know; indeed, we ask and grant this permission turn and turn about. But it doesn't mean that fierce and gentle can be united, snakes paired with birds or lambs with tigers.

Serious and ambitious designs often have a purple patch or two sewn on to them just to make a good show at a distance—a description of a grove and altar of Diana, the meanderings of a stream running through pleasant meads, the River Rhine, the rainbow: but the trouble is, it's not the place for them.

20   Maybe you know how to do a picture of a cypress tree? What's the good of that, if the man who is paying for the picture* is a desperate ship-wrecked mariner swimming to safety? The job began as a wine-jar: the wheel runs round—why is that a tub that's coming out? In short, let it be what you will, but let it be simple and unified.

Most of us poets—father and worthy sons—are deceived by appearances of correctness. I try to be concise, but I become obscure; my aim is smoothness, but sinews and spirit fail; professions of grandeur end in bombast; the over-cautious who fear the storm creep along the ground. Similarly, the writer who

30   wants to give fantastic variety to his single theme paints a dolphin in his woods and a wild boar in his sea. If art is wanting, the flight from blame leads to faults. The poorest smith near the School of Aemilius* will reproduce nails and mimic soft hair in bronze, though he has no luck with the over-all effect of his work, because he won't know how to organize the whole. If I were

anxious to put anything together, I would as soon be that man as I would live with a mis-shapen nose when my black eyes and black hair had made me a beauty.

You writers must choose material equal to your powers. Consider long what your shoulders will bear and what they will refuse. The man who chooses his subject with full control will not be abandoned by eloquence or lucidity of arrangement. 40

As to arrangement: its excellence and charm, unless I'm very wrong, consist in saying at this moment what needs to be said at this moment, and postponing and temporarily omitting a great many things. An author who has undertaken a poem must be choosy—cling to one point and spurn another.

As to words: if you're delicate and cautious in arranging them, you will give distinction to your style if an ingenious combination makes a familiar word new. If it happens to be necessary to denote hidden mysteries by novel symbols, it will fall to you to invent terms the Cethegi in their loin-cloths* never heard—and 50 the permission will be granted if you accept it modestly—and, moreover, your new and freshly invented words will receive credit, if sparingly derived from the Greek springs. Is the Roman to give Caecilius and Plautus privileges denied to Virgil and Varius? Why am I unpopular if I can make a few acquisitions, when the tongue of Cato and Ennius so enriched their native language and produced such a crop of new names for things?

It always has been, and always will be, lawful to produce a word stamped with the current mark. As woods change in leaf as 60 the seasons slide on, and the first leaves fall, so the old generation of words dies out, and the newly born bloom and are strong like young men. We and our works are a debt owed to death. Here a land-locked sea protects fleets from the North wind—a royal achievement; here an old barren marsh where oars were plied feeds neighbouring cities and feels the weight of the plough; here again a river gives up a course that damaged the crops and learns a better way. But whatever they are, all mortal works will die; and still less can the glory and charm of words endure for a long life. Many words which have fallen will be born again, many now in 70 repute will fall if usage decrees: for in her hand is the power and the law and the canon of speech.

Histories of kings and generals, dreadful wars: it was Homer who showed in what metre these could be narrated. Lines unequally yoked in pairs* formed the setting first for lamentations, then for the expression of a vow fulfilled; though who first sent these tiny 'elegies' into the world is a grammarians' quarrel and still *sub judice*. Madness armed Archilochus with its own iambus;
80 that too was the foot that the comic sock and tragic buskin held, because it was suitable for dialogue, able to subdue the shouts of the mob, and intended by nature for a life of action. To the lyre, the Muse granted the celebration of gods and the children of gods, victorious boxers, winning race-horses, young men's love, and generous wine. If I have neither the ability nor the knowledge to keep the duly assigned functions and tones of literature, why am I hailed as a poet? Why do I prefer to be ignorant than learn, out of sheer false shame? A comic subject will not be set out in tragic verse; likewise, the Banquet of
90 Thyestes* disdains being told in poetry of the private kind, that borders on the comic stage. Everything must keep the appropriate place to which it was allotted.

Nevertheless, comedy does sometimes raise her voice, and angry Chremes* perorates with swelling eloquence. Often too Telephus and Peleus in tragedy lament in prosaic language, when they are both poor exiles and throw away their bombast and words half a yard long, if they are anxious to touch the spectator's heart with their complaint.

It is not enough for poetry to be beautiful; it must also be
100 pleasing and lead the hearer's mind wherever it will. The human face smiles in sympathy with smilers and comes to the help of those that weep. If you want me to cry, mourn first yourself; *then* your misfortunes will hurt me, Telephus and Peleus. If your words are given you ineptly, I shall fall asleep or laugh. Sad words suit a mournful countenance, threatening words an angry one; sportive words are for the playful, serious for the grave. For nature first shapes us within for any state of fortune—gives us
110 pleasure or drives us to anger or casts us down to the ground with grievous sorrow and pains us—and then expresses the emotions through the medium of the tongue. If the words are out of tune with the speaker's fortunes, the knights and infantry of Rome* will raise a cackle. It will make a lot of difference whether the

speaker is a god or a hero, an old man of ripe years or a hot youth, an influential matron or a hard-working nurse, a travelling merchant or the tiller of a green farm, a Colchian or an Assyrian, one nurtured at Thebes or at Argos.

Either follow tradition or invent a consistent story. If as a writer you are representing Achilles with all his honours, let him   120 be active, irascible, implacable, and fierce; let him say 'the laws are not for me' and set no limit to the claims that arms can make. Let Medea be proud and indomitable, Ino full of tears, Ixion treacherous, Io never at rest, Orestes full of gloom. On the other hand, if you are putting something untried on the stage and venturing to shape a new character, let it be maintained to the end as it began and be true to itself. It is hard to put generalities in an individual way: you do better to reduce the song of Troy to acts than if you were the first to bring out something unknown   130 and unsaid.* The common stock will become your private property if you don't linger on the broad and vulgar round, or anxiously render word for word, a loyal interpreter, or again, in the process of imitation, find yourself in a tight corner from which shame, or the rule of the craft, won't let you move; or, once again, if you avoid a beginning like the cyclic poet—

> Of Priam's fortune will I sing, and war
> well known to fame.

If he opens his mouth as wide as that, how *can* the promiser bring forth anything to match it? The mountains shall be in labour, and there shall be born—a silly mouse. How much better was the way   140 of that poet whose every endeavour is to the point!

> Tell me, O Muse, of him who, after Troy
> had fallen, saw the manners and the towns
> of many men.*

His plan is not to turn fire to smoke, but smoke to light, so as to relate magnificent wonders thereafter—Antiphates and the Cyclops, Scylla and Charybdis.* *He* doesn't start the Return of Diomedes from the death of Meleager, nor begin the Trojan war from the twin egg;* he is always making good speed towards the end of the story, and carries his hearer right into the thick of it as though it were already known. He leaves out anything which he

150 thinks cannot be polished up satisfactorily by treatment, and tells
his fables and mixes truth with falsehood in such a way that the
middle squares with the beginning and the end with the middle.

Let me tell you what I and the public both want, if you're
hoping for an applauding audience that will wait for the curtain
and keep its seat until the epilogue-speaker says 'Pray clap your
hands'. You must mark the manners of each time of life, and
assign the appropriate part to changing natures and ages. The
child, just able to repeat words and planting his steps on the
ground with confidence, is eager to play with his contemporaries,
160 gets in and out of a temper without much cause, and changes
hour by hour. The beardless youth, his tutor at last out of the
way, enjoys his horses and dogs and the grass of the sunny Park.
Moulded like wax into vice, he is surly to would-be advisers, slow
to provide for necessities, prodigal of money, up in the air, eager,
and quick to abandon the objects of his sudden love. Soon
interests change: the grown man's mind pursues wealth and
influential connections, is enslaved to honour, and avoids doing
anything he may soon be trying to change. Many distresses
surround the old man. He is acquisitive, and, poor man, daren't
170 put his hand on what he has laid up; he is afraid to use it. He goes
about his business timidly and coldly, procrastinating, letting
things drag on in hope, lazy yet greedy of his future; he is
awkward and grumbling, given to praising the days when he was
a boy and to criticizing and finding fault with his juniors. Years as
they come bring many blessings with them, and as they go take
many away. To save yourself giving a young man an old man's
role or a boy a grown man's, remember that your character
should always remain faithful to what is associated with his age
and suits it.

Actions may be either performed on the stage or reported
180 when performed. What comes in through the ear is less effective
in stirring the mind than what is put before our faithful eyes and
told by the spectator to himself. However, you are not to bring on
to the stage events which ought to be carried out within; you are
to remove many things from sight, and let them be related in due
course by the eloquence of an eye-witness. Don't let Medea
murder the children before the people's gaze, or wicked Atreus
cook human offal in public or Procne be metamorphosed into a

bird or Cadmus into a snake. Anything you show me like that earns my incredulity and disgust.

A play that wants to be in demand and to be revived must not 190 be shorter or longer than five acts.*

There should be no god to intervene, unless the problem merits such a champion.

No fourth character should attempt to speak.

The chorus should play an actor's part, and do a man's duty. It should not sing between the acts anything which has no relevance to or cohesion with the plot. It should side with the good and give them friendly counsel, restrain the angry, and approve those who scruple to go astray. It should praise a frugal table's fare, sound justice, law, and times of peace when the town's gates stand open. It should keep secrets entrusted to it, and beg and pray the 200 gods that Fortune may return to the wretched and abandon the proud.

The flute used not to be, as it is now, bound with copper and a rival to the trumpet. It was slight and simple, with few apertures, but serviceable to accompany and aid the chorus and to fill with its music the still not too crowded benches, where a population of no great size gathered in numbers easily counted, honest and decent and modest. But when that same population won wars and began to extend its territory, when longer walls came to embrace the cities, and people indulged themselves on holidays 210 by drinking in the daytime, and nobody blamed them, then rhythm and tunes acquired greater licence. For what taste could the uneducated show, the holiday crowd of countrymen and townsmen, honest folk and rogues, all mixed up together? This is how the musician came to add movement and elaboration to his art, and to trail his robe as he roamed the stage. This is how even the austere lyre gained a stronger voice, while lofty eloquence produced strange utterance and thought that shrewdly grasped practical needs and prophesied the future grew indistinguishable from the oracles of Delphi.

The competitor in tragic poetry, who strove for a worthless 220 goat, next showed the rustic Satyrs,* naked. Preserving his seriousness despite his keen wit, he made an attempt at a joke, because the audience, drunk and lawless at the end of the festival, had to be prevented from going away by tricks and

pleasing innovations. But the way to recommend your laughing, joking Satyrs, the way to turn seriousness to jest, is this: no god or hero you bring on the stage, if he was seen not long ago in royal gold and purple, must lower his language and move into a
230 humble cottage; nor, on the other hand, must his efforts to get off the ground lead him to try to grasp clouds and void. Tragedy does not deserve to blurt out trivial lines, but she will modestly consort a little with the forward satyrs, like a respectable lady dancing because she must on a feast day.

As a Satyr-writer, my Piso friends, I shall not limit my liking to plain and proper terms, nor yet try to be so different from the tone of tragedy that there is no difference between Davus talking or bold Pythias, when she's just tricked Simon out of a talent,* and Silenus, at once guardian and servant of the god he has
240 brought up. I shall make up my poem of known elements, so that anyone may hope to do the same, but he'll sweat and labour to no purpose when he ventures: such is the force of arrangement and combination, such the splendour that commonplace words acquire. Your woodland Fauns,* if you take my judgement, should beware of behaving as if they were born at the street corner and were creatures of the Forum—they shouldn't play the gallant in languishing verse or crack dirty and disreputable jokes; possessors of horses or ancestors or property take offence at this sort of thing and don't look kindly on work approved by the fried-
250 peas-and-nuts public, or give it the prize.

A long syllable following a short one makes an iambus. He is a quick foot; this is why he ordered iambic lines to be called trimeters, although he was giving six beats to the line, and was the same in form from first to last. Not all that long ago, wanting to fall rather more slowly and weightily upon our ears, he admitted the stately spondees to family privileges—what a comfortable, easy-going foot he is!—but without being quite so complaisant as to give up the second and fourth positions in the line. Rarely does he appear in Accius' noble trimeters, and his
260 rarity in Ennius' weighty lines as they fly out on the stage damns them with the shocking accusation of hasty and careless craftsmanship—or else sheer ignorance of the trade.*

Of course, it's not every critic that notices lines that aren't tuneful, and Roman poets have enjoyed undeserved licence. But

does that entitle *me* to make mistakes and scribble away
carelessly? Or should I rather expect everyone to see my
mistakes, and so play safe and cautious, keeping within the
bounds of what I can hope to be pardoned for? In that case, all
I've done is to avoid blame; I have not deserved praise.

Study Greek models night and day. Your ancestors praised   270
Plautus' metre and his humour. On both counts their admiration
was too indulgent, not to say childish, if it's true that you and I
know how to distinguish a witless jest from a subtle one and if
we've skill in our fingers and ears to know what sounds are
permitted.

The hitherto unknown genre of the tragic Muse is said to be
Thespis' invention; he is supposed to have carried on a cart
verses to be sung and and acted by performers whose faces were
smeared with wine-lees. After him came Aeschylus, the inventor
of the mask and splendid robe; he gave the stage a floor of
modest boards, and taught the actors to talk big and give
themselves height by their high boots. Next came Old Comedy,*   280
much praised, though its liberty degenerated into vice and
violence deserving restraint of law; the law was accepted, and the
chorus fell silent, its right of shameful insult removed.

Our poets have left nothing unattempted. Not the least part of
their glory was won by venturing to abandon the footsteps of the
Greeks and celebrate our own affairs; some produced historical
plays, some comedies in Roman dress. Latium would have been
as famous for literature as for valour and deeds of arms if the
poets had not, one and all, been put off by the labour and time of   290
polishing their work. Children of Numa,* show your disapproval
of any poem which long time and much correction have not
disciplined and smoothed ten times over, to satisfy the well-
pared nail.

Democritus thinks native talent a happier thing than poor,
miserable art, and banishes sane poets from his Helicon.* That's
why so many don't bother to cut their nails or beard, but seek
solitude and keep away from the bath. For a man is sure to win
the reward and name of poet if he never lets barber Licinus get
hold of that head that three Anticyras* won't make sound. I'm a   300
fool to purge my bile when spring comes round. I could write as
good poetry as any; but nothing is worth that price, and so I'll

play the part of the whetstone, that can sharpen the knife though
it can't itself cut. In other words, without writing myself, I will
teach function and duty—where the poet's resources come from,
what nurtures and forms him, what is proper and what not, in
what directions excellence and error lead.

Wisdom is the starting-point and source of correct writing.
310 Socratic books will be able to point out to you your material, and
once the material is provided the words will follow willingly
enough. If a man has learned his duty to his country and his
friends, the proper kind of love with which parent, brother, and
guest should be cherished, the functions of a senator and a judge,
the task of a general sent to the front—then he automatically
understands how to give each character its proper attributes.
My advice to the skilled imitator will be to keep his eye on the
model of life and manners, and draw his speech living from
there.

320   Sometimes a play devoid of charm, weight, and skill, but
attractive with its commonplaces and with the characters well
drawn, gives the people keener pleasure and keeps them in their
seats more effectively than lines empty of substance and
harmonious trivialities.

The Greeks have the gift of genius from the Muse, and the
power of well-rounded speech. They covet nothing but praise.
Roman boys do long sums and learn to divide their as into a
hundred parts.*

'Young Albinus, subtract one uncia from a quincunx: what's
left? . . . You could have told me by now. . .'

'A triens.'

'Excellent. You'll be able to look after your affairs. Now add an
uncia. What is it now?'

'A semis.'

330   Once this rust and care for cash has tainted the soul, can we
hope for poems to be written that deserve preserving with cedar
oil and keeping safe in smooth cypress?

Poets aim either to do good or to give pleasure—or, thirdly, to
say things which are both pleasing and serviceable for life.

Whatever advice you give, be brief, so that the teachable mind
can take in your words quickly and retain them faithfully.
Anything superfluous overflows from the full mind.

Whatever you invent for pleasure, let it be near to truth. We don't want a play to ask credence for anything it feels like, or draw a living child from the ogress's belly after lunch. The ranks 340 of elder citizens chase things off the stage if there's no good meat in them, and the high-spirited youngsters won't vote for dry poetry. The man who combines pleasure with usefulness wins every suffrage, delighting the reader and also giving him advice; this is the book that earns money for the Sosii,* goes overseas and gives your celebrated writer a long lease of fame.

However, there are some mistakes we are ready to forgive. The string doesn't always give the note that the hand and mind intended: it often returns a high note when you ask for a low. The bow won't always hit what it threatens to hit. But when most 350 features of a poem are brilliant, I shan't be offended by a few blemishes thrown around by carelessness or human negligence. But what then? If a copyist goes on making the same mistake however much he is warned, he is not forgiven; if a lyre-player always gets the same note wrong, people laugh at him; so, in my estimation, if a poet fails to come off a good deal, he's another Choerilus, whom I admire with a smile if he's good two or three times. Why, I'm angry even if good Homer goes to sleep, though 360 a doze is quite legitimate in a long piece of work.

Poetry is like painting. Some attracts you more if you stand near, some if you're further off. One picture likes a dark place, one will need to be seen in the light, because it's not afraid of the critic's sharp judgement. One gives pleasure once, one will please if you look it over ten times.

sustaining audience interest.

Dear elder son of Piso, though your father's words are forming you in the right way and you have wisdom of your own besides, take this piece of advice away with you and remember it. In some things, a tolerable mediocrity is properly allowed. A mediocre 370 lawyer or advocate is a long way from the distinction of learned Messalla and doesn't know as much as Aulus Cascellius, but he has his value. But neither men nor gods nor shop-fronts allow a poet to be mediocre. Just as music out of tune or thick ointment or Sardinian honey with your poppy gives offence at a nice dinner, because the meal could go on without them, so poetry, which was created and discovered for the pleasure of the mind, sinks right to the bottom the moment it declines a little from the

top. The man who doesn't know how to play keeps away from the
380 sporting gear in the park. The man who's never been taught ball
or discus or hoop keeps quiet, so that the packed spectators can't
get a free laugh. But the man who doesn't know how to make
verses still has a go. Why shouldn't he? He's free, and of free
birth, he's assessed at an equestrian property rate, and he's not
got a fault in the world.

You will never do or say anything if Minerva is against you:
your taste and intelligence guarantee us that. But if you do write
something some day, let it find its way to critic Maecius' ears, and
your father's, and mine, and be stored up for eight years in your
390 notebooks at home. You will be able to erase what you haven't
published; words once uttered forget the way home.

Orpheus, who was a holy man and the interpreter of the gods,
deterred the men of the forests from killing and from disgusting
kinds of food. This is why he was said to tame tigers and rabid
lions. This too is why Amphion, the founder of the city of Thebes,
was said to move rocks where he wished by the sound of the lyre
and coaxing prayers. In days of old, wisdom consisted in
separating public property from private, the sacred from the
secular, in checking promiscuity, in laying down rules for the
married, in building cities, in inscribing laws on wooden tablets.
400 And that is how honour and renown came to divine poets and
poetry. After them came the great Homer and Tyrtaeus, who
sharpened masculine hearts for war by their verses. Oracles were
uttered in verse. The path of life was pointed out in verse. Kings'
favours were won by the Muses' tunes. Entertainment was found
there also, and rest after long labour. So there is no call to be
ashamed of the Muse with her skill on the lyre or of Apollo the
singer.

Do good poems come by nature or by art? This is a common
question. For my part, I don't see what study can do without a
410 rich vein of talent, nor what good can come of untrained genius.
They need each other's help and work together in friendship. A
boy who wants to reach the hoped-for goal in the race endures
and does a lot, sweats and freezes, refrains from sex and wine.
The clarinetist who is playing in honour of Apollo learns his
lesson first and stands in awe of his master. But nowadays it's
enough to say: 'I write marvellous poems. The itch take the

hindmost! It's a disgrace for me to be left behind and admit I don't know something that, to be sure, I never learned.'

A poet who is rich in land and investments bids his flatterers 420 'come and better themselves'—just like an auctioneer collecting a crowd to buy his wares. But if he's a man who can set out a good dinner properly and go bail for a poor and impecunious client and get him out of a grim legal tangle, I shall be surprised if the lucky fellow knows how to distinguish a false friend from a true. If you have given a man a present, or if you want to, don't then lead him, full of joy, to your verses. He's bound to say 'Splendid, beautiful, just right'; he'll grow pale here, he'll drip dew from loving eyes, he'll jump about, he'll beat the ground with 430 his foot. Your mocker is more deeply stirred than your true admirer, just as hired mourners at a funeral say and do almost more than those who genuinely grieve. Kings are said to ply a man with many cups and test him with wine if they are trying to discover if he deserves their friendship. If you write poetry, the fox's hidden feelings will never escape you. If you read anything aloud to Quintilius, he'd say 'pray change that, and that'. You would say you couldn't do better, though you'd tried two or three times, to no purpose. Then he'd tell you to scratch it out and put 440 the badly turned lines back on the anvil. If you preferred defending your error to amending it, he wasted no more words or trouble on preventing you from loving yourself and your handiwork without competition. A wise and good man will censure flabby lines, reprehend harsh ones, put a black line with a stroke of the pen beside unpolished ones, prune pretentious ornaments, force you to shed light on obscurities, convict you of ambiguity, mark down what must be changed. He'll be an Aristarchus.* He won't say, 'Why should I offend a friend in 450 trifles?' These trifles lead to serious troubles, if once you are ridiculed and get a bad reception.

Men of sense are afraid to touch a mad poet and give him a wide berth. He's like a man suffering from a nasty itch, or the jaundice, or fanaticism, or Diana's wrath. Boys chase him and follow him round incautiously. And if, while he's belching out his lofty lines and wandering round, he happens to fall into a well or a pit, like a fowler intent on his birds, then, however long he shouts 'Help! Help! Fellow citizens, help!' there'll be no one to 460

bother to pick him up. And if anyone should trouble to help and
let down a rope, my question will be, 'How do you know that he
didn't throw himself down deliberately? Are you sure he wants to
be saved?' And I shall tell the tale of the death of the Sicilian
poet. Empedocles wanted to be regarded as an immortal god, and
so he jumped, cool as you like, into burning Etna. Let poets have
the right and privilege of death. To save a man against his will is
the same as killing him. This isn't the only time he's done it. If
he's pulled out now, he won't become human or lay aside his love
of a notorious end.

470   It's far from clear *why* he keeps writing poetry. Has the villain
pissed on his father's ashes? Or disturbed the grim site of a
lightning-strike? Anyway, he's raving, and his harsh readings put
learned and unlearned alike to flight, like a bear that's broken the
bars of his cage. If he catches anyone, he holds on and kills him
with reading. He's a real leech that won't let go of the skin till it's
full of blood.

TACITUS: *DIALOGUE ON ORATORS*

You often ask me, Fabius Justus, why, while earlier periods were 1
brightened by the lustre and talent of so many outstanding
orators, our own times should find themselves barren, bereft of
distinction in eloquence—scarcely, indeed, even retaining the
name 'orator'. We use the word now only of the old-timers; the
accomplished speakers of our day are dubbed lawyers, advocates,
attorneys—anything rather than orators.

To answer your question is to take up the burden of an
important problem. It reflects on our abilities if we cannot reach
the heights attained by our predecessors, and on our judgement
if we do not wish to; in fact I should hardly venture on to this
topic if I proposed to put forward my own views: actually,
however, I have set myself to recount a conversation between
men as eloquent as you may find nowadays, whom I heard
discussing this very question when I was still quite young. So it's
not talent I need, but power of memory. What I heard from these
brilliant men they had thought out carefully, and they used
considered language, each putting forward different though
convincing reasons, and each marking them with the genuine
stamp of his own personality and interests. My task now is to
retrace what they said, altering no stage of the discussion,
changing no argument, and keeping the same order that the
disputants took. Nor, indeed, was there lacking someone on the
other side, ready to pour abuse and ridicule on the old days and
back modern eloquence against the geniuses of the past.

The day before the discussion Curiatius Maternus had recited 2
his *Cato,** thus offending (it was said) the susceptibilities of
powerful persons; it was felt that in working out the plot of his
tragedy he had forgotten his own situation and thought only of
Cato's. The city was buzzing with the affair when Maternus had
a visit from Marcus Aper and Julius Secundus, the most notable
lawyers of the day—men whom I myself was engaged in
following with all attention not only in the courts but even in their
homes and whenever they made public appearances. For I was in
love with my studies, and it was a sort of youthful passion that led
me to hang on their lightest stories, their discussions, and their

private oratorical exercises; though most people, it must be admitted, regarded them in a less flattering light—found Secundus halting, and thought that Aper had made his reputation by sheer natural force of intellect rather than by any systematic education. In fact, however, Secundus' style was clear, concise, and adequately fluent, while Aper by no means lacked learning—he wasn't without letters, he merely despised them, perhaps visualizing a greater reputation for hard work if his abilities stood in no apparent need of the support of extraneous techniques.

3   Thus it was that we three entered Maternus' room, to find him sitting there holding the very book that he had read aloud the day before.

Secundus said: 'Maternus, don't the spiteful stories that are going around frighten you into loving this unpopular *Cato* of yours a little less? Or perhaps you've taken the book in hand to give it a thorough revision and cut out the parts that have given a handle to misrepresentation: so that *Cato* on publication may turn out, if not better, at least safer?'

'You will find in the book', he replied, 'what Maternus owed it to himself to put there—and you will recognize what you heard at the recitation. If *Cato* left anything out, *Thyestes* will repair the omission at the next recital. I've already got that tragedy organized in my mind—and I'm hurrying on the publication of *Cato* so that I can put that care aside and concentrate whole-heartedly on the new one.'

'You're never tired of these tragedies of yours', said Aper. 'You still neglect oratory and the law-courts, and spend all your time on Medea and now Thyestes, though you're constantly being summoned to the forum by your friends' cases and countless obligations to colonies and municipalities. You'd hardly have time for them even if you hadn't brought this new business on yourself of lumping in Domitius and Cato—Roman names and Roman episodes—with Greek mythology.'

4   'I should be more put off by your harshness', said Maternus, 'if our continual differences of opinion hadn't turned virtually into a habit. You keep harrying poets and hunting them down; *I* have a plea to sustain every day—the defence of poetry against you: so much for my laziness in advocacy. So I'm particularly

glad we find ourselves provided with a judge who can either forbid me writing my verses in future, or lend his own authority to an old dream of mine—to abandon the niceties of the law (I've sweated away quite enough at them) and devote myself to the worship of an eloquence that better deserves my respect and reverence.'

'Before Aper rejects me as a judge', said Secundus, 'I shall do what good honest judges always do—excuse themselves in cases where it's clear that they have an interest on one side. Everybody knows that no one is a closer friend and companion to me than Saleius Bassus, the best of men and the most perfect of poets. If poetry is under attack, I can't think of a more credit-worthy defendant.'

'Saleius Bassus', said Aper, 'can sleep undisturbed—and so can anyone else who seeks a reputation for poetry because he is incapable of pleading cases. I have found someone to judge this dispute; and I shan't allow Maternus to shelter behind the protection of a crowd; I shall accuse him alone—in this company—on the following count: he was born with an orator's manly eloquence, that he could use to win friends and keep them, form connections, put provinces in his debt; yet he neglects a study that in our state is inconceivably more useful than any other, more pleasurable, more prestigious, more brilliantly productive of fame in Rome and reputation empire-wide, even world-wide.

'If we must put all our thoughts and actions to the test of utility, what could be safer than to pursue an art that provides an unfailing weapon to bring help to your friends, comfort to strangers, safety to the endangered, and yet also strike terror into your enemies and detractors, while you yourself remain calm behind a wall of perpetual power and influence? When all is well, you see its power and usefulness in the refuge and defence it provides for others; but if a note of personal danger sounds, breast-plate and sword in battle are not a stronger defence than eloquence to a defendant at risk—a weapon of offence and defence, enabling you to assail your adversaries or to ward them off, in court or senate or before the emperor. What could Eprius Marcellus use against a hostile senate not long ago other than his own eloquence? *That* was the threatening sword he wore when he

5

parried the philosopher Helvidius, an eloquent speaker perhaps,
but a crude tiro in a contest like that. I don't need to say anything
more on this count; I hardly think my friend Maternus will try to
contradict me here.

6   'To pass to the pleasures of oratory. Its delights are not
confined to one particular moment—they are available almost
daily, even hourly. What is more agreeable for a free-born
gentleman, bred to appreciate something higher than vulgar
pleasures, than to see his house always full, thronged with crowds
of important persons: and to know that this popularity is a tribute
paid not to his money or his childlessness or his job, but to
himself? And indeed to be aware that very often the childless, the
moneyed, and the powerful come to a mere poor youth to interest
him in their own or their friends' troubles? Can huge riches and
vast influence afford such pleasure as the sight of men, old and
experienced, who bask in worldly prestige, having to confess,
amid their material luxuries, that they lack the best thing of all?
Think of the soberly-clad escort when you leave your house and
walk the streets; the show you make on the public scene; the
adoration displayed in the courts; the luxury of rising and taking
up your position, the spectators silent, concentrating on you and
you only! Think of the crowds gathering, pressing close to you,
ready to feel any emotion the orator may assume!

       'Those are the common-or-garden pleasures of oratory, ones
that the most inexperienced eye can register; as for the more
arcane delights, known only to orators themselves—these are the
greater. If he is delivering a carefully rehearsed speech, the
speaker's pleasure—like his words—has weight and lasting
strength. If he has brought a new composition, hardly glanced at,
he may feel a slight flutter of anxiety: but this very concern
enhances his success, and adds to the joy success brings. But the
highest pleasure by far is that of the extemporary speaker, daring
and even rash in his invention. In the mind, as in the soil, other
things may be sown and worked over for a long time—but it is
the spontaneous growths that are more satisfying.

7   'I will make a personal confession. The day I received my
stripe as a senator, the day I won the quaestorship or tribunate or
praetorship, despite being an unknown from a town which could
offer me no advantages, was not more happy than the days I have

been privileged to use what moderate ability I have as a speaker to get a defendant off, or plead some case successfully in the centumviral court,* or defend his own procurators and freedmen before the emperor himself. On those occasions I feel that I am rising above tribunates and praetorships and consulships, that I possess something that, if it is not innate, cannot be granted by letters patent or supplied by influence. No art can give fame and prestige that could be compared with the glory accruing to an orator. Orators are well known in Rome—aren't they?—not only to the busy men of affairs, but to the idlest youth—at least any youth of character and ambition. Their names are the first that children are taught to utter: no one is more often pointed out and addressed by name in the street by ordinary people. Even visitors and foreigners have heard of them back in their municipalities and colonies: and as soon as they get to the city, they ask after them and are agog to recognize them.

'I would be prepared to say that Eprius Marcellus—whom I 8 just mentioned—and Vibius Crispus (you see, I prefer up-to-date examples to far-off forgotten ones) are as great in the furthest corners of the world as at Capua and Vercellae, where I gather they were born. And this fame is the result not of Eprius' two millions, or Crispus' three, though one could argue that they attained this very wealth by their eloquence, but of that eloquence itself. Eloquence is something awesome and super-natural, and over the centuries it gives many instances of men reaching the heights by sheer natural ability; but the examples I have just given are not remote—we don't have to trust to hearsay, but can see them with our own eyes. The more humbly-born they were, and the more shameful the constricting poverty that surrounded their births, the more striking examples they present of the usefulness of oratory. Without advantage of birth or financial resources, neither principled, one of them even physically despicable, they have been the most powerful men in the country for many years; while it pleased them, they dominated the courts—now they dominate Caesar's intimate circle, carry all before them, and are regarded even by the emperor with respect as well as liking: for Vespasian, that decent and fair-minded old gentleman, knows perfectly well that his other 'friends' depend on things which they received from himself and which it is easy for him to accumulate and distribute to others; but that Marcellus and Crispus brought to their relationship with him something they did not receive from the emperor—and could not have received from anyone.

'It may seem trivial in this context of magnificence to mention portraits, inscriptions, statues—but such things are not to be despised, any more than money, at which many rail, but not so many (you will find) turn up their noses. And it is these signs of fame and riches that we see thronging the homes of those who from their earliest youth have devoted themselves to law-courts and oratory.

9   'As for poems and verses, on which Maternus wants to spend his whole life—that was where all this started from—they win their authors no respectable position and bring them no advantages; the pleasure they give is fleeting, the fame empty and fruitless. Maternus' ears may reject this and what I am going on to say: but what good is it to anybody if your Agamemnons and Jasons wax eloquent? Does it mean that anyone can return home successfully defended and in your debt? Does anyone escort Saleius, our friend and excellent poet—most distinguished bard (is that more impressive?)—or pay him visits or throng around him in the street? If he himself, or a friend of his, or a relation gets into difficulty, he will come running to Secundus here, or to you, Maternus—but not in your capacity as poet, and not wanting you to write verses for him. Verses Bassus can supply for himself—they grow in his garden, very pretty and agreeable too: but the upshot of it all is that after burning the midnight oil for a whole year, working all day and most of the night, and contriving to knock together one volume, he has to go round begging and canvassing to find someone who will condescend to listen to it— at a price. He has to borrow a house and equip a recital-hall, hire seats and distribute advertisements. And even if the recitation is a high success, the praise he wins for it is the matter of a day or two, something plucked in leaf or flower that cannot go on to give real tangible fruit; he gains no 'friendship', acquires no clients, leaves no grateful memory; the applause is fleeting, the compliments empty, the pleasure swiftly gone. The other day we thought Vespasian was being wonderfully and outstandingly generous when he gave Bassus five thousand. Of course, it's nice

to find one's abilities paying off with the emperor; but it's even nicer, in a domestic emergency, to be able to look to oneself, draw on one's own resources, test one's own generosity. And after all, if they want to produce anything worthwhile, poets have to leave the society of their friends and the pleasures of the city, throw up all their other responsibilities, and withdraw, as they put it, 'to the woodland groves'—that is, to a life of solitude.

'They are enslaved to fame and reputation alone, and agree 10 that this is the only reward they get for their labours: but fame hardly attends poets as assiduously as orators. Nobody knows the third-rate poet, few the first-rate. Recitations, however successful, are hardly ever reported round the whole city, let alone the provinces of this great empire. Few arrivals from Spain or Asia— to forget about my native Gaul—ask for Saleius Bassus. And if anyone does, he passes on after seeing him once, quite contented, just as if he'd viewed a picture or a statue.

'I don't want you to think that I'm trying to turn away from poetry those who have been denied a natural talent for oratory, if they can in fact pass their spare time agreeably in this field and even make a bit of a name. I regard all branches of eloquence as sacred and holy; not only your tragic style and the thunder of epic, but pleasing lyrics, saucy elegiacs, bitter iambics, playful epigrams, and all other types are to be preferred to other artistic fields. My quarrel is with you personally, Maternus; your constitution destines you for the heights of eloquence, yet you prefer to wander below: you could reach the top, but you potter over trivia. If you were Greek—for in Greece sport too is a respectable career—and were fortunate enough to have the strength of a Nicostratus, I shouldn't be content that your immense arms, obviously meant for wrestling, should squander themselves on tossing light javelins and discuses. In the same way now I can only summon you to leave your halls and theatres and come to the forum, to lawsuits and real contests, especially as you can't take refuge in the plea which many shelter behind, that poetry is less liable to offend than oratory. Your splendid natural energy bubbles out, and you give offence—not for some personal friend, but for Cato—which is more dangerous. *You* can't minimize the offence by appealing to the ties of duty or an advocate's responsibilities or the impulse of extemporary speech.

You obviously took care to pick a character that was notorious and would speak with authority. I can see a possible reply—such a move brings immense applause, special praise in the recital-hall, and soon a topic for all tongues. But that destroys the argument that a poet has a quiet, safe life. You are taking on an adversary too big for you. *We* are satisfied to take up non-political disputes—and ones of our own century: if it were ever necessary to offend great men because a friend is on trial, our loyalty to him would be approved of, and our freedom of speech excused.'

11   Aper had said all this pretty pungently, as usual, and with a serious face. Maternus was relaxed and smiling. 'I was getting ready,' he said, 'to start accusing orators as thoroughly as Aper praised them; for I supposed that he would pass on from his eulogy to a disparagement of poets and the overthrow of the pursuit of poetry. But he has cunningly disarmed me by allowing people who couldn't plead at the bar to write poetry. I may, with an effort, be able to make some impression in law-cases; but it was by reciting tragedy that I put myself on the road to fame, when, in Nero's reign, I broke Vatinius' evil influence that was polluting even literature: and if I have any name or fame today, I think it's due to my poetry rather than my speeches. And now I've decided to disengage myself from work at the bar—I don't *want* the escorts and ceremonious departures and crowds of callers that you talk of, any more than the bronzes and portraits that have pushed their way into my house despite myself. Innocence is a better safeguard of a man's position than eloquence: no fears in *my* case that I may find myself speaking in the senate—except when someone else is in a fix.

12   'As for the woodland groves, and the solitary life Aper was jeering at, they bring me such joy that I count it among the principal rewards of poetry that it is composed away from the bustle and the litigant at the door and the shabby and weeping defendants: the mind is free to withdraw to fresh innocent places, and enjoy a holy world. This is where true eloquence had its beginnings and its shrine—this the guise in which it first won over mortals and flowed into hearts still chaste and uncorrupted. This was the language of oracles. The profiteering and bloodstained eloquence of today is a new thing, born of evil habits and—as Aper said—a substitute for the sword. But the

old happy and (as a poet may be allowed to put it) golden era had neither orators nor accusations, but it swarmed with inspired poets to sing of good deeds, not to defend bad ones. Nobody received greater fame or more reverent honour, either from the gods, whose oracles they passed on and whose feasts they attended (as the story goes), or from kings who were themselves sacred and descended from gods. We hear of no pleader then, but of Orpheus and Linus and, further back, Apollo himself. This may seem tendentious fiction: but you won't deny, Aper, that the fame of Homer with posterity doesn't yield to that of Demosthenes: the reputation of Euripides or Sophocles isn't narrower than Lysias' or Hyperides'. You will come across more people nowadays to carp at Cicero's reputation than at Virgil's: Ovid's *Medea* and Varius' *Thyestes* are more famous than any volume of Pollio or Corvinus.

'I have no worries about the contrast of the poet's lot, and his happy relationship to the Muses, with the anxious troubled life of an orator. *They* may be brought by their struggles and their perils to the consulship; *I* prefer the quiet security of Virgil's retreat— and he didn't go without imperial favour or popular fame. You need only look at Augustus' letters, or remember the day when the people rose as one man in the theatre on hearing lines by Virgil quoted, and rapturously applauded the poet—who happened to be present as a spectator—as though he was Augustus himself. And in our time too Pomponius Secundus was every bit as respectable and lastingly famous as Domitius Afer.

'What is there to envy in the fortunes of Crispus and Marcellus, on whom you want me to model myself? Is it the fear they feel or the fear they inspire? Is it that they are every day at the mercy of the importunate, who turn on them as soon as they get what they want? Or that they are fettered by every sort of obsequiousness, always too free for the emperor and too servile for us? How does all this give them supreme power? Freedmen have as much. I should prefer to be carried by Virgil's 'sweet Muses'* to their sacred haunts and fountains, far from troubles and cares and the daily compulsion to act against one's inclinations: and have no further truck with the mad slippery life of the forum, trembling and pale in the pursuit of fame. I don't want to be woken up by shouting clients or breathless freedmen,

13

or worry so much about the future that I have to write safeguards into my will,* or own more than I could safely leave to the heir I choose. For 'some day my hour too will come'—I trust the statue on my grave will be cheerful and garlanded, not sad and grim. No debates, no petitions about my memorial, please.'

14   Maternus, excited and even inspired, had scarcely stopped when Vipstanus Messalla entered the room. He realized from the intent expression on all their faces that a serious discussion was in progress, and he said: 'Have I come at a bad moment, and disturbed you in a private conversation on the preparation of some case?'

'Not at all, not at all', said Secundus. 'In fact, I wish you had come earlier. You would have had the pleasure of hearing the very detailed remarks of our friend Aper exhorting Maternus to turn all his attentions to lawsuits—and Maternus defending his poems in a brilliant speech: one—as as only right in a defence of poets—that was pretty bold and more poetic than oratorical.'

'I should have been infinitely delighted by such a debate,' said Messalla, 'and I'm pleased by the very fact that important people like you, the foremost orators of our age, should be prepared not to employ your gifts only on legal business and declamation practice, but to take up discussions of this kind. They feed the mind—and bring the most agreeable pleasures of learning and literature to yourselves, the disputants, and to all who hear of them. It is admirable that Secundus has written a life of Julius Africanus and given us the hope that he may produce more books like it; though less admirable that Aper hasn't yet deserted the exercises of the schools, but prefers to spend his leisure as the new rhetoricians do, rather than as the old orators did.'

15   Aper said: 'You're always showing your admiration for the old and antique, Messalla, and laughing present-day pursuits to scorn. I've often heard you in this vein: forgetting your own eloquence, and your brother's,* and affirming that nobody nowadays is an orator—and particularly boldly because you don't fear to be called envious: the glory you deny to yourself others concede to you.'

'I don't repent of my words,' Messalla replied, 'and I don't believe Secundus or Maternus or even you, Aper, despite your occasional arguments to the contrary, really differ from me. I should like one of you to consent to investigate the causes of the infinite gulf between old and new, and expound them to me—for I often find myself reflecting on the problem. What consoles others only increases my puzzlement—I mean that the Greeks too have declined: there's a greater difference between Aeschines and Demosthenes on the one hand, and Nicetes Sacerdos or any of the others who shake Ephesus and Mytilene with the shrieked applause of their pupils, than between Afer or Africanus or yourselves and Cicero or Pollio.'

'It's a big question you bring up,' said Secundus, 'and one well worth discussing. But who is more qualified to take it up than you? You have supreme learning and outstanding powers, and you've taken trouble to consider the problem beforehand.'

Messalla said: 'I will tell you what I have thought—so long as I get you to agree in advance to help me in my speech.'

'I promise for both of us', said Maternus. 'Secundus and I will both take up the sections that we see you have left—not left *out*, but left to us. Aper is a habitual dissentient, as you said just now: and it's been obvious for some time that he's girding himself for the opposition, and won't easily put up with this alliance of ours in praise of the ancients.'

'No,' said Aper, 'I certainly shall not allow our own century to go unheard and undefended, and so be condemned by your conspiracy.

'My first question is this: who do you mean by "ancients"? What generation of orators do you mark off by this term? When I hear the word, I think of old-timers born long ago, and Ulysses and Nestor come into my mind—men living perhaps thirteen hundred years ago. But you bring up Demosthenes and Hyperides, who without a doubt flourished under Philip and Alexander—and outlived both. So that little more than three hundred years separate us from the age of Demosthenes. This may seem a long time set against the frailty of human life. But it is very short—merely yesterday—in comparison with the passage of the centuries and the immeasurable past. Remember Cicero's *Hortensius*:* the true 'great' year has passed when the same position of the stars in the heavens comes round again—and this year embraces twelve thousand, nine hundred and fifty-four of the years *we* speak of. If that is true, Demosthenes, your great

16

hero, whom you make out to be old and ancient, is in the same
year—and the same month—as us.

17   'Well, to pass to Latin authors. You don't, I suppose, usually
class as superior to present-day speakers Menenius Agrippa, who
really could be counted an ancient—you mean Cicero, Caesar,
Caelius, Calvus, Brutus, Pollio, Corvinus; but I don't see why
you regard these as belonging to ancient times rather than our
own. To take Cicero himself: he was killed—as Tiro his
freedman writes—on the seventh of December in the consulship
of Hirtius and Pansa, the year Augustus made himself and
Quintus Pedius suffect-consuls in place of Pansa and Hirtius.
Reckon fifty-six years for the deified Augustus' rule over the
state: add Tiberius' twenty-three, nearly four for Caligula,
fourteen each for Claudius and Nero, the one long year divided
between Galba, Otho, and Vitellius, and the six years that have so
far passed in the present happy reign in which Vespasian is
protecting the country—that makes a hundred and twenty years*
from the death of Cicero up to this year: a single lifetime—for I
myself once saw a man in Britain who volunteered that he'd been
present at the battle in which they tried to keep Caesar from
British shores and drive him away when he invaded. If this man
who stood in arms against Caesar had found his way to Rome
because of captivity or his own choice or some chance, he could
perfectly well have heard speeches by Caesar himself and by
Cicero, and yet also attended orations given by us. At the recent
largess you yourselves saw plenty of old men who told how they
had received money once or twice from Augustus as well. The
inference is that they could have heard Corvinus and Pollio
speaking: Corvinus lasted till the middle of Augustus' principate,
Pollio almost to the end of it. You can't split up time like this, and
go on using 'ancients' and 'old-timers' of men whom the same
hearers could have recognized and thus joined to us in a single
life-span.

18   'This is all by way of preface, to show that any credit that may
accrue to their times from these famous orators is the common
possession of all—and more nearly available to us than to Servius
Galba or Gaius Carbo or others we could justly call ancients.
They are uncouth, unpolished, crude, coarse speakers—and your
hero Calvus, or Caelius, or Cicero himself would have done well

not to imitate them at all. I want to take a bolder and more daring line: but let it be said first that types and styles of oratory vary with the period. Compared with the elder Cato, Gaius Gracchus is fuller and richer: compared with Gracchus Crassus is more refined and decorative: Cicero is more clear, witty, and sublime than either—and Corvinus surpasses Cicero in gentleness and sweetness and care in the use of words. I am not looking for the most eloquent among them; I am for the moment content with proving that eloquence has no single face. In those you call 'ancients', too, more than one type can be discerned, and a thing isn't automatically worse because it's different. But men are so jealous that the old always receives praise, the new scorn. There have doubtless been those who admired Appius Caecus more than Cato. It is beyond question that Cicero too had his critics, who found him inflated, swollen, verbose, exuberant, redundant—and not 'Attic'* enough. You must have read Calvus' and Brutus' letters to Cicero: it's easy enough to see from them that Cicero thought Calvus bloodless and dry, Brutus flat and disjointed: and on the other hand Cicero was criticized by Calvus as lax and spineless, and by Brutus—to use his own words—as "feeble and hamstrung". If you ask me, *all* these criticisms were true; but I shall come to individuals in a moment—meanwhile my business is with the general trend.

'Admirers of antiquity tend to draw a firm line where it ends— 19 at Cassius Severus: him they make the scapegoat, asserting that he was the first to stray from the old straight path of oratory. My contention is that he changed to a new style by an intelligent act of judgement, and not because of any lack of ability or education. He saw what I said just now—that as times change and audiences vary, the style and appearance of oratory must change too. The people in the old days were inexperienced and ill-educated: they were quite ready to tolerate long speeches, cluttered up with irrelevancies, and regarded it as a virtue if a speaker took all day. *Then* there was applause for long introductions, and narratives delving deep in the past, elaborate divisions put in merely for show, innumerable interconnected arguments, and all the other items prescribed in the dry-as-dust handbooks of Hermagoras and Apollodorus: as for anyone who had an inkling of philosophy, and inserted a philosophic passage in his speech, he was lauded to the skies. And no wonder: these things were new then and unknown, and very few even of the orators themselves were acquainted with rhetorical precept or philosophical dogma. But now that all this is commonplace, and scarcely anyone finds himself in the public seats who isn't at least a dabbler in these studies, if not an expert, one needs new and less obvious routes for eloquence to follow. Only so can an orator escape boring his hearers, especially where judges can decide on their own authority, not under a legal code, and can make their own provisions about the length of speeches, without having this dictated to them. They don't have to wait on the orator's pleasure until he cares to talk about the actual matter in hand: they often go out of their way to warn him and call him back when he digresses and affirm that they are in a hurry.

20   'Who nowadays would tolerate a proem on the bad health of the speaker—a normal theme for Corvinus? Who would wait while five volumes of speeches against Verres* unrolled themselves? Who would endure the immense books on our shelves—the speech for Tullius or Caecina—all about objections and legal forms? Nowadays the judge is always ahead of the speaker, and he grows hostile unless he is lured on and seduced by fluent arguments, brilliant reflections, refined and colourful description. The crowds of by-standers, too, and spectators who casually drift in, have by now got used to demanding cheerful and agreeable oratory: they're no longer prepared to put up with gloom and unshaven antiquity in the courts any more than they would be to applaud the reproduction of Roscius' or Ambivius Turpio's gestures on the stage. Indeed youths still on the educational anvil, who pursue orators for their own scholastic advantage, want not only to listen, but to take something splendid and memorable back home with them. They swop things among themselves, often put them into letters back to their colonies and provinces—some short, sharp, brilliant epigram, or a passage resplendent with out-of-the-way poetic colouring. Yes, an orator now has to provide poetic beauty as well, not the Accius or Pacuvius variety, mildewed with age, but drawn from the shrines of Horace, Virgil, and Lucan. These are the ears and these the judgements that contemporary orators have to pander to—and it is for this reason that they have become more pretty and more

ornate in style. And if our speeches do bring pleasure to their hearers, that doesn't make them any less effective: to think that would be as illogical as to suppose that modern temples are flimsier because they are bright with marble and brilliant with gold, rather than constructions of rough stone and unsightly tile.

'I tell you frankly that when I read some of the ancients, I can 21 hardly suppress my laughter—and in some I can hardly stay awake. I don't mean the rank and file—Canutius, Attius, Furnius, Toranius, and other patients in the same hospital who enjoy desiccation and anaemia: but even Calvus, who, I suppose, left twenty-one or so books behind him, comes up to the mark for me in hardly a single speech. I don't see any general dissent from this view. Very few read Calvus' speeches against Asitius or Drusus. Nevertheless all serious students have to reckon with the speeches against Vatinius, and particularly the second: it is brilliant in language and in content, and it was entirely suited to the tastes of the jury—so you can see that Calvus too realized where his style required improving; he didn't lack the desire to speak more loftily and with more refinement—only the talent and the strength. Again, it is just those speeches of Caelius in which we recognize modern colour and sublimity that please us, in whole or part. But his shabby language, disjointed rhythm, and lack of periodic structure are the symptoms of the old oratory; and no one, I think, can be such an antiquarian that he approves of the side of Caelius that is antique.

'We may surely agree that it was because of his multifarious cares and occupations that Caesar accomplished less in oratory than his miraculous talents suggested. Equally, we may leave Brutus to his philosophy—even his admirers confess that in his oratory he fell short of his reputation. I hardly suppose anyone still reads Caesar's *For Decius the Samnite* or Brutus' *For King Deiotarus* and all the other volumes of like flatness and tedium— except, perhaps, somebody who also admires their poetry. Yes, they did write poetry, and sent it to private collectors: they were no greater poets than Cicero, but they had more luck—fewer know about it. Pollio too—he was born more recently, but he looks to me like a fellow student of the Meneniuses and the Appiuses. He reproduced Pacuvius and Accius in his speeches as well as in his tragedies: such a hard dry writer is he.

'But oratory is like the human body—it is beautiful only when the veins don't stand out and the bones can't be counted; when good sound blood fills the limbs and pulses in the muscles. The sinews are covered in fine red flesh, and shown off by the attractive surface. I won't harry Corvinus: it wasn't his fault that he couldn't provide the brilliant luxuriance of our day. We can all see how far his mind and talent fell short of his judgement.

22   'I come to Cicero. He had the same battle with his contemporaries as I have with you. They admired the ancients, he preferred the eloquence of his own day. And there is nothing in which he outstripped the orators of that period more decisively than in his judgement. He was the first to *cultivate* oratory, the first to apply choice to words and artifice to structure. He even attempted more flowery passages, and happened on a number of epigrams, at least in the speeches he wrote as an old man at the end of his life—after, that is, he had developed, and discovered by practice and experience what the best style was. For his early speeches have the faults of the ancients. He is slow in his proems, verbose in his narrative, lax in his digressions; he is slow to be moved, rarely catches fire; few sentences end neatly and with a punch. Nothing here to excerpt, nothing to take home—it's like a rough building, with a firm wall that will last but with no proper polish or splendour.

'I think of an orator as a family man of substance and taste: I don't want him to have a house that merely keeps wind and rain off, but one that catches the eye and pleases it. His furniture shouldn't be confined to necessities—he should have gold and jewels in his store, so that one enjoys frequently taking him down and admiring him. Some things are out of date and smelly—let them be kept out: we want no word tarnished with rust, no sentences put together in the slow sluggish manner of the annalists: he must avoid tasteless and disagreeable pleasantry, vary his structure, and use more than one kind of clausula.

23   'I have no wish to laugh at Cicero's "wheel of fortune"* and "boar-sauce"*—or the *esse videatur** which appears instead of an epigram at the end of every other sentence throughout his speeches. I bring this up unwillingly, and I ignore many further instances that monopolize the admiration and even imitation of those who call themselves 'ancient' orators. No names—I am

quite happy just to make the type clear. But in any case you can picture the people I mean: they read Lucilius in preference to Horace and Lucretius rather than Virgil; they find the eloquence of Aufidius Bassus and Servilius Nonianus tame in comparison with Sisenna's or Varro's; they scorn and even hate the model speeches published by rhetoricians—but admire Calvus'. These people go on chatting in front of the judge in the old style, but they have lost their audience's attention; the spectators don't bother to listen, and even the litigant can scarcely put up with them, so gloomy and unpolished are they. They may attain the healthiness they boast of, but they do so by starving, not by building up their strength. Even as far as the body is concerned, doctors hesitate to recommend a state of health that involves mental anxiety. It's not enough not to be unwell: I want a man to be strong, cheerful, and active. One who is praised only for his health is not far off illness.

'But you—my very eloquent friends—go on brightening this age of ours with beauty of speech as you can, and as you do. You, Messalla, I observe, choose out the brightest passages of the ancients for your imitation: and you, Maternus and Secundus, mix with your grave sentiments brilliant and refined language. Such is your choice of material, such your ordering of it, such your copiousness when the case demands, such your conciseness when the case permits, such your agreeable rhythm, such the clarity of your thought, such the vividness of the emotions you portray, such the discretion of your outspokenness, that even if the judgement of our own period is dulled by envy and jealousy, our descendants will surely speak the truth of you.'

After Aper's speech, Maternus said: 'One recognizes our 24 friend Aper's force and ardour. What an irresistible torrent of eloquence he brought to the aid of our century! How fully, on how many fronts he harried the ancients! He showed not merely brilliance of inspiration, but learning and technique, borrowing from the ancients the weapons with which to go on and attack them. I trust, however, Messalla, that he hasn't put you off your promise. We aren't looking for a defender of the ancients—and despite his praise just now we don't put any of ourselves in the class of the men he attacked. Of course, he isn't being candid: it's an old trick, and one often used by our friends the philosophers,

to take on oneself the role of opponent. So produce for us not so
much a eulogy of the ancients—their fame is enough praise for
them—as the reasons why we have lagged so far behind their
standards of eloquence: particularly when chronology has proved
that only a hundred and twenty years have passed since the death
of Cicero.'

25   Then Messalla said: 'I shall follow the line you suggest,
Maternus. There is certainly no need for a long refutation of
Aper—indeed, his first point was in my view a verbal quibble: I
mean, that it's improper to call men ancients who have quite
certainly been dead a hundred years. I am not fighting about a
word; he can call them ancients or elders or anything else he
prefers, so long as it's granted that the oratory of those days was
superior. And I'm not disposed to argue with the part where he
came to grips with the problem and pronounced that you get
more than one style of oratory even at the same time—let alone
in different centuries. Now among the orators of Attica
Demosthenes take the crown. Aeschines and Hyperides and
Lysias and Lycurgus are in next place: but it is that *period* which is
by universal consent regarded as the peak. Similarly at Rome
Cicero outstripped all other eloquent speakers of his time, but
Calvus and Pollio and Caesar and Caelius and Brutus are rightly
regarded as superior to those who came before and after. It
makes no difference that their species differ—the genus is the
same. Calvus is more concise, Pollio more vigorous, Caesar more
impressive, Caelius more bitter, Brutus more serious, Cicero
more vehement and full and powerful than his contemporaries;
but they all display the same *health* of eloquence: if you turn over
all their books together, you can tell that, however much their
talents differed, there is a certain similarity and kinship between
their judgement and intentions. They carped at each other, to be
sure—and there are traces of reciprocated malice in their letters;
but that is a fault they were subject to as men, not as orators.
Certainly Calvus, Pollio, and Cicero too were wont to envy and
be jealous and to be afflicted by other human weaknesses; alone
among them Brutus, I think, laid bare his inmost convictions with
no malice or envy, but with simplicity and candour. It's hardly
likely he could envy Cicero when he didn't (I think) envy even
Caesar. As for Servius Galba and Gaius Laelius and other

ancients that Aper couldn't stop chasing, the defence can be waived; I agree that their eloquence, still growing and adolescent, lacked much.

'But if we leave out of account supreme and perfect oratory, 26 and look round for a style to choose, I should distinctly prefer Gaius Gracchus' impetuosity or Lucius Crassus' ripeness to Maecenas' curling-tongs or Gallio's jingles: better clothe oratory in a hairy toga than prink it out in gaudy and meretricious costumes. That sort of refinement doesn't suit oratory—or even a real man: I mean the sort many pleaders of our day so abuse that they come to reproduce the rhythms of the stage: language obscene, thoughts frivolous, rhythm licentious. Many people actually boast, as if it were a step towards fame and a sign of their genius, that their model speeches are sung or danced: it ought to be almost out of the question even to listen to talk like this. Hence the common remark—shameful and perverse though it is—that modern orators speak lasciviously, modern actors dance eloquently.

'I don't wish to deny that Cassius Severus—the only name Aper dared to mention—could be called an orator, if we compare him with his successors: though he has more bile than good red blood in the great majority of his speeches. He was the first to despise order in his material, to lay aside shame and modesty in language. He is inept even in the use of such arms as he does employ, often so eager to strike a blow that he loses his balance altogether. He doesn't fight—he brawls. But, as I say, compared with his successors he is superior by far to the others whom Aper couldn't bring himself to name or deploy in the battle—superior in variety of learning, wit, charm, and sheer strength.

'I was certainly expecting that Aper, having condemned Pollio, Caelius, and Calvus, would bring up a fresh division for us, and give even more names, or at least as many, so that we could find a pair for Cicero and Caesar and so on, one by one. As it is, he confines himself to criticizing the ancients by name—but hasn't dared to praise any of their successors except in a generalized manner. I suppose he was afraid that if he picked only a few out, he would offend many others. Every man jack of today's rhetoricians labours under the illusion that he can class himself Cicero's superior—though at the same time altogether inferior to Gabinianus. I shan't hesitate to name individuals; if I put forward examples, it becomes easier to see by what stages eloquence has been broken and enfeebled.'

27   'Spare us that', said Maternus. 'Just keep your promise. We don't need a demonstration that the ancients are more eloquent—I for one am quite convinced of that: we're looking for the causes which you mentioned you frequently thought about. That of course was when you were in a quieter frame of mind a little while ago and hadn't been provoked by Aper's criticisms of your ancestors* into getting angry with the oratory of today.'

'I haven't been provoked by Aper's point of view,' he said, 'and *you* mustn't be provoked if anything happens to grate on your ears. You know the rule of conversations of this kind: give your honest opinion and don't worry about giving offence.'

'Go on, then,' said Maternus, 'and since you speak of the ancients, employ the ancient habit of plain speaking—we've got even further away from that than from eloquence.'

28   Messalla went on: 'The causes you are looking for, Maternus, are by no means abstruse—you and Secundus and Aper know them quite well, even if you have given me the role of expounding publicly things we all feel. Everybody knows that eloquence, and the other arts too, have declined from their old heights not for any lack of exponents, but because the young are lazy, their parents neglectful, their teachers ignorant—and because the old ways are forgotten. The rot started in Rome, then spread through Italy—and now is seeping into the provinces. You know better than I the situation there; I shall talk about the city, and its own individual and home-bred vices that are on hand to welcome a child as soon as he's born, and pile up as he grows older. First of all, I must say a few words about our ancestors' strict methods in the education and moulding of their children.

'In the old days everyone had his son—born in wedlock of a chaste mother—brought up not in the room of some hired nurse but on his mother's lap; and the mother's especial claim to praise was to look after her household and slave for her children. Or some older relation was selected, of tried and proved character, and the whole brood committed to her charge; in her presence it was not allowed to say anything that was shameful or do anything that was wrong. She brought an element of purity and modesty not only to their tasks and studies but to their games and relaxations as well. This is the way Cornelia, as is well known, took charge of the upbringing of the Gracchi, and educated these distinguished children; so Aurelia with Caesar, Atia with Augustus. The object of this austere training was that each child's nature, open, honest, untwisted by any vice, should immediately and whole-heartedly seize on good arts. And whether the child inclined to the army or to law or to eloquence he concentrated on that alone and made it his whole diet.

'But nowadays a child is delivered on birth to some Greek 29 maid, who is helped by one or other of the slaves—and generally a quite worthless one at that, unfit for any serious duty. Their nursery stories and superstitions give the first colour to green and untrained minds. Nobody in the whole house cares what he does or says in the presence of the young master; even the parents don't trouble to get their little ones used to goodness and propriety—they substitute wantonness and pertness: hence very soon impudence creeps in, and contempt for one's own property and everyone else's. The peculiar and private vices of this city seem to be implanted in children while they're still in the womb, stage fever and enthusiasm for gladiators and race-horses. The mind gets taken over and besieged by these activities, and no room is left for better attainments. Do you often find people talking of anything else at home? All the youths are chatting about such things when we go into the lecture room. Even teachers have no more frequent topic of discussion with their pupils: indeed they attract students not by being disciplinarians or showing proof of their attainments, but by servile greetings and the enticements of flattery.

'I won't stop to discuss elementary education, though here too 30 insufficient trouble is taken; not enough time is spent either on getting to know authors or studying history or acquiring knowledge of events, people, and times. They're all agog for the so-called rhetoricians. I shall shortly tell you when the profession was introduced into this city, and how it had no sort of standing in the eyes of our ancestors; but first let me draw your attention to the training that we know was undergone by those old orators: for their endless pains, their daily practice, their constant exercise in all kinds of study are mentioned in their own books.

'You will, of course, be acquainted with Cicero's *Brutus*, at the end of which, after his recital of the old orators one by one, he relates* his own beginnings, the steps he took towards eloquence, what one may call his oratorical education. He relates how he studied civil law at the feet of Quintus Mucius and took a deep draught of all kinds of philosophy from the Academic Philo and the Stoic Diodotus. He was by no means content with the teachers to whom he had access in Rome, and so he traversed Greece and Asia also, in order to take in the widest variety of accomplishment. This, obviously, is why one can diagnose from Cicero's books that neither mathematics nor music nor grammar nor any other gentlemanly branch of knowledge fell outside his range. He was acquainted with the subtleties of dialectic, the practical teachings of ethics, and the physical causes and changes of events. This is the point I am making, my friends: that wonderful eloquence is the lavish overflow from great learning, wide skills, and universal knowledge. There is no narrow boundary circumscribing oratorical potentiality and ability, as there is in other fields: he only is a true orator who can speak on any question brilliantly and splendidly and persuasively, with equal regard for the importance of the subject, the circumstances of the time, and the pleasure of the audience.

31   'This was the conviction of those old-time orators. They realized that it was therefore essential not to declaim in the rhetoricians' schools, not to exercise one's tongue and one's vocal chords in imaginary debates that have no sort of relation to reality, but to fill their minds with those high accomplishments that necessitate discussion of Good and Evil, Right and Wrong, Just and Unjust: this is the material that is the orator's stock-in-trade. In law-courts we are generally talking about equity, in deliberations about what is expedient, in eulogy about the Good. But often these distinctions are blurred: and no one can talk fluently and widely and elegantly on such topics unless he has acquainted himself with human nature, the power of virtue and the depravity of vice, and can understand the class of things that are neither virtue nor vice. Hence other advantages: the man who knows what anger is can more easily arouse or calm a judge's anger, and a knowledge of the nature of pity and the emotions by which it is aroused can enable one to move it more freely. If an

orator is conversant with these arts and this training, whether he has to speak to hostile or prejudiced or envious or morose or frightened men he will be able to feel his hearers' pulses, and proceed to adapt his speech as their characters require. He will have all the means available, stored up for every conceivable use. There are audiences with whom a concise, brief, one-argument-at-a-time style will carry more conviction; here a training in dialectic pays off. Others are pleased rather by oratory that is wordy, level, appealing to common feelings: to influence them we shall borrow from the Peripatetics* commonplaces ready and available for any controversy. The Academics will provide belligerence, Plato sublimity, Xenophon sweetness. An orator won't regard it as outside this province to bring into action good remarks even of Epicurus and Metrodorus, and employ them where appropriate. I am trying to model not a sage, or some disciple of the Stoics, but someone who must take a sip of all the arts, while draining only some of them down. So it was that the old orators included legal knowledge in their studies, and learnt the elements of grammar, music, and mathematics. Many of the cases one comes up against—indeed virtually all of them—require a knowledge of the law; and there are a large number that call for acquaintance with those other attainments, too.

'I don't want to hear the retort that it's enough for us to receive 32 straightforward special briefings as each occasion requires. First of all, we make different uses of our own and borrowed materials; it's obvious that it matters a lot if one owns what one puts on display or merely hires it. Moreover the very fact that we have wide knowledge of the arts lends us distinction even when we're on quite another tack—it stands out brilliantly when you least expect it. This is noticed by ordinary people as well as by a learned and observant listener; and their instantaneous praise means that they agree that here is a true orator, who has had a proper training and has gone through all the right hoops. Such a man cannot be, I maintain, and never has been anyone but somebody who goes into the forum armed with all the arts like a fully-equipped soldier striding into battle. But this point is so ignored by modern speakers that you may catch them in their cases uttering phrases with all the disgraceful and shaming faults of our every-day conversation. They have no knowledge of the laws, no acquaintance with decrees of the senate, no respect, even, for the Roman code; as for philosophy and the precepts of the wise they shudder at the very thought of them. They squeeze eloquence into a handful of bright ideas and a narrow range of epigrams—dethroning it, one may say; for once it was the mistress of all the arts, and filled men's hearts with the beauty of its retinue. Now it is circumscribed and crippled, with no attendants and no respect shown it, without—I could almost say—any claim to breeding, and is learnt as though it were a mere low-class trade. This is, I think, the first and foremost cause for the extent to which we have fallen short of the old oratory.

'If you want witnesses, who better to call than Demosthenes among the Greeks, whom history relates to have been a most attentive student of Plato? And Cicero, I seem to remember, committed himself to the statement that anything he may have attained in eloquence he attained thanks not to the workshops of the rhetoricians but to the wide spaces of the Academy.* There are other reasons, weighty and important ones—but it's only fair that *you* should expose them; I have done my job, and according to my habit, offended quite enough people who, hearing my arguments, will certainly say that in praising the knowledge of law and philosophy as essential for an orator, I merely pander to my own foolish pursuits.'

33   Maternus said: 'Personally, I don't think you have yet completed the task you undertook—indeed you seem merely to have begun it, and drawn a few preparatory lines and sketches. You've told us what arts the old orators were normally trained in, and you've contrasted our ignorance and sloth with their vigorous and fruitful studies. But I'm waiting for the rest: I've learnt what they knew—or what we don't know—but I want also to find out what exercises youths about to enter the forum generally used to strengthen and nourish their talents. Eloquence is a matter of art and knowledge—but far more of capacity and experience: you won't, I'm sure, dispute that, and I judge from the faces of our friends that they agree.'

Aper and Secundus assented, and Messalla made a sort of fresh start.

'I think I've given a sufficient exposition of the roots and beginnings of the old eloquence, showing you in what arts the ancient orators were normally trained and brought up: now for their exercises. Of course, there is exercise in the arts themselves; no one can grasp such recondite and varied matters unless theory is backed by practice, practice by capacity, capacity by actual experience. From which it can be inferred that there is no distinction between understanding what you are to express and expressing what you understood. This may seem a little obscure; but anyone who tries to separate theory and practice will at any rate concede that a mind that is full and trained in these arts comes much more prepared to those exercises that are characteristic of oratorical education.

'Well, in the time of our ancestors the youth who was preparing for the forum and an oratorical career, after a thorough training at home and stuffed with desirable knowledge, was led off by his father or relations to an orator who held a high position in the state. He got used to following this man about, escorting him, being present at all his speeches in law-court or public assembly: he was on hand to listen to his legal cross-talk and observe his tiffs: he learnt to fight, you might say, in the battle-line. Hence vast experience, vast patience, and immense power of judgement came the way of youths right from the start. They studied in the full glare of daylight, amid actual crises where no one says anything stupid or inconsistent and gets away with it—he faces rejection by the judge, abuse from his adversaries, scorn even from his own supporters. Thus they straight away became imbued with an eloquence that was real and unspoilt. They might follow one man in particular, but they got to know all the advocates of the time in constant law-suits and actions. Moreover, they had a chance to observe the variations of public taste, and so easily discovered what in each man found favour or disfavour. Thus they had available a teacher—and a very good select one at that—who presented the actual face of eloquence to them, not a mere reflection, and opponents and rivals fighting with swords of steel, not of wood, and an auditorium never empty, never the same, consisting of hearers for and against them, with the result that nothing that was said, good or bad, could go unnoticed. For you know that really great and lasting distinction in oratory has its source as much in the benches opposite as in those on your side: there indeed it grows more

34

firmly, and gains strength more surely. Under this sort of supervisor the youth of whom I am speaking—pupil of orators, spectator in the forum, follower of law-cases, trained and hardened in the experience of others, familiar with the laws from daily hearing of them, one to whom the faces of the judges did not seem strange—constantly observing the habits of assemblies, constantly aware of the taste of the people—such a man in prosecution or defence, from the start was by himself and alone equal to the demands of any case. Lucius Crassus prosecuted Gaius Carbo at eighteen, Caesar Dolabella at twenty, Pollio Gaius Cato at twenty-one, Calvus Vatinius when not much older—and those speeches we read even today with admiration.

35   'But now our poor young men are led off to the schools of the so-called rhetors. That these people emerged a little before the time of Cicero and displeased our ancestors is clear from the fact that they were ordered by the censors Crassus and Domitius to close—as Cicero says—their "schools for shamelessness".*But as I was saying: youths are led off to schools in which it is difficult to say what has the worst effect on their progress—the place, their fellow students, or the studies they go through. There is no respect in a place where no one not of equal ignorance ever goes; the other students are no help—boys among boys and youths among youths, they speak and are heard with equal irresponsibility; but the exercises themselves are to a large extent positively harmful.

    'Two types of subject, of course, are dealt with in the rhetors' schools: *suasoriae** and *controversiae.** The former are regarded as much the less serious and as demanding less experience, and so they are assigned to the boys; but the older ones get the *controversiae*—God, how do I describe those! They are fantastically put together; and moreover these deliberately unreal subjects are treated with declamatory bombast. So it comes about that the most grandiose language is lavished on rewards for tyrannicides or choices by the raped or remedies for plague or adultery by matrons or any of the other topics that come up daily in school, in the forum rarely or never: but when they come to speak before real judges. . .*

36   '. . . consider the matter. He could utter nothing sordid,

nothing low. Great eloquence is like a flame: it needs fuel to feed it; it is roused by movement; and it brightens as it burns.

'It was the same principle in our city also that carried the oratory of the ancients to its heights. Modern orators have attained what influence they reasonably may in a settled, calm, and contented state; but *they* saw that they could reap advantages from the confusion and licence then prevailing; all was in turmoil, there was no single ruler, and an orator had prestige to the extent that he could carry a fickle people with him. Hence the continual passing of laws to win popular acclaim, hence the addresses by magistrates ready to spend pretty well all night on the rostrum, hence the prosecutions of leading men and the feuds handed down like family heirlooms, hence the quarrels of the great and the incessant rivalry of senate and people. These contributed to the dismemberment of the state: but they meant practice for the eloquence of those times and ensured that it was heaped with great rewards; the better at speaking one was, the more easily one could attain public office, the more when holding it one could outdistance one's colleagues, the more influence one could wield with leading men, the more authority in the senate, the more fame and glory with the public. These people were flooded with clients—even foreign nations counted as that; they were the object of respect from magistrates about to go to their provinces and of attentions from the same men on their return; they seemed to be at the beck and call of praetorships and consulships, and even when out of office they did not lack power, for their counsel and authority lent them control of senate and people alike. They had convinced themselves that no one could attain or preserve an outstanding and pre-eminent place in the city without eloquence. And no wonder, when they found themselves addressing the people even when they did not want to, when it was not enough just to give a brief explanation of your position in the senate, but you had to defend your opinion with all your powers of eloquence; when they regarded it as essential to reply in person if one was summoned to face some charge or calumny; when one had to give evidence at public trials not in absence or in writing, but present and personally. Eloquence was not just the route to the highest rewards—it was a vital necessity:

it was splendid and glorious to be thought eloquent, and shameful to be called dumb and tongueless.

37   'So shame as much as reward urged them on, to avoid being petty clients rather than patrons, to ensure that inherited connections did not pass to others, and that they did not, by a reputation for sloth and incompetence, fail to achieve office—or come to grief in it when achieved. I don't know whether you have handled those old documents, still available in the libraries of antiquarians and just now being collected by Mucianus: eleven books of *Proceedings* and three of *Letters* have already come out, haven't they? Anyway from these you can judge that Pompey and Crassus excelled in oratorical talent as well as in military prowess; the Lentuli, Metelli, Luculli, Curios, and the other top people took a great deal of trouble over the same pursuits: no one in those days attained to great power without some eloquence.

'Remember too the distinction of the defendants and the importance of the cases, themselves a considerable spur to eloquence. For it makes a lot of difference whether you have to speak about a theft or a rule of procedure or an interdict—or about electoral bribery, the robbery of allies, and the slaughter of citizens. No doubt it is better that such things should not happen; no doubt the best state of affairs for a country is one in which we don't have to put up with such evils; but seeing that they *did* happen, they provided immense scope for eloquence. A talent swells with the size of the events it has to deal with; no one can produce a famous and notable oration unless he finds a case equal to his powers. Demosthenes is not famous, surely, for the speeches he wrote against his guardians, Cicero isn't a great orator because he defended Publius Quintius or Licinius Archias. It was Catiline, Milo, Verres, and Antony who covered him with glory. Don't think I'm saying that it was worth it that the state should produce such criminal citizens merely to give orators rich scope for their oratory. But, as I keep saying, let us remember the question under discussion, and realize that we are speaking of something that flourishes more easily in stormy and troubled times. It's better (everyone knows that) and more advantageous to enjoy peace than to be harassed by war: it remains true that wars produce more good fighters than peace. So it is with oratory. The more often it stands in the firing-line, the more knocks it gives and receives, the greater adversaries and the more bitter battles it takes on, the higher and more sublime it reigns, ennobled by those crises, in the mouths of men, who are so made that they desire safety but have a penchant for danger.

'I turn now to the shape and customs of the old law-courts. 38 The present pattern is more convenient, but the forum in its old guise gave more practice to eloquence. No one then was forced to keep his speech down to a meagre ration of hours; there was free scope for postponements; every speaker fixed his own time-limit, and there was no limitation on the number of days or of advocates in attendance. Pompey, during his third consulship,* was the first to bring in restrictions and to put the bit on eloquence: all the same everything continued to be conducted in the forum and according to the laws and before the praetors. For the praetors presided over far greater cases then, as can most strikingly be seen from the fact that the centumviral cases, which now hold first place, were so overshadowed by the prestige of other courts that we now read no speech delivered before the Centumviri by Cicero, Caesar, Brutus, Caelius, Calvus, or any great orator—only the speeches of Pollio entitled *For the Heirs of Urbinia*: but *they* were delivered as late as the middle of Augustus' reign, at a time when a long period of peace, continuous public calm, unbroken tranquillity in the senate, and particularly the restraining influence of the emperor had combined to pacify eloquence herself, like everything else.

'What I am going to say may perhaps seem ridiculously trivial, 39 but I'll say it all the same to get a laugh purposely. Don't we agree that eloquence has been brought into disrepute by those tight cloaks that enclose and fetter us when we chat away to the judges? Hasn't it been emasculated by the recital halls and public record offices where cases are now normally disposed of? Well-bred horses are proved by spacious race-tracks: and there is similarly a kind of unfenced field where orators must run free and unshackled if eloquence is not to be weakened and broken. We even find ourselves thwarted by the very trouble we take over careful style, because the judge often asks when you propose to begin—and you have to begin there, the moment he asks. Often the judge orders silence when proofs or evidence are being given. Only one or two people are present amidst all this, and matters

proceed in a sort of vacuum. But what an orator needs is noise
and applause, a theatre for his performance: the old orators had
all that every day. An audience large (and well-bred too) packed
the forum; clients, fellow tribesmen, municipal delegations, a
good proportion of the population of Italy came to support
defendants—for in many cases the Roman people believed that
what was decided mattered to *them*. It is well known that when
Gaius Cornelius, Marcus Scaurus, Titus Milo, Lucius Bestia,
and Publius Vatinius were prosecuted and defended* the whole
state came running to listen: even the most tepid orator might
have been excited and inflamed by the enthusiasm of the partisan
public. And this is why, surely, these speeches are extant, and are
so fine that their authors need cite no other evidence to be put in
their true class.

40   'Moreover, the constant public assemblies, the opportunity to
harass any powerful man, the fact that vendettas could bring
actual fame—for many eloquent speakers did not scruple to
attack even Scipio, Sulla, or Pompey, and even actors used their
control of the public ear to assault grave personages (such is
malice!)—all this made speakers eager, and gave the spur to
oratory.

'It is no inert and passive thing I speak of, that rejoices in
probity and modesty. The great and famous eloquence I have in
mind is the nurseling of licence—which fools call liberty—and
the companion of sedition: it unbridles and spurs on the people;
it has no respect for persons, no proper dignity; it is insolent,
rash, arrogant; in well-organized states it does not arise. What
Spartan or Cretan orators have we heard of? Yet those states
reputedly had the severest constitutions and the severest laws.
We know of no eloquence that flourished among the Macedonians
or Persians or any race that was content not to challenge its
rulers. There were some Rhodian orators, and many Athenian
ones—and in their cities everything was in the power of the
people, everything under the control of the inexperienced:
everyone, you might almost say, had a hand in everything. Our
state, so long as it drifted, so long as it sapped itself by faction,
dissension, and discord, so long as there was no peace in the
forum, no agreement in the senate, no settled routine in the
courts, no respect for superiors, no restriction imposed on

magistrates, produced no doubt a stronger eloquence, just as an untilled field has some more luxuriant plants. But the eloquence of the Gracchi was not worth to the republic the price it had to pay—the laws of the Gracchi: and Cicero, by the end he met, bought his fame in eloquence at too high a cost.

'And what remains of the old forum only goes to prove that the 41 state is not yet healed, not yet settled as we should wish. Who needs our advocacy except the guilty or the unfortunate? What town becomes our client unless it is harassed by a neighbouring people or by internal discord? Do we defend a province unless it has been despoiled and plundered? It would have been better not to have to complain than to have the complaint rectified. If a state in which no one committed any crime could be found, the orator would be superfluous amidst those innocent men, like a doctor among the healthy. And just as medicine has little practice and has made little progress in races that have the best health and the soundest constitutions, so among dutiful citizens ready to serve their ruler orators have less honour and a more obscure name. What need of long speeches in the senate? Our great men swiftly reach agreement. What need of constant harangues to the people? The deliberations of state are not left to the ignorant many—they are the duty of one man, the wisest. What need of prosecutions? Crime is rare and trivial. What need of long and unpopular defences? The clemency of the judge meets the defendants half way. Believe me, my excellent friends, who are as eloquent as our day requires: if you had been born in earlier ages and those men we so much admire had been born in our times, some god having suddenly switched round your lives and periods, you would not have missed the highest distinction in eloquence—and they would not have failed to observe moderation. As it is, since no one can at the same time enjoy both great fame and great peace, let each group enjoy the blessings of his own age without carping at the other's.'

Maternus had finished. Messalla said: 'I should have liked to 42 contradict some things and hear more about others. But the day is over.'

'Let that be later on, as you like,' said Maternus, 'and if anything seemed obscure in what I said, we can discuss it again.'

And he got up, and embraced Aper, saying: 'I will denounce you to the poets, and Messalla will to the antiquarians.'

'And I will denounce both of you to the rhetoricians and the professors.'

They laughed; and we went our ways.

handwritten annotations at top:
gender + these dichotimy.
18 C painting circles
sweep them away
w/ emotion
Friedrich
moment of
sublimity

'LONGINUS': *ON SUBLIMITY*

PREFACE

My dear Postumius Terentianus,*

You will recall that when we were reading together Caecilius'* 1.1
monograph *On Sublimity*, we felt that it was inadequate to its high
subject, and failed to touch the essential points. Nor indeed did it
appear to offer the reader much practical help, though this ought
to be a writer's principal object. Two things are required of any
textbook: first, that it should explain what its subject is; second,
and more important, that it should explain how and by what
methods we can achieve it. Caecilius tries at immense length to
explain to us what sort of thing 'the sublime' is, as though we did
not know; but he has somehow passed over as unnecessary the
question how we can develop our nature to some degree of
greatness. However, we ought perhaps not so much to blame our 2
author for what he has left out as to commend him for his
originality and enthusiasm.

You have urged me to set down a few notes on sublimity for
your own use. Let us then consider whether there is anything in
my observations which may be thought useful to public men. You
must help me, my friend, by giving your honest opinion in detail,
as both your natural candour and your friendship with me
require. It was well said that what man has in common with the
gods is 'doing good and telling the truth'.

Your education dispenses me from any long preliminary 3
definition. Sublimity is a kind of eminence or excellence of
discourse. It is the source of the distinction of the very greatest
poets and prose writers and the means by which they have given
eternal life to their own fame. For grandeur produces ecstasy 4
rather than persuasion in the hearer; and the combination of
wonder and astonishment always proves superior to the merely
persuasive and pleasant. This is because persuasion is on the
whole something we can control, whereas amazement and
wonder exert invincible power and force and get the better of
every hearer. Experience in invention and ability to order and
arrange material cannot be detected in single passages; we begin

handwritten at bottom left: divine frenzy? suddenness

to appreciate them only when we see the whole context. Sublimity, on the other hand, produced at the right moment, tears everything up like a whirlwind, and exhibits the orator's whole power at a single blow.

2.1 Your own experience will lead you to these and similar considerations. The question from which I must begin is whether there is in fact an art of sublimity or profundity.* Some people think it is a complete mistake to reduce things like this to technical rules. Greatness, the argument runs, is a natural product, and does not come by teaching. The only art is to be born like that. They believe moreover that natural products are very much weakened by being reduced to the bare bones of a textbook.

2 In my view, these arguments can be refuted by considering three points:

(i) Though nature is on the whole a law unto herself in matters of emotion and elevation, she is not a random force and does not work altogether without method.

(ii) She is herself in every instance a first and primary element of creation, but it is method that is competent to provide and contribute quantities and appropriate occasions for everything, as well as perfect correctness in training and application.

(iii) Grandeur is particularly dangerous when left on its own, unaccompanied by knowledge, unsteadied, unballasted, abandoned to mere impulse and ignorant temerity. It often needs the curb as well as the spur.

3 What Demosthenes* said of life in general is true also of literature: good fortune is the greatest of blessings, but good counsel comes next, and the lack of it destroys the other also. In literature, nature occupies the place of good fortune, and art that of good counsel. Most important of all, the very fact that some things in literature depend on nature alone can itself be learned only from art.

If the critic of students of this subject will bear these points in mind, he will, I believe, come to realize that the examination of the question before us is by no means useless or superfluous.

[Lacuna equivalent to about two of these printed pages]

FAULTS INCIDENT TO THE EFFORT TO ACHIEVE SUBLIMITY: TURGIDITY, PUERILITY, FALSE EMOTION, FRIGIDITY

> . . . restrain the oven's mighty glow.   3.1
> For if I see but one beside his hearth,
> I'll thrust in just one tentacle of storm,
> and fire his roof and turn it all to cinders.
> I've not yet sung my proper song.*

This is not tragedy; it is a parody of the tragic manner—tentacles, vomiting to heaven, making Boreas a flute-player, and so on. The result is not impressiveness but turbid diction and confused imagery. If you examine the details closely, they gradually sink from the terrifying to the contemptible.

Now if untimely turgidity is unpardonable in tragedy, a genre which is naturally magniloquent and tolerant of bombast, it will scarcely be appropriate in writing which has to do with real life. Hence the ridicule attaching to Gorgias of Leontini's 'Xerxes,   2 the Persians' Zeus' and 'their living tombs, the vultures', or to various things in Callisthenes, where he has not so much risen to heights as been carried off his feet. Clitarchus is an even more striking example; he is an inflated writer, and, as Sophocles has it,

> blows at his tiny flute, the mouth-band off.

Amphicrates, Hegesias, Matris—they are all the same.* They often fancy themselves possessed when they are merely playing the fool.

Turgidity is a particularly hard fault to avoid, for it is one to   3 which all who aim at greatness naturally incline, because they seek to escape the charge of weakness and aridity. They act on the principle that 'to slip from a great prize is yet a noble fault'. In   4 literature as in the body, puffy and false tumours are bad, and may well bring us to the opposite result from that which we expected. As the saying goes, there is nothing so dry as a man with dropsy.

While turgidity is an endeavour to go above the sublime, puerility is the sheer opposite of greatness; it is a thoroughly low,

[margin annotations:] charges levied against mannerist painting

find fault with

over-determined insincere

mean, and ignoble vice. What do I mean by 'puerility'? A pedantic thought, so over-worked that it ends in frigidity. Writers slip into it through aiming at originality, artifice, and (above all) charm, and then coming to grief on the rocks of tawdriness and affectation.

5 A third kind of fault—what Theodorus called 'the pseudo-bacchanalian'—corresponds to these in the field of emotion. It consists of untimely or meaningless emotion where none is in place, or immoderate emotion where moderate is in place. Some people often get carried away, like drunkards, into emotions unconnected with the subject, which are simply their own pedantic invention. The audience feels nothing, so that they inevitably make an exhibition of themselves, parading their ecstasies before an audience which does not share them.

4.1 But I reserve the subject of emotion for another place, returning meanwhile to the second fault of those I mentioned: frigidity. This is a constant feature in Timaeus, who is in many ways a competent writer, not without the capacity for greatness on occasion, learned and original, but as unconscious of his own faults as he is censorious of others', and often falling into the grossest childishness through his passion for always starting

2 exotic ideas. I will give one or two examples; Caecilius has already cited most of those available.

(i) In praise of Alexander the Great, Timaeus writes: 'He conquered all Asia in fewer years than it took Isocrates to write the *Panegyricus** to advocate the Persian war.' What a splendid comparison this is—the Macedonian king and the sophist! On the same principle, the Lacedaemonians were very much less brave than Isocrates: it took them thirty years to capture Messene, whereas he took only ten to write the *Panegyricus*!

3 (ii) Listen also to Timaeus' comment on the Athenians captured in Sicily.* 'They were punished for their impiety to Hermes and mutilation of his statues, and the main agent of their punishment was one who had a family connection with their victim, Hermocrates the son of Hermon.' I cannot help wondering, my dear Terentianus, why he does not also write about the tyrant Dionysius, 'Because he was impious towards Zeus and Heracles, Dion and Heraclides robbed him of his throne.'

But why speak of Timaeus, when those heroes of letters, 4
Xenophon and Plato, for all that they were trained in Socrates'
school, forget themselves sometimes for the sake of similar petty
pleasures? Thus Xenophon writes in *The Constitution of the
Lacedaemonians*: 'You could hear their voice less than the voice of
stone statues, you could distract their eyes less than the eyes of
bronze images: you would think them more bashful than the very
maidens in the eyes.' It would have been more in keeping with
Amphicrates' manner than Xenophon's to speak of the pupils of
our eyes as bashful maidens.* And what an absurd misconception
to think of everybody's pupils as bashful! The shamelessness of a
person, we are told, appears nowhere so plainly as in the eyes.
Remember the words Achilles uses to revile Agamemnon's
violent temper: 'Drunken sot, with a dog's *eyes*!'* Timaeus, 5
unable to keep his hands off stolen property, as it were, has not
left the monopoly of this frigid conceit to Xenophon. He uses
it in connection with Agathocles, who eloped with his cousin
from the unveiling ceremony of her marriage to another: 'Who
would have done this, if he had not harlots in his eyes for
pupils?'

And what of Plato,* the otherwise divine Plato? He wants to 6
express the idea of writing-tablets. 'They shall write', he says,
'and deposit in the temples memorials of cypress.' Again: 'As for
walls, Megillus, I should concur with Sparta in letting walls sleep
in the earth and not get up.' Herodotus' description* of beautiful 7
women as 'pains on the eyes' is the same sort of thing, though it is
to some extent excused by the fact that the speakers are
barbarians and drunk—not that it is a good thing to make an
exhibition of the triviality of one's mind to posterity, even through
the mouths of characters like these.

All such lapses from dignity arise in literature through a single 5.1
cause: that desire for novelty of thought which is all the rage
today. Evils often come from the same source as blessings; and
so, since beauty of style, sublimity, and charm all conduce to
successful writing, they are also causes and principles not only of
success but of failure. Variation, hyperbole, and the use of plural
for singular are like this too; I shall explain below the dangers
which they involve.

SOME MARKS OF TRUE SUBLIMITY

6.1 At this stage, the question we must put to ourselves for discussion is how to avoid the faults which are so much tied up with sublimity. The answer, my friend, is: by first of all achieving a genuine understanding and appreciation of true sublimity. This is difficult; literary judgement comes only as the final product of long experience. However, for the purposes of instruction, I think we can say that an understanding of all this can be acquired. I approach the problem in this way:

7.1 In ordinary life, nothing is truly great which it is great to despise; wealth, honour, reputation, absolute power—anything in short which has a lot of external trappings—can never seem supremely good to the wise man because it is no small good to despise them. People who could have these advantages if they chose but disdain them out of magnanimity are admired much more than those who actually possess them. It is much the same with elevation in poetry and literature generally. We have to ask ourselves whether any particular example does not give a show of grandeur which, for all its accidental trappings, will, when dissected, prove vain and hollow, the kind of thing which it does a 2 man more honour to despise than to admire. It is our nature to be elevated and exalted by true sublimity. Filled with joy and pride, we come to believe we have created what we have only heard. 3 When a man of sense and literary experience hears something many times over, and it fails to dispose his mind to greatness or to leave him with more to reflect upon than was contained in the mere words, but comes instead to seem valueless on repeated inspection, this is not true sublimity; it endures only for the moment of hearing. Real sublimity contains much food for reflection, is difficult or rather impossible to resist, and makes a 4 strong and ineffaceable impression on the memory. In a word, reckon those things which please everybody all the time as genuinely and finely sublime. When people of different trainings, ways of life, tastes, ages, and manners all agree about something, the judgement and assent of so many distinct voices lends strength and irrefutability to the conviction that their admiration is rightly directed.

THE FIVE SOURCES OF SUBLIMITY; THE PLAN OF THE BOOK

There are, one may say, five most productive sources of sublimity. (Competence in speaking is assumed as a common foundation for all five; nothing is possible without it.)

(i) The first and most important is the power to conceive great thoughts; I defined this in my work on Xenophon.*

(ii) The second is strong and inspired emotion.* (These two sources are for the most part natural; the remaining three involve art.)

(iii) Certain kinds of figures. (These may be divided into figures of thought and figures of speech.)

(iv) Noble diction. This has as subdivisions choice of words and the use of metaphorical and artificial language.

(v) Finally, to round off the whole list, dignified and elevated word-arrangement.

Let us now examine the points which come under each of these heads.

I must first observe, however, that Caecilius has omitted some of the five—emotion, for example. Now if he thought that sublimity and emotion were one and the same thing and always existed and developed together, he was wrong. Some emotions, such as pity, grief, and fear, are found divorced from sublimity and with a low effect. Conversely, sublimity often occurs apart from emotion. Of the innumerable examples of this I select Homer's bold account of the Aloadae:*

Ossa upon Olympus they sought to heap; and on Ossa
Pelion with its shaking forest, to make a path to heaven—

and the even more impressive sequel—

and they would have finished their work . . .

In orators, encomia and ceremonial or exhibition pieces always involve grandeur and sublimity, though they are generally devoid of emotion. Hence those orators who are best at conveying emotion are least good at encomia, and conversely the experts at encomia are not conveyers of emotions. On the other hand, if Caecilius thought that emotion had no contribution to make to

Longinus does not omit emotion

sublimity and therefore thought it not worth mentioning, he was again completely wrong. I should myself have no hesitation in saying that there is nothing so productive of grandeur as noble emotion in the right place. It inspires and possesses our words with a kind of madness and divine spirit.

(I) GREATNESS OF THOUGHT

9.1 The first source, natural greatness, is the most important. Even if it is a matter of endowment rather than acquisition, we must, so far as is possible, develop our minds in the direction of greatness and make them always pregnant with noble thoughts. You ask

2 how this can be done. I wrote elsewhere something like this: 'Sublimity is the echo of a noble mind.' This is why a mere idea, without verbal expression, is sometimes admired for its nobility— just as Ajax's silence* in the Vision of the Dead is grand and

3 indeed more sublime than any words could have been. First then we must state where sublimity comes from: the orator must not have low or ignoble thoughts. Those whose thoughts and habits are trivial and servile all their lives cannot possibly produce anything admirable or worthy of eternity. Words will be great if thoughts are weighty. This is why splendid remarks come

4 naturally to the proud; the man who, when Parmenio* said, 'I should have been content'. . .

[Lacuna equivalent to about six pages.]

SUCCESSFUL AND UNSUCCESSFUL WAYS OF REPRESENTING SUPERNATURAL BEINGS AND OF EXCITING AWE

5 . . . the interval between earth and heaven. One might say that this is the measure not so much of Strife* as of Homer.

Contrast the line about Darkness in Hesiod—if the *Shield* is by Hesiod:

Mucus dripped from her nostrils.*

This gives a repulsive picture, not one to excite awe. But how does Homer magnify the divine power?

> As far as a man can peer through the mist,
> sitting on watch, looking over the wine-dark sea,
> so long is the stride of the gods' thundering horses.*

He uses a cosmic distance to measure their speed. This enormously impressive image would make anybody say, and with reason, that, if the horses of the gods took two strides like that, they would find there was not enough room in the world.

The imaginative pictures in the Battle of the Gods are also 6 very remarkable:

> And the great heavens and Olympus trumpeted around them.
> Aïdoneus, lord of the dead, was frightened in his depths;
> and in fright he leapt from his throne, and shouted,
> for fear the earth-shaker Poseidon might break through the
>   ground,
> and gods and men might see
> the foul and terrible halls, which even the gods detest.*

Do you see how the earth is torn from its foundations, Tartarus laid bare, and the whole universe overthrown and broken up, so that all things—Heaven and Hell, things mortal and things immortal—share the warfare and the perils of that ancient battle? But, terrifying as all this is, it is blasphemous and indecent 7 unless it is interpreted allegorically; in relating the gods' wounds, quarrels, revenges, tears, imprisonments, and manifold misfortunes, Homer, or so it seems to me, has done his best to make the men of the Trojan war gods, and the gods men. If men are unhappy, there is always death as a harbour in trouble; what he has done for his gods is to make them immortal indeed, but immortally miserable.

Much better than the Battle of the Gods are the passages 8 which represent divinity as genuinely unsoiled and great and pure. The lines about Poseidon, much discussed by my predecessors, exemplify this:

> The high hills and the forest trembled,
> and the peaks and the city of Troy and Achaean ships
> under the immortal feet of Poseidon as he went his way.
> He drove over the waves, the sea-monsters gambolled around
>   him,

coming up everywhere out of the deep; they recognized their
  king.
The sea parted in joy; and the horses flew onward.

9   Similarly, the lawgiver of the Jews,* no ordinary man—for he
understood and expressed God's power in accordance with its
worth—writes at the beginning of his *Laws*: 'God said'—now
what?—'"Let there be light", and there was light; "Let there be
earth", and there was earth.'

10   Perhaps it will not be out of place, my friend, if I add a further
Homeric example—from the human sphere this time—so that
we can see how the poet is accustomed to enter into the greatness
of his heroes. Darkness falls suddenly. Thickest night blinds the
Greek army. Ajax is bewildered. 'O Father Zeus!',* he cries,

> 'Deliver the sons of the Achaeans out of the mist,
> make the sky clear, and let us see;
> in the light—kill us.'

The feeling here is genuinely Ajax's. He does not pray for life—
that would be a request unworthy of a hero—but having no good
use for his courage in the disabling darkness, and so angered at
his inactivity in the battle, he prays for light, and quickly: he will
at all costs find a shroud worthy of his valour, though Zeus be
arrayed against him.

COMPARISON BETWEEN THE *ILIAD* AND THE *ODYSSEY*

11   In this passage, the gale of battle blows hard in Homer; he

> rages like Ares, spear-brandishing, or the deadly fire
> raging in the mountains, in the thickets of the deep wood.
> Foam shows at his mouth.*

In the *Odyssey*, on the other hand—and there are many reasons
for adding this to our inquiry—he demonstrates that when a
great mind begins to decline, a love of story-telling characterizes
12 its old age. We can tell that the *Odyssey* was his second work from
various considerations, in particular from his insertion of the
residue of the Trojan troubles in the poem in the form of
episodes, and from the way in which he pays tribute of

lamentation and pity to the heroes, treating them as persons long known. The *Odyssey* is simply an epilogue to the *Iliad*:

> There lies warlike Ajax, there Achilles,
> there Patroclus, the gods' peer as a counsellor,
> and there my own dear son.*

For the same reason, I maintain, he made the whole body of the 13 *Iliad*, which was written at the height of his powers, dramatic and exciting, whereas most of the *Odyssey* consists of narrative, which is a characteristic of old age. Homer in the *Odyssey* may be compared to the setting sun: the size remains without the force. He no longer sustains the tensions as it was in the tale of Troy, nor that consistent level of elevation which never admitted any falling off. The outpouring of passions crowding one on another has gone; so has the versatility, the realism, the abundance of imagery taken from the life. We see greatness on the ebb. It is as though the Ocean were withdrawing into itself and flowing quietly in its own bed. Homer is lost in the realm of the fabulous 14 and incredible. In saying this, I have not forgotten the storms in the *Odyssey*, the story of Cyclops, and a few other episodes; I am speaking of old age—but it is the old age of a Homer. The point about all these stories is that the mythical element in them predominates over the realistic.

I digressed into this topic, as I said, to illustrate how easy it is for great genius to be perverted in decline into nonsense. I mean things like the story of the wineskin, the tale of the men kept as pigs in Circe's palace ('howling piglets', Zoilus called them), the feeding of Zeus by the doves (as though he were a chick in the nest), the ten days on the raft without food, and the improbabilities of the murder of the suitors. What can we say of all this but that it really is 'the dreaming of a Zeus'?

There is also a second reason for discussing the *Odyssey*. I 15 want you to understand that the decline of emotional power in great writers and poets turns to a capacity for depicting manners. The realistic description of Odysseus' household forms a kind of comedy of manners.

SELECTION AND ORGANIZATION OF MATERIAL

10.1 Now have we any other means of making our writing sublime?
Every topic naturally includes certain elements which are
inherent in its raw material. It follows that sublimity will be
achieved if we consistently select the most important of these
inherent features and learn to organize them as a unity by
combining one with another. The first of these procedures
attracts the reader by the selection of details, the second by the
density of those selected.

Consider Sappho's treatment of the feelings involved in the
madness of being in love. She uses the attendant circumstances
and draws on real life at every point. And in what does she show
her quality? In her skill in selecting the outstanding details and
making a unity of them:

2   To me he seems a peer of the gods, the man who sits
facing you and hears your sweet voice
    and lovely laughter; it flutters my heart in my breast. When
I see you only for a moment, I cannot speak;
    my tongue is broken, a subtle fire runs under my skin; my
eyes cannot see, my ears hum;
    cold sweat pours off me; shivering grips me all over; I am
paler than grass; I seem near to dying;
    but all must be endured. . .*

3 Do you not admire the way in which she brings everything
together—mind and body, hearing and tongue, eyes and skin?
She seems to have lost them all, and to be looking for them as
though they were external to her. She is cold and hot, mad and
sane, frightened and near death, all by turns. The result is that
we see in her not a single emotion, but a complex of emotions.
Lovers experience all this; Sappho's excellence, as I have said,
lies in her adoption and combination of the most striking details.

A similar point can be made about the descriptions of storms
4 in Homer, who always picks out the most terrifying aspects. The
author of the *Arimaspea** on the other hand expects these lines to
excite terror:

This too is a great wonder to us in our hearts:
there are men living on water, far from land, on the deep sea:
miserable they are, for hard is their lot;
they give their eyes to the stars, their lives to the sea;
often they raise their hands in prayer to the gods,
as their bowels heave in pain.

Anyone can see that this is more polished than awe-inspiring. 5
Now compare it with Homer (I select one example out of many):

He fell upon them as upon a swift ship falls a wave,
huge, wind-reared by the clouds. The ship
is curtained in foam, a hideous blast of wind
roars in the sail. The sailors shudder in terror:
they are carried away from under death, but only just.*

Aratus tried to transfer the same thought: 6

A little plank wards off Hades.

But this is smooth and unimpressive, not frightening. Moreover,
by saying 'a plank wards off Hades', he has got rid of the danger.
The plank *does* keep death away. Homer, on the other hand, does
not banish the cause of fear at a stroke; he gives a vivid picture of
men, one might almost say, facing death many times with every
wave that comes. Notice also the forced combination of naturally use
uncompoundable prepositions: *hupek*, 'from under'. Homer has word
tortured the words to correspond with the emotion of the choice
moment, and expressed the emotion magnificently by thus manner
crushing words together. He has in effect stamped the special & order
character of the danger on the diction: 'they are carried away to convey
from under death'. meaning

Compare Archilochus on the shipwreck, and Demosthenes* 7
on the arrival of the news ('It was evening . . .').

In short, one might say that these writers have taken only the
very best pieces, polished them up and fitted them together.
They have inserted nothing inflated, undignified, or pedantic.
Such things ruin the whole effect, because they produce, as it
were, gaps or crevices, and so spoil the impressive thoughts
which have been built into a structure whose cohesion depends
upon their mutual relations.

AMPLIFICATION

11.1 The quality called 'amplification' is connected with those we have been considering. It is found when the facts or the issues at stake allow many starts and pauses in each section. You wheel up one impressive unit after another to give a series of increasing
2 importance. There are innumerable varieties of amplification: it may be produced by commonplaces, by exaggeration or intensification of facts or arguments, or by a build-up of action or emotion. The orator should realize, however, that none of these will have its full effect without sublimity. Passages expressing pity or disparagement are no doubt an exception; but in any other instance of amplification, if you take away the sublime element, you take the soul away from the body. Without the strengthening influence of the sublimity, the effective element in the whole loses all its vigour and solidity.
3   What is the difference between this precept and the point made above about the inclusion of vital details and their combination in a unity? What in general is the difference between amplification and sublimity? I must define my position briefly on these points, in order to make myself clear.

12.1 I do not feel satisfied with the definition given by the rhetoricians: 'amplification is expression which adds grandeur to its subject'. This might just as well be a definition of sublimity or emotion or tropes. All these add grandeur of some kind. The difference lies, in my opinion, in the fact that sublimity depends on elevation, whereas amplification involves extension; sublimity exists often in a single thought, amplification cannot exist without
2 a certain quantity and superfluity. To give a general definition, amplification is an aggregation of all the details and topics which constitute a situation, strengthening the argument by dwelling on it; it differs from proof in that the latter demonstrates the point made. . .

[Lacuna equivalent to about two pages.]

SAME GENERAL SUBJECT CONTINUED: A COMPARISON
BETWEEN PLATO AND DEMOSTHENES, WITH A WORD ON
CICERO

. . . spreads out richly in many directions into an open sea of 3
grandeur. Accordingly, Demosthenes, the more emotional of the
two, displays in abundance the fire and heat of passion, while
Plato, consistently magnificent, solemn, and grand, is much less
intense—without of course becoming in the least frigid. These 4
seem to me, my dear Terentianus—if a Greek is allowed an
opinion—to be also the differences between the grandeur of
Cicero and the grandeur of Demosthenes. Demosthenes has an
abrupt sublimity; Cicero spreads himself. Demosthenes burns
and ravages; he has violence, rapidity, strength, and force, and
shows them in everything; he can be compared to a thunderbolt
or a flash of lightning. Cicero, on the other hand, is like
a spreading conflagration. He ranges everywhere and rolls
majestically on. His huge fires endure; they are renewed in
various forms from time to time and repeatedly fed with fresh
fuel.—But this is a comparison which your countrymen can 5
make better than I.

Anyway, the place for the intense, Demosthenic kind of
sublimity is in indignant exaggeration, in violent emotion, and in
general wherever the hearer has to be struck with amazement.
The place for expansiveness is where he has to be deluged with
words. This treatment is appropriate in *loci communes*, epilogues,
digressions, all descriptive and exhibition pieces, historical or
scientific topics, and many other departments.

To return to Plato, and the way in which he combines the 13.1
'soundless flow' of his smooth style with grandeur. A passage of
the *Republic** you have read makes the manner quite clear: 'Men
without experience of wisdom and virtue but always occupied
with feasting and that kind of thing naturally go downhill and
wander through life on a low plane of existence. They never look
upwards to the truth and never rise, they never taste certain or
pure pleasure. Like cattle, they always look down, bowed
earthwards and tablewards; they feed and they breed, and their
greediness in these directions make them kick and butt till they

kill one another with iron horns and hooves, because they can
never be satisfied.'

IMITATION OF EARLIER WRITERS AS A MEANS
TO SUBLIMITY

2 Plato, if we will read him with attention, illustrates yet another
road to sublimity, besides those we have discussed. This is the
way of imitation and emulation of great writers of the past. Here
too, my friend, is an aim to which we must hold fast. Many are
possessed by a spirit not their own. It is like what we are told of
the Pythia* at Delphi: she is in contact with the tripod near the
cleft in the ground which (so they say) exhales a divine vapour,
and she is thereupon made pregnant by the supernatural power
and forthwith prophesies as one inspired. Similarly, the genius of
the ancients acts as a kind of oracular cavern, and effluences flow
from it into the minds of their imitators. Even those previously
not much inclined to prophesy become inspired and share the
enthusiasm which comes from the greatness of others. Was
3 Herodotus the only 'most Homeric' writer? Surely Stesichorus
and Archilochus earned the name before him. So, more than any,
did Plato, who diverted to himself countless rills from the
Homeric spring. (If Ammonius had not selected and written up
detailed examples of this, I might have had to prove the point
4 myself.) In all this process there is no plagiarism. It resembles
rather the reproduction of good character in statues and works of
art. Plato could not have put such a brilliant finish on his
philosophical doctrines or so often risen to poetical subjects and
poetical language, if he had not tried, and tried wholeheartedly,
to compete for the prize against Homer, like a young aspirant
challenging an admired master. To break a lance in this way may
well have been a brash and contentious thing to do, but the
competition proved anything but valueless. As Hesiod says, 'this
strife is good for men.'* Truly it is a noble contest and prize of
honour, and one well worth winning, in which to be defeated by
one's elders is itself no disgrace.

14.1 We can apply this to ourselves. When we are working on
something which needs loftiness of expression and greatness of
thought, it is good to imagine how Homer would have said the

same thing, or how Plato or Demosthenes or (in history) Thucydides would have invested it with sublimity. These great figures, presented to us as objects of emulation and, as it were, shining before our gaze, will somehow elevate our minds to the greatness of which we form a mental image. They will be even 2 more effective if we ask ourselves 'How would Homer or Demosthenes have reacted to what I am saying, if he had been here? What would his feelings have been?' It makes it a great occasion if you imagine such a jury or audience for your own speech, and pretend that you are answering for what you write before judges and witnesses of such heroic stature. Even more 3 stimulating is the further thought: 'How will posterity take what I am writing?' If a man is afraid of saying anything which will outlast his own life and age, the conceptions of his mind are bound to be incomplete and abortive; they will miscarry and never be brought to birth whole and perfect for the day of posthumous fame.

VISUALIZATION (*PHANTASIA*)

Another thing which is extremely productive of grandeur, 15.1 magnificence and urgency, my young friend, is visualization (*phantasia*). I use this word for what some people call image-production. The term *phantasia* is used generally for anything which in any way suggests a thought productive of speech; but the word has also come into fashion for the situation in which enthusiasm and emotion make the speaker *see* what he is saying and bring it *visually* before his audience. It will not escape you 2 that rhetorical visualization has a different intention from that of the poets: in poetry the aim is astonishment, in oratory it is clarity. Both, however, seek emotion and excitement.

> Mother, I beg you, do not drive them at me,
> the women with the blood in their eyes and the snakes—
> they are here, they are here, jumping right up to me*

Or again:

> O! O! She'll kill me. Where shall I escape?

The poet himself saw the Erinyes, and has as good as made his audience see what he imagined.

3   Now Euripides devotes most pains to producing a tragic effect with two emotions, madness and love. In these he is supremely successful. At the same time, he does not lack the courage to attempt other types of visualization. Though not formed by nature for grandeur, he often forces himself to be tragic. When the moment for greatness comes, he (in Homer's words)

> whips flank and buttocks with his tail
> and drives himself to fight.*

4 For example, here is Helios handing the reins to Phaethon:*

> 'Drive on, but do not enter Libyan air—
> it has no moisture in it, and will let
> your wheel fall through—'

and again:

> 'Steer towards the seven Pleiads.'
> The boy listened so far, then seized the reins,
> whipped up the winged team, and let them go.
> To heaven's expanse they flew.
> His father rode behind on Sirius,
> giving the boy advice: 'That's your way, there:
> turn here, turn here.'

May one not say that the writer's soul has mounted the chariot, has taken wing with the horses and shares the danger? Had it not been up among those heavenly bodies and moved in their courses, he could never have visualized such things.

    Compare, too, his Cassandra:

> Ye Trojans, lovers of horses. . .*

5   Aeschylus, of course, ventures on the most heroic visualizations; he is like his own Seven against Thebes*—

> Seven men of war, commanders of companies,
> killing a bull into a black-bound shield,
> dipping their hands in the bull's blood,
> took oath by Ares, by Enyo, by bloodthirsty Terror—

in a joint pledge of death in which they showed themselves no mercy. At the same time, he does sometimes leave his thoughts unworked, tangled and hard. The ambitious Euripides does not shirk even these risks. For example, there is in Aeschylus a 6 remarkable description of the palace of Lycurgus* in its divine seizure at the moment of Dionysus' epiphany:

> the palace was possessed, the house went bacchanal.

Euripides expresses the same thought less harshly:

> the whole mountain went bacchanal with them.

There is another magnificent visualization in Sophocles'* 7 account of Oedipus dying and giving himself burial to the accompaniment of a sign from heaven, and in the appearance of Achilles over his tomb at the departure of the Greek fleet. Simonides has perhaps described this scene more vividly than anyone else; but it is impossible to quote everything.

The poetical examples, as I said, have a quality of exaggeration 8 which belongs to fable and goes far beyond credibility. In an orator's visualizations, on the other hand, it is the element of fact and truth which makes for success; when the content of the passage is poetical and fabulous and does not shrink from any impossibility, the result is a shocking and outrageous abnormality. This is what happens with the shock orators of our own day; like tragic actors, these fine fellows *see* the Erinyes, and are incapable of understanding that when Orestes says

> Let me go; you are one of my Erinyes,
> you are hugging me tight, to throw me into Hell,*

he visualizes all this *because he is mad*.

What then is the effect of rhetorical visualization? There is 9 much it can do to bring urgency and passion into our words; but it is when it is closely involved with factual arguments that it enslaves the hearer as well as persuading him. 'Suppose you heard a shout this very moment outside the court, and someone said that the prison had been broken open and the prisoners had escaped—no one, young or old, would be so casual as not to give what help he could. And if someone then came forward and said "This is the man who let them out", our friend would never get a hearing; it would be the end of him.'* There is a similar instance 10 in Hyperides' defence of himself when he was on trial for the

[handwritten margin notes:] the more vivid the more holds on to the audience

[handwritten note at bottom:] evoking visual image.

proposal to liberate the slaves which he put forward after the defeat. 'It was not the proposer', he said, 'who drew up this decree: it was the battle of Chaeronea.'* Here the orator uses a visualization actually in the moment of making his factual argument, with the result that his thought has taken him beyond

11 the limits of mere persuasiveness. Now our natural instinct is, in all such cases, to attend to the stronger influence, so that we are diverted from the demonstration to the astonishment caused by the visualization, which by its very brilliance conceals the factual aspect. This is a natural reaction: when two things are joined together, the stronger attracts to itself the force of the weaker.

12 This will suffice for an account of sublimity of thought produced by greatness of mind, imitation, or visualization.

(iii) FIGURES: AN EXAMPLE TO ILLUSTRATE THE RIGHT USE OF FIGURES: THE 'OATH' IN 'ON THE CROWN'

16.1 The next topic* is that of figures. Properly handled, figures constitute, as I said, no small part of sublimity. It would be a vast, or rather infinite, labour to enumerate them all; what I shall do is to expound a few of those which generate sublimity, simply in order to confirm my point.

2 Here is Demosthenes* putting forward a demonstrative argument on behalf of his policy. What would have been the natural way to put it? 'You have not done wrong, you who fought for the liberty of Greece; you have examples to prove this close at home: the men of Marathon, of Salamis, of Plataea did not do wrong.' But instead of this he was suddenly inspired to give voice to the oath by the heroes of Greece: 'By those who risked their lives at Marathon, you have not done wrong!' Observe what he effects by this single figure of conjuration, or 'apostrophe' as I call it here. He deifies his audience's ancestors, suggesting that it is right to take an oath by men who fell so bravely, as though they were gods. He inspires the judges with the temper of those who risked their lives. He transforms his demonstration into an extraordinary piece of sublimity and passion, and into the convincingness of this unusual and amazing oath. At the same time he injects into his hearers' minds a healing specific, so as to lighten their hearts by these paeans of praise and make them as

proud of the battle with Philip as of the triumphs of Marathon and Salamis. In short, the figure enables him to run away with his audience.

Now the origin of this oath is said to be in the lines of 3 Eupolis:*

> By Marathon, by *my* battle,
> no one shall grieve me and not suffer for it.

But the greatness depends not on the mere form of the oath, but on place, manner, occasion, and purpose. In Eupolis, there is nothing but the oath; he is speaking to the Athenians while their fortunes are still high and they need no comfort; and instead of immortalizing the men in order to engender in the audience a proper estimation of their valour, he wanders away from the actual people who risked their lives to an inanimate object, namely the battle. In Demosthenes, on the other hand, the oath is addressed to a defeated nation, to make them no longer think of Chaeronea as a disaster. It embraces, as I said, a demonstration that they 'did no wrong', an illustrative example, a confirmation, an encomium, and an exhortation. Moreover, 4 because he was faced with the possible objection 'your policies brought us to defeat—and yet you swear by victories!' he brings his thought back under control and makes it safe and unanswerable, showing that sobriety is needed even under the influence of inspiration: 'By those who *risked their lives* at Marathon, and *fought in the ships* at Salamis and Artemisium, and *formed the line* at Plataea!' He never says *conquered*; throughout he withholds the word for the final issue, because it was a happy issue, and the opposite to that of Chaeronea. From the same motives he forestalls his audience by adding immediately: 'all of whom were buried at the city's expense, Aeschines—all, not only the successful.'

THE RELATION BETWEEN FIGURES AND SUBLIMITY

At this point, my friend, I feel I ought not to pass over an 17.1 observation of my own. It shall be very brief: figures are natural allies of sublimity and themselves profit wonderfully from the alliance. I will explain how this happens.

Playing tricks by means of figures is a peculiarly suspect procedure. It raises the suspicion of a trap, a deep design, a fallacy. It is to be avoided in addressing a judge who has power to decide, and especially in addressing tyrants, kings, governors, or anybody in a high place. Such a person immediately becomes angry if he is led astray like a foolish child by some skilful orator's figures. He takes the fallacy as indicating contempt for himself. He becomes like a wild animal. Even if he controls his temper, he is now completely conditioned against being convinced by what is said. A figure is therefore generally thought to be best when the fact that it is a figure is concealed.

2   Thus sublimity and emotion are a defence and a marvellous aid against the suspicion which the use of figures engenders. The artifice of the trick is lost to sight in the surrounding brilliance of beauty and grandeur, and it escapes all suspicion. 'By the men of Marathon . . .' is proof enough. For how did Demosthenes conceal the figure in that passage? By sheer brilliance, of course. As fainter lights disappear when the sunshine surrounds them, so the sophisms of rhetoric are dimmed when they are enveloped in encircling grandeur. Something like this happens in painting: when light and shadow are juxtaposed in colours on the same plane, the light seems more prominent to the eye, and both stands out and actually appears much nearer. Similarly, in literature, emotional and sublime features seem closer to the mind's eye, both because of a certain natural kinship and because of their brilliance. Consequently, they always show up above the figures, and overshadow and eclipse their artifice.

RHETORICAL QUESTIONS

18.1   What are we to say of inquiries and questions? Should we not say that they increase the realism and vigour of the writing by the actual form of the figure?

'Or—tell me—do you want to go round asking one another "Is there any news?"? What could be hotter news than that a Macedonian is conquering Greece? "Is Philip dead?" "No, but he's ill." What difference does it make to you? If anything happens to him, you will soon create another Philip.'

Again: 'Let us sail to Macedonia. "Where shall we anchor?" says someone. The war itself will find out Philip's weak spots.'* Put in the straightforward form, this would have been quite insignificant; as it is, the impassioned rapidity of question and answer and the device of self-objection have made the remark, in virtue of its figurative form, not only more sublime but more credible. For emotion carries us away more easily when it seems 2 to be generated by the occasion rather than deliberately assumed by the speaker, and the self-directed question and its answer represent precisely this momentary quality of emotion. Just as people who are unexpectedly plied with questions become annoyed and reply to the point with vigour and exact truth, so the figure of question and answer arrests the hearer and cheats him into believing that all the points made were raised and are being put into words on the spur of the moment.

Again—this sentence in Herodotus* is believed to be a particularly fine example of sublimity. . .

[Lacuna equivalent to about two pages.]

ASYNDETON

. . . the words tumble out without connection, in a kind of stream, 19.1 almost getting ahead of the speaker. Xenophon* says: 'Engaging their shields, they pushed, fought, slew, died'.

'We went as you told us, noble Odysseus, up the woods, 2
we saw a beautiful palace built in the glades',

says Homer's Eurylochus.*
Disconnected and yet hurried phrases convey the impression of an agitation which both obstructs the reader and drives him on. Such is the effect of Homer's asyndeta.

ASYNDETON COMBINED WITH ANAPHORA

The conjunction of several figures in one phrase also has a very 20.1 stirring effect. Two or three may be joined together in a kind of team, jointly contributing strength, persuasiveness, charm. An example is the passage in *Against Midias*,* where asyndeton is

combined with anaphora and vivid description. 'The aggressor would do many things—some of which his victim would not even be able to tell anyone else—with gesture, with look, with voice.'
2 Then, to save the sentence from monotony and a stationary effect—for this goes with inertia, whereas disorder goes with emotion, which is a disturbance and movement of the mind—he leaps immediately to fresh instances of asyndeton and epanaphora: 'With gesture, with look, with voice, when he insults, when he acts as an enemy, when he slaps the fellow, when he slaps him on the ears. . .' The orator is doing here exactly what the bully
3 does—hitting the jury in the mind with blow after blow. Then he comes down with a fresh onslaught, like a sudden squall: '. . . when he slaps the fellow, when he slaps him on the ears. That rouses a man, that makes him lose control, when he is not used to being insulted. No one could bring out the horror of such a moment by a mere report.' Here Demosthenes keeps up the natural effect of epanaphora and asyndeton by frequent variation. His order becomes disorderly, his disorder in turn acquires a certain order.

POLYSYNDETON

21.1 Now add the conjunctions, as Isocrates' school does. 'Again, one must not omit this point, that the aggressor would do many things, first with gesture, then with look, and finally with voice.' As you proceed with these insertions, it will become clear that the urgent and harsh character of the emotion loses its sting and becomes a spent fire as soon as you level it down to smoothness
2 by the conjunctions. If you tie a runner's arms to his side, you take away his speed; likewise, emotion frets at being impeded by conjunctions and other additions, because it loses the free abandon of its movement and the sense of being, as it were, catapulted out.

HYPERBATON

22.1 Hyperbaton belongs to the same general class. It is an arrangement of words or thoughts which differs from the normal sequence. . .* It is a very real mark of urgent emotion. People who in real life feel anger, fear, or indignation, or are distracted by jealousy or some other emotion (it is impossible to say how many emotions there are; they are without number), often put one thing forward and then rush off to another, irrationally inserting some remark, and then hark back again to their first point. They seem to be blown this way and that by their excitement, as if by a veering wind. They inflict innumerable variations on the expression, the thought, and the natural sequence. Thus hyperbaton is a means by which, in the best authors, imitation approaches the effect of nature. Art is perfect when it looks like nature, nature is felicitous when it embraces concealed art. Consider the words of Dionysius of Phocaea in Herodotus.* 'Now, for our affairs are on the razor's edge, men of Ionia, whether we are to be free or slaves—and worse than slaves, runaways—so if you will bear hardships now, you will suffer temporarily but be able to overcome your enemies.' The natural order of thought would have been: 'Men of Ionia, now is the time for you to bear hardships, for our affairs are on the razor's edge.' The speaker has displaced 'men of Ionia'; he begins with the cause of fear, as though the alarm was so pressing that he did not even have time to address the audience by name. He has also diverted the order of thought. Before saying that they must suffer hardship themselves (that is the gist of his exhortation), he first gives the reason why it is necessary, by saying 'our affairs are on the razor's edge'. The result is that he seems to be giving not a premeditated speech but one forced on him by the circumstances.

It is even more characteristic of Thucydides to show ingenuity in separating by transpositions even things which are by nature completely unified and indivisible.

Demosthenes is less wilful in this than Thucydides, but no one uses this kind of effect more lavishly. His transpositions produce not only a great sense of urgency but the appearance of extemporization, as he drags his hearers with him into the hazards of his long hyperbata. He often holds in suspense the meaning which he set out to convey and, introducing one extraneous item after another in an alien and unusual place before getting to the main point, throws the hearer into a panic lest the sentence collapse altogether, and forces him in his excitement to share the speaker's peril, before, at long last and beyond all expectation, appositely paying off at the end the long due conclusion; the very audacity and hazardousness of the hyperbata add to the astounding effect. There are so many examples that I forbear to give any.

CHANGES OF CASE, TENSE, PERSON, NUMBER, GENDER; PLURAL FOR SINGULAR AND SINGULAR FOR PLURAL

23.1 What is called polyptoton,* like accumulation, variation, and climax, is, as you know, extremely effective and contributes both to ornament and to sublimity and emotion of every kind.

2 How do variations in case, tense, person, number, and gender diversify and stimulate the style? My answer to this is that, as regards variations of number, the lesser effect (though a real one) is produced by instances in which singular forms are seen on reflection to be plural in sense:

> The innumerable host
> were scattered over the sandy beach, and shouted.*

More worthy of note are the examples in which plurals give a more grandiose effect, and court success by the sense of 3 multitude expressed by the grammatical number. An example comes in Sophocles,* where Oedipus says:

> Weddings, weddings,
> you bred me and again released my seed,
> made fathers, brothers, children, blood of the kin,
> brides, wives, mothers—all
> the deeds most horrid ever seen in men.

All this is about Oedipus on the one hand and Jocasta on the other, but the expansion of the number to the plural forms pluralizes the misfortunes also.

Another example is:

> Hectors and Sarpedons came forth.*

4 Another is the Platonic passage about the Athenians, which I have quoted elsewhere: 'No Pelopses or Cadmuses or Aegyptuses or Danauses or other barbarians by birth have settled

among us; we are pure Greeks, with no barbarian blood',* and so on. Such an agglomeration of names in crowds naturally makes the facts sound more impressive. But the practice is only to be followed when the subject admits amplification, abundance, hyperbole, or emotion—one or more of these. Only a sophist has bells on his harness wherever he goes.

24.1 The contrary device—the contraction of plurals into singulars— also sometimes produces a sublime effect. 'The whole Peloponnese was divided.'* 'When Phrynichus* produced *The Capture of Miletus* the theatre burst into tears' ('theatre' for 'spectators'). To compress the separate individuals into the corresponding unity produces a more solid effect.

2 The cause of the effect is the same in both cases. Where the nouns are singular, it is a mark of unexpected emotion to pluralize them. Where they are plural, to unite the plurality under one well-sounding word is again surprising because of the opposite transformation of the facts.

VIVID PRESENT TENSE

25.1 To represent past events as present is to turn a narrative into a thing of immediate urgency. 'A man who has fallen under Cyrus' horse and is being trampled strikes the horse in the belly with his sword. The horse, convulsed, shakes Cyrus off. He falls' (Xenophon).* This is common in Thucydides.

IMAGINARY SECOND PERSON

26.1 Urgency may also be conveyed by the replacement of one grammatical person by another. It often gives the hearer the sense of being in the midst of the danger himself.

'You would say they were tireless, never wearied in war,
so eagerly they fought' (Homer).*

'May you never be drenched in the sea in that month!' (Aratus).*

2 'You will sail upstream from Elephantine, and then you will come to a smooth plain. After crossing this, you will embark on

another boat and sail for two days. Then you will come to a great
city called Meroe' (Herodotus.).*

Do you see, my friend, how he grips your mind and takes it on
tour through all these places, making hearing as good as seeing?
All such forms of expression, being directed to an actual person,
bring the hearer into the presence of real events.

3   Moreover, if <u>you speak as though to an individual and not to a</u>
<u>large company, you will affect him more and make him more</u>
<u>attentive and excited</u>, because the personal address stimulates:

> You could not tell with whom Tydides stood.*

LAPSES INTO DIRECT SPEECH

27.1 Sometimes a writer, in the course of a narrative in the third
person, makes a sudden change and speaks in the person of his
character. This kind of thing is an outburst of emotion.

> Hector shouted aloud to the Trojans
> to rush for the ships, and leave the spoils of the dead.
> 'If I see anyone away from the ships of his own accord,
> I will have him killed on the spot.'*

Here the poet has given the narrative to himself, as appropriate to
him, and then suddenly and without warning has put the abrupt
threat in the mouth of the angry prince. It would have been flat if
he had added, 'Hector said'. As it is, the change of construction
is so sudden that it has outstripped its creator.

2   Hence the use of this figure is appropriate when the urgency of
the moment gives the writer no chance to delay, but forces on
him an immediate change from one person to another. 'Ceyx was
distressed at this, and ordered the children to depart. "For I am
unable to help you. Go therefore to some other country, so as to
save yourselves without harming me"' (Hecataeus).*

3   Somewhat different is the method by which Demosthenes in
*Against Aristogiton** makes variation of person produce the effect
of strong emotion and rapid change of tone: 'Will none of you be
found to feel bile or anger at the violence of this shameless
monster, who—you vile wretch, your right of free speech is
barred not by gates and doors which can be opened, but. . .!' He

makes the change before the sense is complete, and in effect divides a single thought between two persons in his passion ('who—you vile wretch. . .!'), as well as turning to Aristogiton and giving the impression of abandoning the course of his argument—with the sole result, so strong is the emotion, of giving it added intensity.

So also Penelope:*   4

Herald, why have the proud suitors sent you here?
Is it to tell Odysseus' maidservants
to stop their work and get dinner for them?
After their wooing, may they never meet again!
May this be their last dinner here—
you who gather together so often and waste wealth,
who never listened to your fathers when you were children
and they told you what kind of man Odysseus was!

PERIPHRASIS

No one, I fancy, would question the fact that periphrasis is a   28.1
means to sublimity. As in music the melody is made sweeter by
what is called the accompaniment, so periphrasis is often heard
in concert with the plain words and enhances them with a new
resonance. This is especially true if it contains nothing bombastic
or tasteless but only what is pleasantly blended. There is a   2
sufficient example in Plato, at the beginning of the Funeral
Speech:* 'These men have received their due, and having
received it they go on their fated journey, escorted publicly by
their country and privately each by his own kindred.' Plato here
calls death a 'fated journey' and the bestowal of regular funeral
rites a public escort by the country. This surely adds no
inconsiderable impressiveness to the thought. He has lyricized
the bare prose, enveloping it in the harmony of the beautiful
periphrases.

'You believe labour to be the guide to a pleasant life; you have   3
gathered into your souls the noblest and most heroic of
possessions: you enjoy being praised more than anything else in
the world' (Xenophon).* In this passage 'you make labour the
guide to a pleasant life' is put for 'you are willing to labour'. This

and the other expansions invest the praise with a certain grandeur of conception.

4 Another example is the inimitable sentence of Herodotus:* 'The goddess inflicted a feminine disease on the Scythians who plundered the temple.'

29.1 Periphrasis, however, is a particularly dangerous device if it is not used with moderation. It soon comes to be heavy and dull, smelling of empty phrases and coarseness of fibre. This is why Plato*—who is fond of the figure and sometimes uses it unseasonably—is ridiculed for the sentence in the *Laws* which runs: 'Neither silvern wealth nor golden should be permitted to establish itself in the city.' If he had wanted to prohibit cattle, says the critic, he would have talked of 'ovine and bovine' wealth.

CONCLUSION OF THE SECTION ON FIGURES

2 So much, my dear Terentianus, by way of digression on the theory of the use of those figures which conduce to sublimity. They all make style more emotional and excited, and emotion is as essential a part of sublimity as characterization is of charm.

(iv) DICTION: GENERAL REMARKS

30.1 Thought and expression are of course very much involved with each other. We have therefore next to consider whether any topics still remain in the field of diction. The choice of correct and magnificent words is a source of immense power to entice and charm the hearer. This is something which all orators and other writers cultivate intensely. It makes grandeur, beauty, old-world charm, weight, force, strength, and a kind of lustre bloom upon our words as upon beautiful statues; it gives things life and makes them speak. But I suspect there is no need for me to make

2 this point; you know it well. It is indeed true that beautiful words are the light that illuminates thought.

Magniloquence, however, is not always serviceable: to dress up trivial material in grand and solemn language is like putting a huge tragic mask on a little child. In poetry and history, however . . .

[Lacuna equivalent to about four pages.]

USE OF EVERYDAY WORDS

... and productive, as is Anacreon's 'I no longer turn my mind to 31.1
the Thracian filly'.* Similarly, Theopompus' much-admired phrase
seems to me to be particularly expressive because of the aptness
of the analogy, though Caecilius manages to find fault with it:
'Philip was excellent at stomaching facts.' An idiomatic phrase is
sometimes much more vivid than an ornament of speech, for it is
immediately recognized from everyday experience, and the
familiar is inevitably easier to credit. 'To stomach facts' is thus
used vividly of a man who endures unpleasantness and squalor
patiently, and indeed with pleasure, for the sake of gain. There 2
are similar things in Herodotus.* 'Cleomenes in his madness cut
his own flesh into little pieces with a knife till he had sliced
himself to death', 'Pythes continued fighting on the ship until he
was cut into joints.' These phrases come within an inch of being
vulgar, but they are so expressive that they avoid vulgarity.

METAPHORS

As regards number of metaphors, Caecilius seems to agree with 32.1
the propounders of the rule that not more than two or at most
three may be used of the same subject. Here too Demosthenes is
our canon. The right occasions are when emotions come
flooding in and bring the multiplication of metaphors with them
as a necessary accompaniment. 'Vile flatterers, mutilators of 2
their countries, who have given away liberty as a drinking
present, first to Philip and now to Alexander, measuring
happiness by the belly and the basest impulses, overthrowing
liberty and freedom from despotism, which Greeks of old
regarded as the canons and standards of the good.'* In this
passage the orator's anger against traitors obscures the multiplicity
of his metaphors.

This is why Aristotle and Theophrastus say that there are ways 3
of softening bold metaphors—namely by saying 'as if', 'as it
were', 'if I may put it so', or 'if we may venture on a bold
expression'. Apology, they say, is a remedy for audacity. I accept 4
this doctrine, but I would add—and I said the same about
figures—that strong and appropriate emotions and genuine

sublimity are a specific palliative for multiplied or daring metaphors, because their nature is to sweep and drive all these other things along with the surging tide of their movement. Indeed it might be truer to say that they *demand* the hazardous. They never allow the hearer leisure to count the metaphors, because he too shares the speaker's enthusiasm.

5   At the same time, nothing gives distinction to commonplaces and descriptions so well as a continuous series of tropes. This is the medium in which the description of man's bodily tabernacle is worked out so elaborately in Xenophon and yet more superlatively by Plato.* Thus Plato calls the head the 'citadel' of the body; the neck is an 'isthmus' constructed between the head and the chest; the vertebrae, he says, are fixed underneath 'like pivots'. Pleasure is a 'lure of evil' for mankind; the tongue is a 'taste-meter'. The heart is a 'knot of veins' and 'fountain of the blood that moves impetuously round', allocated to the 'guard-room'. The word he uses for the various passages of the canals is 'alleys'. 'Against the throbbing of the heart,' he continues, 'in the expectation of danger and in the excitation of anger, when it gets hot, they contrived a means of succour, implanting in us the lungs, soft, bloodless, and with cavities, a sort of cushion, so that when anger boils up in the heart, the latter's throbbing is against a yielding obstacle, so that it comes to no harm.' Again: he calls the seat of the desires 'the women's quarters', and the seat of anger 'the men's quarters'. The spleen is for him 'a napkin for the inner parts, which therefore grows big and festering through being filled with secretions'. 'And thereafter', he says again, 'they buried the whole under a canopy of flesh', putting the flesh on 'as a protection against dangers from without, like felting'. Blood he called 'fodder of the flesh'. For the purpose of nutrition, he says also, 'they irrigated the body, cutting channels as in gardens, so that the streams of the veins might flow as it were from an incoming stream, making the body an aqueduct'. Finally: when the end is at hand, the soul's 'ship's cables' are 'loosed', and she herself 'set free'.

6   The passage contains countless similar examples; but these are enough to make my point, namely that tropes are naturally grand, that metaphors conduce to sublimity, and that passages involving
7   emotion and description are the most suitable field for them. At

the same time, it is plain without my saying it that the use of tropes, like all other good things in literature, always tempts one to go too far. This is what people ridicule most in Plato, who is often carried away by a sort of literary madness into crude, harsh metaphors or allegorical fustian. 'It is not easy to understand that a city ought to be mixed like a bowl of wine, wherein the wine seethes with madness, but when chastened by another, sober god, and achieving a proper communion with him, produces a good and moderate drink.'* To call water 'a sober god', says the critic, and mixture 'chastening', is the language of a poet who is far from sober himself.

DIGRESSION: GENIUS VERSUS MEDIOCRITY

Faults of this kind formed the subject of Caecilius' attack in his 8 book on Lysias, in which he had the audacity to declare Lysias in all respects superior to Plato. He has in fact given way without discrimination to two emotions: loving Lysias more deeply than he loves himself, he yet hates Plato with an even greater intensity. His motive, however, is desire to score a point, and his assumptions, are not, as he believed, generally accepted. In preferring Lysias to Plato he thinks he is preferring a faultless and pure writer to one who makes many mistakes. But the facts are far from supporting his view.

Let us consider a really pure and correct writer. We have then 33.1 to ask ourselves in general terms whether grandeur attended by some faults of execution is to be preferred, in prose or poetry, to a modest success of impeccable soundness. We must also ask whether the greater *number* of good qualities or the greater good qualities ought properly to win the literary prizes. These questions are relevant to a discussion of sublimity, and urgently require an answer.

I am certain in the first place that great geniuses are least 2 'pure'. Exactness in every detail involves a risk of meanness; with grandeur, as with great wealth, there ought to be something overlooked. It may also be inevitable that low or mediocre abilities should maintain themselves generally at a correct and safe level, simply because they take no risks and do not aim at the heights, whereas greatness, just because it is greatness, incurs danger.

3   I am aware also of a second point. All human affairs are, in the nature of things, better known on their worse side; the memory
4 of mistakes is ineffaceable, that of goodness is soon gone. I have myself cited not a few mistakes in Homer and other great writers, not because I take pleasure in their slips, but because I consider them not so much voluntary mistakes as oversights let fall at random through inattention and with the negligence of genius. I do, however, think that the greater good qualities, even if not consistently maintained, are always more likely to win the prize— if for no other reason, because of the greatness of spirit they reveal. Apollonius makes no mistakes in the *Argonautica*; Theocritus is very felicitous in the *Pastorals*, apart from a few passages not connected with the theme; but would you rather be Homer or Apollonius? Is the Eratosthenes of that flawless little poem *Erigone** a greater poet than Archilochus, with his abundant, uncontrolled flood, that bursting forth of the divine spirit which is so hard to bring under the rule of law? Take lyric poetry: would you rather be Bacchylides or Pindar? Take tragedy: would you rather be Ion of Chios or Sophocles? Ion and Bacchylides are impeccable, uniformly beautiful writers in the polished manner; but it is Pindar and Sophocles who sometimes set the world on fire with their vehemence, for all that their flame often goes out without reason and they collapse dismally. Indeed, no one in his senses would reckon all Ion's works put together as the equivalent of the one play *Oedipus*.

34.1   If good points were totted up, not judged by their real value, Hyperides would in every way surpass Demosthenes. He is more versatile, and has more good qualities. He is second-best at everything, like a pentathlon competitor; always beaten by the others for first place, he remains the best of the non-specialists.
2 In fact, he reproduces all the good features of Demosthenes, except his word-arrangement, and also has for good measure the excellences and graces of Lysias. He knows how to talk simply where appropriate; he does not deliver himself of everything in the same tone, like Demosthenes. His expression of character has sweetness and delicacy. Urbanity, sophisticated sarcasm, good breeding, skill in handling irony, humour neither rude nor tasteless but flavoured with true Attic salt, an ingenuity in attack with a strong comic element and a sharp sting to its apt fun—all

this produces inimitable charm. He has moreover great talents for exciting pity, and a remarkable facility for narrating myths with copiousness and developing general topics with fluency. For example, while his account of Leto* is in his more poetic manner, his Funeral Speech is an unrivalled example of the epideictic style. Demosthenes, by contrast, has no sense of 3 character. He lacks fluency, smoothness, and capacity for the epideictic manner; in fact he is practically without all the qualities I have been describing. When he forces himself to be funny or witty, he makes people laugh at him rather than with him. When he wants to come near to being charming, he is furthest removed from it. If he had tried to write the little speech on Phryne or that on Athenogenes,* he would have been an even better advertisement for Hyperides. Yet Hyperides' beauties, though numerous, are 4 without grandeur: 'inert in the heart of a sober man', they leave the hearer at peace. Nobody feels frightened reading Hyperides.

But when Demosthenes begins to speak, he concentrates in himself excellences finished to the highest perfection of his sublime genius—the intensity of lofty speech, living emotions, abundance, acuteness, speed where speed is vital, all his unapproachable vehemence and power. He concentrates it all in himself—they are divine gifts, it is almost blasphemous to call them human—and so outpoints all his rivals, compensating with the beauties he has even for those which he lacks. The crash of his thunder, the brilliance of his lightning make all other orators, of all ages, insignificant. It would be easier to open your eyes to an approaching thunderbolt than to face up to his unremitting emotional blows.

To return to Plato and Lysias, there is, as I said, a further 35.1 difference between them. Lysias is much inferior not only in the importance of the good qualities concerned but in their number; and at the same time he exceeds Plato in the number of his failings even more than he falls short in his good qualities.

What then was the vision which inspired those divine writers 2 who disdained exactness of detail and aimed at the greatest prizes in literature? Above all else, it was the understanding that nature made man to be no humble or lowly creature, but brought him into life and into the universe as into a great festival, to be both a spectator and an enthusiastic contestant in its competitions. She implanted in our minds from the start an irresistible desire for anything which is great and, in relation to ourselves, supernatural.

3   The universe therefore is not wide enough for the range of human speculation and intellect. Our thoughts often travel beyond the boundaries of our surroundings. If anyone wants to know what we were born for, let him look round at life and contemplate the splendour, grandeur, and beauty in which it

4   everywhere abounds. It is a natural inclination that leads us to admire not the little streams, however pellucid and however useful, but the Nile, the Danube, the Rhine, and above all the Ocean. Nor do we feel so much awe before the little flame we kindle, because it keeps its light clear and pure, as before the fires of heaven, though they are often obscured. We do not think our flame more worthy of admiration than the craters of Etna, whose eruptions bring up rocks and whole hills out of the depths, and sometimes pour forth rivers of the earth-born, spontaneous

5   fire. A single comment fits all these examples: the useful and necessary are readily available to man, it is the unusual that always excites our wonder.

36.1   So when we come to great geniuses in literature—where, by contrast, grandeur is not divorced from service and utility—we have to conclude that such men, for all their faults, tower far above mortal stature. Other literary qualities prove their users to be human; sublimity raises us towards the spiritual greatness of god. Freedom from error does indeed save us from blame, but it

2   is only greatness that wins admiration. Need I add that every one of those great men redeems all his mistakes many times over by a single sublime stroke? Finally, if you picked out and put together all the mistakes in Homer, Demosthenes, Plato, and all the other really great men, the total would be found to be a minute fraction of the successes which those heroic figures have to their credit. Posterity and human experience—judges whose sanity envy cannot question—place the crown of victory on their heads. They keep their prize irrevocably, and will do so

so long as waters flow and tall trees flourish.*

3   It has been remarked that 'the failed Colossus is no better than the Doryphorus of Polyclitus'.* There are many ways of

answering this. We may say that accuracy is admired in art and grandeur in nature, and it is *by nature* that man is endowed with the power of speech; or again that statues are expected to represent the human form, whereas, as I said, something higher than human is sought in literature.

At this point I have a suggestion to make which takes us back 4 to the beginning of the book. Impeccability is generally a product of art; erratic excellence comes from natural greatness; therefore, art must always come to the aid of nature, and the combination of the two may well be perfection.

It seemed necessary to settle this point for the sake of our inquiry; but everyone is at liberty to enjoy what he takes pleasure in.

SIMILES

We must now return to the main argument. Next to metaphors 37.1 come comparisons and similes. The only difference is . . .

[Lacuna equivalent to about two pages.]

HYPERBOLE

. . . such expressions as: 'Unless you've got your brains in your 38.1 heels and are walking on them'.* The important thing to know is how far to push a given hyperbole; it sometimes destroys it to go too far; too much tension results in relaxation, and may indeed end in the contrary of the intended effect. Thus Isocrates' zeal for 2 amplifying everything made him do a childish thing. The argument of his *Panegyricus** is that Athens surpasses Sparta in services to the Greek race. Right at the beginning we find the following: 'Secondly, the power of speech is such that it can make great things lowly, give grandeur to the trivial, say what is old in a new fashion, and lend an appearance of antiquity to recent events.' Is Isocrates then about to reverse the positions of Athens and Sparta? The encomium on the power of speech is equivalent to an introduction recommending the reader not to believe what he is told! I suspect that what we said of the best 3 figures is true of the best hyperboles: they are those which avoid being seen for what they are. The desired effect is achieved when they are connected with some impressive circumstance and with moments of high emotion. Thucydides' account* of those killed in Sicily is an example: 'The Syracusans came down and massacred them, especially those in the river. The water was stained; but despite the blood and the dirt, men continued to drink it, and many still fought for it.' It is the intense emotion of the moment which makes it credible that dirt and blood should

4　still be fought for as drink. Herodotus* has something similar about Thermopylae: 'Meanwhile though they defended themselves with swords (those who still had them), and with hands and mouths, the barbarians buried them with their missiles.' What is meant by fighting armed men with mouths or being buried with missiles? Still, it is credible; for we form the impression that the hyperbole is a reasonable product of the situation, not that the

5　situation has been chosen for the sake of the hyperbole. As I keep saying, acts and emotions which approach ecstasy provide a justification for, and an antidote to, any linguistic audacity. This is why comic hyperboles, for all their incredibility, are convincing because we laugh at them so much: 'He had a farm, but it didn't stretch as far as a Laconic letter.' Laughter is emotion in amusement.

6　　　There are hyperboles which belittle as well as those which exaggerate. Intensification is the factor common to the two species, vilification being in a sense an amplification of lowness.

(v) WORD-ARRANGEMENT OR COMPOSITION

39.1　There remains the fifth of the factors contributing to sublimity which we originally enumerated. This was a certain kind of composition or word-arrangement. Having set out my conclusions on this subject fully in two books, I shall here add only so much as is essential for our present subject.

EFFECT OF RHYTHM

Harmony is a natural instrument not only of conviction and pleasure but also to a remarkable degree of grandeur and
2　emotion. The oboe fills the audience with certain emotions and

makes them somehow beside themselves and possessed. It sets a rhythm, it makes the hearer move to the rhythm and assimilate himself to the tune, 'untouched by the Muses though he be'.* The notes of the lyre, though they have no meaning, also, as you know, often cast a wonderful spell of harmony with their varied sounds and blended and mingled notes. Yet all these are but spurious images and imitations of persuasion, not the genuine activities proper to human nature of which I spoke. Composition, on the other hand, is a harmony of words, man's natural instrument, penetrating not only the ears but the very soul. It arouses all kinds of conceptions of words and thoughts and objects, beauty and melody—all things native and natural to mankind. The combination and variety of its sounds convey the speaker's emotions to the minds of those around him and make the hearers share them. It fits his great thoughts into a coherent structure by the way in which it builds up patterns of words. Shall we not then believe that by all these methods it bewitches us and elevates to grandeur, dignity, and sublimity both every thought which comes within its compass and ourselves as well, holding as it does complete domination over our minds? It is absurd to question facts so generally agreed. Experience is proof enough. 3

The idea which Demosthenes used in speaking of the decree* is reputed very sublime, and is indeed splendid. 'This decree made the danger which then surrounded the city pass away like a cloud (*touto to psēphisma ton tote tē polei peristanta kindūnon parelthein epoiēsen hōsper nephos*).' But the effect depends as much on the harmony as on the thought. The whole passage is based on dactylic rhythms, and these are very noble and grand. (This is why they form the heroic, the noblest metre we know.)... 4

[A short phrase missing.]

... but make any change you like in the order:

touto to psēphisma hōsper nephos epoiēse ton tote kindūnon parelthein,

or cut off a syllable:

epoiēse parelthein hōs nephos.

You will immediately see how the harmony echoes the sublimity. The phrase *hōsper nephos* rests on its long first unit (– –) which measures four shorts; the removal of a syllable (*hōs nephos*) at once curtails and mutilates the grand effect.

Now lengthen the phrase:

parelthein epoiēsen hōsperei nephos.

It still means the same, but the effect is different, because the sheer sublimity is broken up and undone by the breaking up of the run of long syllables at the end.

EFFECT OF PERIOD STRUCTURE

40.1   I come now to a principle of particular importance for lending grandeur to our words. The beauty of the body depends on the way in which the limbs are joined together, each one when severed from the others having nothing remarkable about it, but the whole together forming a perfect unity. Similarly great thoughts which lack connection are themselves wasted and waste the total sublime effect, whereas if they co-operate to form a unity and are linked by the bonds of harmony, they come to life and speak just by virtue of the periodic structure. It is indeed generally true that, in periods, grandeur results from the total contribution of many elements.

2   I have shown elsewhere that many poets and other writers who are not naturally sublime, and may indeed be quite unqualified for grandeur, and who use in general common and everyday words which carry with them no special effect, nevertheless acquire magnificence and splendour, and avoid being thought low or mean, solely by the way in which they arrange and fit together their words. Philistus, Aristophanes sometimes,
3   Euripides generally, are among the many examples. Thus Heracles* says after the killing of the children:

I'm full of troubles, there's no room for more.

This is a very ordinary remark, but it has become sublime, as the situation demands. If you re-arrange it, it will become apparent that it is in the composition, not in the sense, that Euripides' greatness appears.

Dirce is being pulled about by the bull: 4

> And where it could, it writhed and twisted round,
> dragging at everything, rock, woman, oak,
> juggling with them all.*

The conception is fine in itself, but it has been improved by the fact that the word-harmony is not hurried and does not run smoothly; the words are propped up by one another and rest on the intervals between them; set wide apart like that, they give the impression of solid strength.

FEATURES DESTRUCTIVE OF SUBLIMITY

(1) *Bad and Affected Rhythm*

Nothing is so damaging to a sublime effect as effeminate and 41.1 agitated rhythm, pyrrhics ($\cup\cup$), trochees ($-\cup$ or $\cup\cup\cup$) and dichorei ($-\cup-\cup$); they turn into a regular jig. All the rhythmical elements immediately appear artifical and cheap, being constantly repeated in a monotonous fashion without the slightest emotional effect. Worst of all, just as songs distract an 2 audience from the action and compel attention for themselves, so the rhythmical parts of speech produce on the hearer the effect not of speech but of rhythm, so that they foresee the coming endings and sometimes themselves beat time for the speaker and anticipate him in giving the step, just as in a dance.

(2) *The 'Chopped Up' Style*

Phrases too closely knit are also devoid of grandeur, as are those 3 which are chopped up into short elements consisting of short syllables, bolted together, as it were, and rough at the joins.

(3) *Excessive Brevity*

Excessively cramped expression also does damage to sublimity. It 42.1 cripples grandeur to compress it into too short a space. I do not mean proper compression, but cutting up into tiny pieces. Cramping mutilates sense; brevity gives directness. Conversely with fully extended expressions: anything developed at unseasonable length falls dead.

(4) *Undignified Vocabulary*

43.1 Lowness of diction also destroys grandeur.

The description of the storm in Herodotus* is magnificent in
conception, but includes expressions which are below the dignity
of the subject. 'The sea seethed' is one instance: the cacophony
does much to dissipate the sublime effect. 'The wind slacked' is
another example; yet another is the 'unpleasant end' which
awaited those who were thrown against the wreckage. 'Slack' is
an undignified, colloquial word; 'unpleasant' is inappropriate to
such an experience.

2   Similarly, Theopompus* first gives a magnificent setting to the
descent of the Persian king on Egypt, and then ruins it all with a
few words.

'What city or nation in Asia did not send its embassy to the
King? What thing of beauty or value, product of the earth or work
of art, was not brought him as a gift? There were many precious
coverlets and cloaks, purple, embroidered, and white; there were
many gold tents fitted out with all necessities; there were many
robes and beds of great price. There were silver vessels and
worked gold, drinking cups and bowls, some studded with jewels,
some elaborately and preciously wrought. Countless myriads of
arms were there, Greek and barbarian. There were multitudes of
pack animals and victims fattened for slaughter, many bushels of
condiments, many bags and sacks and pots of onions and every
other necessity. There was so much salt meat of every kind that
travellers approaching from a distance mistook the huge heaps
for cliffs or hills thrusting up from the plain.'

3   He passes from the sublime to the mean; the development of
the scene should have been the other way round. By mixing up
the bags and the condiments and the sacks in the splendid
account of the whole expedition, he conjures up the vision of a
kitchen. Suppose one actually had these beautiful objects before
one's eyes, and then dumped some bags and sacks in the middle
of the gold and jewelled bowls, the silver vessels, the gold tents,
and the drinking-cups—the effect would be disgusting. It is the
same with style: if you insert words like this when they are not
4   wanted, they make a blot on the context. It was open to
Theopompus to give a general description of the 'hills' which he

says were raised, and, having made this change, to proceed to the rest of the preparations, mentioning camels and multitudes of beasts of burden carrying everything needed for luxury and pleasure of the table, or speaking of 'heaps of all kinds of seeds and everything that makes for fine cuisine and dainty living'. If he had wanted at all costs to make the king self-supporting, he could have talked of 'all the refinements of *maîtres-d'hôtel* and chefs'.

It is wrong to descend, in a sublime passage, to the filthy and 5 contemptible, unless we are absolutely compelled to do so. We ought to use words worthy of things. We ought to imitate nature, who, in creating man, did not set our private parts or the excretions of our body in the face, but concealed them as well as she could, and, as Xenophon* says, made the channels of these organs as remote as possible, so as not to spoil the beauty of the creature as a whole.

CONCLUSION

There is no urgent need to enumerate in detail features which 6 produce a low effect. We have explained what makes style noble and sublime; the opposite qualities will obviously make it low and undignified.

APPENDIX: CAUSES OF THE DECLINE OF LITERATURE

I shall not hesitate to add for your instruction, my dear 44.1 Terentianus, one further topic, so as to clear up a question put to me the other day by one of the philosophers.

'I wonder,' he said, 'and so no doubt do many others, why it is that in our age there are minds which are strikingly persuasive and practical, shrewd, versatile, and well-endowed with the ability to write agreeably, but no sublime or really great minds, except perhaps here and there. There is a universal dearth of literature.

'Are we to believe', he went on, 'the common explanation that 2 democracy nurtures greatness, and great writers flourished with democracy and died with it? Freedom, the argument goes, nourishes and encourages the thoughts of the great, as well as exciting their enthusiasm for rivalry with one another and their

3 ambition for the prize. In addition the availability of political reward sharpens and polishes up orators' talents by giving them exercise; they shine forth, free in a free world. We of the present day, on the other hand,' he continued, 'seem to have learned in infancy to live under justified slavery, swathed round from our first tender thoughts in the same habits and customs, never allowed to taste that fair and fecund spring of literature, freedom. We end up as flatterers in the grand manner.'

4 He went on to say how the same argument explained why, unlike other capacities, that of the orator could never belong to a slave.

'The inability to speak freely and the consciousness of being a prisoner at once assert themselves, battered into him as they have been by the blows of habit. As Homer* says, "The day of slavery takes half one's manhood away". I don't know if it's true, but I understand that the cages in which dwarfs or Pygmies are kept not only prevent the growth of the prisoners but cripple them because of the fastening which constricts the body. One might describe all slavery, even the most justified, as a cage for the soul, a universal prison.'

6 'My good friend,' I replied, 'it is easy to find fault with the present situation; indeed it is a human characteristic to do so. But I wonder whether what destroys great minds is not the peace of the world, but the unlimited war which lays hold on our desires, and all the passions which beset and ravage our modern life. Avarice, the insatiable disease from which we all suffer, and love of pleasure—these are our two slave-masters; or perhaps one should say that they sink our ship of life with all hands. Avarice is

7 a mean disease; love of pleasure is base through and through. I cannot see how we can honour, or rather deify, unlimited wealth as we do without admitting into our souls the evils which attach to it. When wealth is measureless and uncontrolled, extravagance comes with it, sticking close beside it, and, as they say, keeping step. The moment wealth opens the way into cities and houses, extravagance also enters and dwells therein. These evils then become chronic in people's lives, and, as the philosophers say, nest and breed. They are soon busy producing offspring: greed, pride, and luxury are their all-too-legitimate children. If these offspring of wealth are allowed to mature, they breed in turn

those inexorable tyrants of the soul, insolence, lawlessness, and shamelessness. It is an inevitable process. Men will no longer 8 open their eyes or give thought to their reputation with posterity. The ruin of their lives is gradually consummated in a cycle of such vices. Greatness of mind wanes, fades, and loses its attraction when men spend their admiration on their mortal parts and neglect to develop the immortal. One who has been bribed to 9 give a judgement will no longer be a free and sound judge of rightness and nobility. The corrupt man inevitably thinks his own side's claim just and fair. Yet nowadays bribery is the arbiter of the life and fortunes of every one of us—not to mention chasing after other people's deaths and conspiring about wills. We are all so enslaved by avarice that we buy the power of making profit out of everything at the price of our souls. Amid such pestilential corruption of human life, how can we expect that there should be left to us any free, uncorrupt judge of great things of permanent value? How can we hope not to lose our case to the corrupt practices of the love of gain?

'Perhaps people like us are better as subjects than given our 10 freedom. Greed would flood the world in woe, if it were really released and let out of the cage, to prey on its neighbours.'

Idleness, I went on to say, was the bane of present-day minds. 11 We all live with it. Our whole regime of effort and relaxation is devoted to praise and pleasure, not to the useful results that deserve emulation and honour.

'Best to let these things be',* and proceed to our next subject. 12 This was emotion, to which we promised to devote a separate treatise. It occupies, as I said, a very important place among the constituents of literature in general, and sublimity in particular . . .

[A few words missing at the end.]

DIO OF PRUSA: *PHILOCTETES IN THE TRAGEDIANS*

I got up about an hour after daybreak, partly because I was unwell, and partly because the dawn air was cooler—more like autumn, though it was the middle of the summer. I attended to my toilet and said my prayers. Then I got into the carriage and took a number of turns on the racecourse, driving as gently and quietly as possible. I followed this up with a walk and a little rest; then I oiled myself and bathed and after a light meal began to read tragedies. They were all treatments of a single subject by the three great names, Aeschylus, Sophocles, and Euripides: the theft—or perhaps one should say violent robbery—of Philoctetes' bow. Anyway, Philoctetes is deprived of his weapon by Odysseus and himself taken to Troy, to a certain extent voluntarily, but with a degree of compulsion about it too, because he had been deprived of the weapon that gave him his livelihood on the island and confidence to face his disease, apart from being his claim to fame. I feasted on the performance, and reflected that if I had lived in Athens in those days I should not have been able to participate in a competition between these writers. Some indeed were present at competitions between the young Sophocles and the old Aeschylus, and again between Sophocles in his latter days and the young Euripides; but Euripides was altogether too late to encounter Aeschylus.

Moreover, they rarely if ever competed with plays on the same theme. So I thought I was much indulged, and had discovered a new way of consoling myself for being ill. I produced the plays for myself (in my mind's eye) very splendidly, and tried to give them my whole attention, like a judge of the first tragic choruses. But had I been on oath, I could never have come to a decision. So far as I was concerned, none of them could have been beaten.

Aeschylus' grandeur and archaic splendour, and the originality of his thought and expression, seemed appropriate to tragedy and the antique manners of the heroes; it had nothing subtle, nothing facile, nothing undignified. Even his Odysseus, though shrewd and crafty for the times, was miles away from present-day

standards of malevolence. He would seem an old-fashioned
fellow indeed by the side of those who in our age claim to be
simple and magnanimous. He did not need Athena to disguise
him in order to prevent him from being recognized by
Philoctetes, as Homer and (after him) Euripides have it. A hostile
critic might perhaps say that Aeschylus was not concerned to
make Philoctetes' failure to recognize Odysseus plausible. There
is a possible defence, I think, against such an objection. The time
was indeed perhaps not long enough for the features to fail to
come to mind after a lapse of only ten years, but Philoctetes'
illness and incapacity and the solitary life he had led so long also
contribute to make the situation possible. Many people have
suffered such a failure of memory as a result of illness or
misfortune.

Nor did Aeschylus' chorus need to apologize, like that of
Euripides. Both made up their choruses of inhabitants of Lemnos,
but Euripides began by making them apologize for their neglect
in not having come to see Philoctetes or given him any help for so
many years, while Aeschylus simply brought the chorus on
without comment. This is altogether simpler and more tragic, in
contrast with Euripides' more sophisticated and painstaking
treatment. If it had been possible to avoid every irrationality in
tragedy, it might have been reasonable not to let this one pass
either; but in fact poets often, for example, represent heralds as
making several days' journey in one day. Secondly, it simply
wasn't possible for none of the inhabitants of Lemnos to have
approached Philoctetes or taken care of him. He could never
have survived ten years without help. Probably therefore he did
get some, but rarely and not on any great scale, and no one chose
to receive him in their house and nurse him because of the
unpleasant nature of his illness. Indeed Euripides himself
introduces one Actor, a Lemnian, who visits Philoctetes as an
acquaintance who has often met him. Nor do I think it right to
find fault with Aeschylus' making Philoctetes relate to an
apparently ignorant chorus his desertion by the Achaeans and his
whole history. The unfortunate often recall their troubles and
weary their listeners, who know it well and don't want to hear it
again, with their perpetual narrations. Again, Odysseus' deception
of Philoctetes and the arguments by which he wins him are not

only more respectable—suitable to a hero, not a Eurybatus or a Pataecion*—but also, as it seems to me, more convincing. What was the need of elaborate art and guile in dealing with a sick man—and an archer too, whose prowess was useless the moment one came near him? To relate the disasters of the Achaeans, the death of Agamemnon, the death of Odysseus for a shocking crime, and the total destruction of the army, was not only useful for cheering up Philoctetes and making him more willing to accept Odysseus' company, but also not implausible in view of the length of the campaign and the recent events consequent on the anger of Achilles, when Hector came near to burning the fleet.

Euripides' intelligence and care for every detail—nothing unconvincing or negligent is allowed to pass, and instead of bare facts he gives us the whole force of his eloquence—is the opposite of Aeschylus' simplicity. This is the style of the man of affairs and the orator; the reader can learn many valuable lessons from it. For example, Odysseus in the prologue is represented as revolving in his mind many rhetorically effective thoughts. He wonders about his own position. May he perhaps appear wise and intelligent to many people but in fact be the opposite? He could be living a secure, untroubled life—and here he is voluntarily involved in affairs and dangers! The cause, he says, is the ambition of talented and noble men; it is because they want reputation and fame among all mankind that they voluntarily undertake great and arduous tasks:

> Nothing so vain as man was ever born.

Then he clearly and accurately explains the plot of the play, and why he has come to Lemnos. Athena has disguised him so that he shall not be recognized by Philoctetes when he meets him. (This is an imitation of Homer, who makes Athena disguise Odysseus when he meets various people, such as Eumaeus and Penelope).* He says an embassy is going to come from the Trojans to Philoctetes, to offer him the kingdom of Troy in exchange for his own services and those of his bow. This complicates the story, and affords a starting-point for a speech in which he shows himself resourceful and eloquent enough to stand comparison with anyone in developing the opposite position. Nor does he make Odysseus come alone; Diomedes is with him, another Homeric touch. In short, he shows throughout the play great intelligence and convincingness in incident, and wonderful, hardly credible, skill of language. The iambics are clear, natural, rhetorically effective. The lyrics afford not only pleasure but many exhortations to virtue.*

Sophocles comes between the two. He possesses neither Aeschylus' originality and simplicity, nor the craftsmanship, shrewdness, and rhetorical effectiveness of Euripides. His verse is dignified and grand, tragic and euphonious to the highest degree, combining great charm with sublimity and dignity. At the same time, his management of the story is excellent and convincing. He makes Odysseus arrive with Neoptolemus because it was ordained that Troy should be captured by Neoptolemus and Philoctetes with the bow of Heracles, but conceal himself while sending Neoptolemus to Philoctetes, telling him what he must do. Moreover, the chorus is made up not, as in Aeschylus and Euripides, of natives, but of the crew of Odysseus' and Neoptolemus' ship. The characters are wonderfully dignified and gentlemanly. Odysseus is much gentler and more straightfoward than in Euripides, Neoptolemus is simple and noble to excess, unwilling to win his point over Philoctetes by guile and deceit, but insisting on strength and openness, and afterwards, when Odysseus has persuaded him and he has deceived Philoctetes and got possession of the bow, unable to endure his victim's complaints and demands, and quite capable of giving him the bow back, despite Odysseus' appearance and attempt to stop him. Indeed, he does give it back in the end; and having done so then tries to persuade Philoctetes to go with him voluntarily to Troy. Philoctetes refuses to give way or comply, but begs Neoptolemus to take him home to Greece, as he had promised. The young man agrees and is ready to perform his promise, until Heracles appears and persuades Philoctetes to sail to Troy voluntarily. The lyrics are without the general reflections and exhortations to virtue which we saw in Euripides, but they possess extraordinary charm and grandeur. It was not without cause that Aristophanes wrote:

He licked the lip of the jar, as it were, of honey-covered Sophocles.*

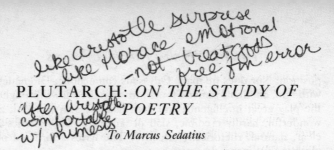

like aristotle surprise
like Horace emotional
— not treat gods
free from error

after aristotle
comfortable
w/ mimesis

PLUTARCH: *ON THE STUDY OF POETRY*

To Marcus Sedatius

p. 14d   'The nicest meat', said the poet Philoxenus, 'is what is not meat, and the nicest fish is what is not fish.' Let us leave the discussion of this to the people who, in Cato's phrase, have more sensibility in their palates than in their heads. What is plain is that in philosophy very young students enjoy more what does not appear to be philosophical or serious; to this they are ready to submit and subject themselves. In going through not only Aesop's fables and tales from the poets but Heraclides' *Abaris* and Ariston's *Lycon*,* they take a passionate delight in the doctrines about the soul which are mixed with the mythology. Thus we must preserve the decency of the young not only in the pleasures of food and drink; more important, we must accustom them in their readings and lectures to make use of the pleasurable element sparingly, as a kind of sauce, and to pursue the profit and salvation that derives from it. Locked gates do not preserve a city if one door is open to let in the enemy; continence in other pleasures does not save a young man if he lets himself go inadvertently through the pleasures of the ear. Indeed, the more firmly these delights take

p. 15   hold of the sensible and intelligent, the more they are overlooked and damage and destroy their host.

Now it is neither useful nor perhaps possible to keep boys of the age of my Soclaros or your Cleandros* away from poetry. Let us therefore protect them. They need an escort in reading even more than they do in the street.

I have decided therefore to send you in written form the thoughts which came into my mind the other day when I had been talking about poetry. If they strike you as equal to those prophylactics against drunkenness which people hang round themselves or take at drinking parties, share them with Cleandros and get a grip on his character. It is all the more amenable to the sort of thing we are speaking of because he is never slow but always so vigorous and alert.

In the polyp's head is good and bad:

it is nice to eat, but results in sleep disturbed by dreams, with confused and outlandish visions, or so they say. Similarly with poetry: it contains much that is pleasant and profitable to the young mind, but just as much that is confusing and misleading, if study is not properly directed. It can be said of poetry as of the land of Egypt:

> Many drugs it bears that are good, and many that are
> hurtful to its cultivators;
>
> therein is love and desire and the intimacies
> that cheat and steal the hearts even of the wise.*

The deceitfulness of poetry does not affect the really stupid and foolish. This is why, when Simonides was asked: 'Why are the Thessalians the only people you do not deceive?', he replied: 'Because they are too ignorant to be deceived by me.' Similarly, Gorgias said that tragedy was 'a deceit in which the deceiver does his duty better than the non-deceiver, and the deceived is wiser than the undeceived'.

What then ought we to do? Stop the young men's ears, like the Ithacan sailors',* with some hard, insoluble wax, and force them to set sail with Epicurus* and steer clear of poetry? Or fix and settle their judgment with rational arguments, not letting pleasure distract it into harm, and so protect them and guide them aright?

> For not even the son of Dryas, mighty Lycurgus*

was a sane man, when, because many people were getting drunk and behaving badly in their cups, he went round cutting down vines, instead of bringing the water nearer and (to use Plato's expression)* chastening a mad god with another and sober one. Mixing destroys the harm in wine, but not its usefulness. Let us not therefore cut out or destroy the vine of the Muses. When unmixed pleasure makes its fabulous and theatrical elements wax wanton and luxuriant, blustering violently for reputation, let us take hold and prune and constrain: but when it touches poetry with its grace, and the sweet attractions of the style are fruitful and purposeful, let us introduce some admixture of philosophy. For just as mandragora planted beside vines and transmitting its qualities to the wine makes the effect on the drinker milder, so poetry, by taking some arguments from philosophy and combining them with an element of fable, makes learning easy and agreeable to young people. Future philosophers therefore must not avoid poetry. Rather should they be initiated into philosophy through it, becoming accustomed to seek and enjoy truth in pleasant

p. 16 surroundings—or to protest and be annoyed at the lack of it. This is the beginning of education, and

> work well begun is like to finish well

as Sophocles says.

THE DECEITFULNESS OF POETRY

2 When we first introduce our young men to poetry, there is nothing they should have learned so thoroughly, nothing so readily springing to their mind, as the proverbial saying that

> poets tell many lies,

whether deliberate or not. The deliberate lies of the poets are due to their thinking truth drier than fiction, from the point of view of pleasure to the hearer and charm, which is what most of them aim at. Truth is real, and does not change course, however unpleasant the outcome. Fiction easily deviates and turns from the painful to the pleasant. Metre, trope, grand language, timely metaphor, harmony, and word-order* possess nothing like the beguiling charm of a well-contrived plot. In painting, colour is more exciting than line because it is colour that represents flesh and deceives the eye; and similarly in poetry a convincing fiction produces admiration and satisfaction more than any device of metre or diction deficient in plot and story. This is why Socrates,* the lifelong striver for truth, found himself, when he set about composing poetry in obedience to a dream, no very convincing or gifted maker of lies; he therefore put Aesop's fables into verse, on the principle that where there is no fiction there is no poetry. For there can be sacrifices without dances and music, but poetry without plot and fiction is impossible. Empedocles,* Parmenides, the *Theriaca* of Nicander, and the wise saws (*gnōmologiai*) of Theognis have borrowed from poetry the vehicle, as it were, of grandeur and metre, so as to avoid the pedestrian.

Now consider any absurd or unpalatable statement, in poetry, about gods or demigods or virtue, put into the mouth of a man of distinction and reputation. The reader who accepts it as true is lost, and his judgement ruined. The reader who remembers and clearly bears in mind the magic of fiction that poetry possesses, and can say to it every time,

> 'You tricksy beast, more subtle than the lynx,

why do you contract your brows in fun? Why do you pretend to teach when in fact you deceive?'—he will come to no harm and believe no evil. He will check himself when he feels afraid of Poseidon* and dreads his bursting the earth open and laying Hades bare. He will hold himself back when he feels angry with Apollo on behalf of the first man among the Greeks—

> he who sang the hymn, he who was at the feast,
> he who said all this, he was the killer.*

He will stop weeping for the dead Achilles and Agamemnon in Hades, stretching out their feeble and powerless hands in their longing for life. Or if he is disturbed by their sufferings and drugged into submission, he will not hesitate to say to himself:

> Make haste towards the light. Know all these things
> to tell your wife hereafter.*

This is a neat touch of Homer's: the visit to Hades is aptly described as a tale for women because of its fabulous content.

VOLUNTARY AND INVOLUNTARY ERRORS OF POETS

So much for the poets' deliberate inventions. More often, however, it is not invention but false belief and opinion that produce the falsehood they then rub off on us. For example: Homer says of Zeus

> He put in two dooms of death that lays men low,   p. 17
> one for Achilles, one for Hector, tamer of horses;
> he seized the middle, and poised it. Down
>   went Hector's day of doom;

and he was away to Hades, and Phoebus Apollo
    abandoned him.*

And Aeschylus built a whole tragedy around the story, calling it
'The Weighing of the Souls', and presenting Thetis on one side
of Zeus' scale and Eos on the other, praying on behalf of their
sons as they fought. Now this is plainly a myth or fiction
constructed to please or astonish the hearer. By contrast,

        Zeus, who dispenses war among mankind,*

and

                    God breeds a crime in men
        when he would utterly overthrow a house,*

are written in accordance with the poets' own opinion and belief;
they express and impart to us their own misconception and
ignorance about the gods.

    Again, few readers fail to realize that the portentous tales and
descriptions found in accounts of Hades, where horrifying names
are used to produce graphic images and pictures of burning
rivers, savage places, and grim punishments, contain a large
element of fable and falsehood—poison in the food as it were.
Homer, Pindar, and Sophocles did not believe what they were
saying when they wrote:

        whence the slow streams of murky night
        belch forth unending darkness;

or

and they passed by the streams of Ocean and the White Rock,*

or

        narrows of Hell, and ebb and flow of the abyss.

But what they say in lamentation and fear of the pitifulness of
death or the horror of going unburied comes from genuine
feeling and the prejudices created by common opinion and error:

        Do not go away and leave me unwept and unburied,*

and

> The soul flew from the limbs and went down to Hades;
> lamenting its fate, leaving manhood and youth behind it;

and

> Do not kill me untimely. Sweet is the light to see;
> do not force me to look on what lies under the ground.

This is why they touch us more and disturb us, because we are filled with the emotion and weakness out of which they are spoken. To meet this danger, let us again ensure, right from the beginning, an insistence on the fact that poetry is *not* concerned with truth. Indeed, the truth about these matters is hard to track down or comprehend even for those whose only study is the knowledge and understanding of reality. They admit it themselves. Have ready Empedocles' words:

> not visible to men nor audible,
> nor to be grasped in the mind;

and those of Xenophanes:

> the certainty no man has known or ever shall know
> about the gods and all the things I speak of.

Remember Socrates' disavowal* (in Plato) of knowledge of these things. The young men will be less inclined to pay attention to the poets as sources of knowledge about these matters if they see the philosophers in a daze!

POETRY AS IMITATION

Let us fix our young student's mind even more firmly, by indicating, the moment we introduce him to works of poetry, that poetry is an art of imitation, a capacity analogous to painting. He should of course be given the familiar dictum that 'poetry is speaking painting and painting silent poetry'; but in addition to this, let us explain that when we see a picture of a lizard or a monkey or Thersites'* face we feel pleasure and admiration not because it is beautiful but because it is *like*. Ugliness cannot become beautiful in its essence, but imitation is commended if it achieves likeness, whether of a good or a bad object. Indeed, if it

3

p. 18

produces a beautiful image of an ugly thing, it fails to provide propriety or probability. Some painters do in fact represent disconcerting events: Timomachus did a 'Medea killing her children', Theon an 'Orestes killing his mother', Parrhasius 'Odysseus feigning madness', while Chaerephanes depicted indecent intercourse of men and women. The young student must be educated especially in this kind of thing, and be taught that what we praise is not the action represented by the imitation but the art shown in the appropriate reproduction of the subject. Similarly, since poetry also often narrates by imitation wicked actions and bad emotions or traits of character, the young man must not necessarily accept admirable or successful work of this kind as true, or label it beautiful, but simply commend it as suitable and appropriate to the subject. When we actually hear a pig grunt, a windlass rattle, the wind whistle or the sea roar, we feel annoyance and distress; but if anyone mimics the noise convincingly, as Parmeno did the pig or Theodorus the windlass, we feel pleasure. We avoid a man who is sickly or covered with sores as a disagreeable sight, but we enjoy looking at Aristophon's 'Philoctetes' or Silanion's 'Jocasta', which are made to resemble the sick and dying. Similarly, when the young man reads what Thersites the buffoon or Sisyphus the seducer or Batrachos the brothel-keeper is represented as saying or doing, he should be taught to praise the technique and skill of the imitation, but to censure and abuse the habits and activities represented. To imitate something beautiful is not the same thing as to imitate it beautifully. 'Beautifully' here means fittingly and suitably—and what is fitting and suitable to something ugly is ugly itself. Damonidas the cripple's shoes, which he prayed might fit the feet of the man who stole them, were poor shoes, but they fitted him. Similarly,

> If we *must* do wrong, it's best to do it
> to win a kingdom;*

and

> Win a just man's repute, but act like one
> who will do anything for profit;

and

> The dowry's a talent. Not take it? Can I live
> if I disdain a talent? Shall I sleep
> if I let it go? Shall I not suffer in hell
> for blasphemy against a silver talent?—

all these remarks are wicked and false, but they are in character for Eteocles, Ixion, and an old moneylender. If therefore we remind our children that the poets do not commend or approve this kind of thing but simply attribute vile and shocking words to vile and shocking characters, they will not be harmed by the poets' opinion. Indeed, the suspicion felt towards the character discredits the action and the speech as being the bad act or speech of a bad person. An example is Paris's going to bed with Helen after he ran away from the battle.* By representing no one else as going to bed with a woman in the daytime except the licentious adulterer, Homer obviously intends disgrace and blame to be attached to this kind of indulgence.

HINTS TO BE TAKEN

Attention must be paid in this connection to any hint the poet gives that he disapproves of what is being said. For example, Menander writes in the prologue to *Thais*:

> Sing me a woman, O goddess, pert, pretty, persuasive,
> unfair, demanding, never letting you in,
> loving nobody, but always pretending to love.

Homer is best at this, because he gives advance discredit or recommendation to the bad or good things his characters say. For 'advance recommendation', compare:

> He spoke a sweet and shrewd word,*

or

> He stood by him, and restrained him with gentle words.

In discrediting a remark in advance, Homer virtually gives a solemn warning not to use or attend to it, because it is outrageous and vicious. Thus, when he is about to relate Agamemnon's harsh treatment of the priest, he prefaces it by saying:

4
p. 19

But it did not satisfy Agamemnon, son of Atreus, in his heart,
but he dismissed him evilly—

that is to say, brutally, wantonly, and improperly. Similarly, he
gives Achilles the harsh words

> drunken sot, with a dog's eyes and a hind's heart,

only after stating his own judgement:

> Then Peleus' son again with grim words
> addressed Atrides: he had not yet ceased from his anger.

For nothing said angrily and harshly is likely to be good.
Similarly also with actions:

> He spoke, and planned dire deeds on Hector,
> laying him out on his face by Patroclos' bier.

And he also uses concluding lines to good effect, casting his
own vote as it were on what is said or done. Thus he makes the
gods say of Ares' adultery:

> Bad deeds do not prosper. The slow catches the swift.*

On Hector's pride and boasting, we have:

> So he spake, boasting; but Hera was indignant.

And on Pandarus' archery:

> So spake Athena, and convinced the fool.

Now these verbal assertions and opinions may be observed by
any attentive reader. But other lessons are supplied by the actual
events related. Euripides, for instance, is said to have answered
critics who attacked his Ixion as impious and vile by saying: 'But I
didn't take him off the stage until he was nailed to the wheel.' In
Homer, this kind of instruction is tacit; but it affords a useful
kind of re-interpretation for the most severely criticized myths.
Some critics in fact have so forced and perverted the meaning of
these by using what used to be called *huponoia* and is now called
allegory,* as to interpret the revelation by Helios of Ares' adultery
with Aphrodite as meaning that the planet Mars in conjunction
with the planet Venus produces adulterous births, which are

revealed by the return of the sun on his course to discover them; or again, to interpret the way in which Hera beautified herself for Zeus, and the magic of the cestus,* as symbolizing a purification of the air coming into proximity with the fiery element. As if Homer did not himself give the solution of both these problems! In the story of Aphrodite, he in fact teaches the attentive reader that poor music, bad songs, and speeches with immoral themes produce dissolute character, unmanly life, and a race of men content with luxury, softness, womanishness, and

> changes of clothes, hot baths, and bed.* p. 20

This is why he represents Odysseus as instructing the bard to

> change the tune, and sing the Making of the Horse—

very properly suggesting that musicians and poets should take their subjects from men of sense and wisdom. In the story of Hera, likewise, he demonstrates that the sort of intercourse and pleasure between the sexes that depends on drugs, magic, or deceit, is not only ephemeral, inconstant, and insecure, but turns to hostility and anger as soon as the effects of the pleasure fade. Zeus accordingly threatens Hera:

> So that you can see if love and bed avail you,
> the love you enjoyed when you came from the gods, and
>   deceived me.*

If the description and representation of bad deeds includes as well the disgrace and damage which befalls the doers, it benefits rather than harms the audience. Philosophers use examples, admonishing and instructing from given facts, while poets do the same thing by inventing facts and spinning tales on their own. I am not sure whether Melanthius was joking or in earnest when he said that Athens was preserved by the dissidence and dissensions of the politicians, because they did not all lean to the same side of the boat, but their quarrels somehow counteracted their damaging effects. But it is like that with poets: their differences among themselves produce compensating convictions and prevent any violent swing in a harmful direction. Sometimes, they themselves highlight the contradictions by

putting opposing opinions side by side. We must then support
the better side. For example:

> 'My child, the gods do often trip men up.'
> 'Yes, that's the easiest way—convict the gods';

or

> 'Should you, but not they, glory in wealth of gold?'
> 'Stupid to be wealthy and know nothing else';

or

> 'Why sacrifice, when you are going to die?'
> 'It's better; there's no hardship in piety.'

The solutions of these problems are obvious if, as has been said,
we direct the young by our critical judgement in the better
direction.

HOW TO REFUTE THE POETS OUT OF THEIR OWN MOUTHS

Preposterous statements which are not immediately accounted
for must be refuted by using contradictory statements made by
the poet elsewhere, without showing anger with him or
annoyance at remarks made not in earnest but humorously and in
character. For example, we may answer Homer's episodes in
which the gods are 'hurled down' by one another or wounded by
men, or quarrel or are angry, by saying to the poet:

> You know a better tale than this*—

your thoughts and your words are much better elsewhere: for
instance, 'the easy-living gods', or 'there the blessed gods have
joy all their days', or 'such is the fate the gods give wretched men,
to live in sorrow, while they themselves are carefree'. These are
perfectly sane and truthful opinions about the gods; the other
passages are inventions to amaze men.

Again, when Euripides says

> With many forms of trickery
> the gods, our masters, trip us up,

it is not a bad answer to produce his own better line:

> If gods do ill, they are no gods.

Pindar* says cruelly and provocatively:

> Do anything to blot your enemy out.

'But', we may reply, 'you say yourself

> A bitter end awaits unrighteous pleasure.'

Sophocles says:

> Profit is sweet, even though it comes from falsehood.

'But', we answer, 'we heard you say

> False words bear no fruit.'

Similarly, in reply to the lines about wealth:

> For wealth is strong to travel
> on public and forbidden ground alike
> and places where the poor man, even if lucky,
> could never have his will; it makes the ugly
> look beautiful, the stumbling talker wise—

one can cite many passages of Sophocles:

> Even the poor man can be held in honour,

and

> no worse for being a beggar, if he's wise,

and

> What grace is there in much beauty
> if it is wicked intrigue
> that breeds prosperity of riches?

Menander certainly encouraged and inflated the love of pleasure by the burning eroticism of the lines:

> All things that live and see our common sun
> are slaves to pleasure.

But elsewhere he converts us and draws us towards the good, eradicating the wantonness of our wickedness with the words

> An ugly life is a disgrace, however pleasant.

This is of course quite the opposite, and better and more useful.

ONE POET REFUTED BY ANOTHER

Consideration of juxtaposed opposites like this will either lead us to better views or at least destroy our belief in the worse. But if a poet does not himself provide a resolution of his absurdities, it is just as good to set against him the statements of other authorities of repute in order to turn the scale in the better direction. For example, Alexis disturbs some people when he says:

> The wise man should collect a stock of pleasures:
> and there are three that have the power that really
> contributes to one's life: food, drink, and sex;
> the rest are best regarded as an extra.

To counter this, let us recall that Socrates said the opposite—namely, that bad men live to eat and drink and good men eat and drink to live. Again, against the saying

> Wickedness is no bad weapon against the wicked,

which in a sense invites us to make ourselves resemble them, we may adduce a remark of Diogenes: when he was asked how an enemy might be resisted, he replied 'by becoming a good man oneself'. Diogenes is also useful against Sophocles, who has made myriads despair by saying about the mysteries:

> Thrice blessed they who have beheld these rites
> before they go to Hades. They alone
> live there, the rest endure infinite ill.

'What?' said Diogenes, 'will the thief Pataicion be better off than Epaminondas* when he dies, just because he was initiated?'

p. 22   Timotheus' hymn to Artemis, performed in the theatre, contained the words:

> maddened maenad, raving ranting.

'I wish you a daughter like that!' was Cinesias' impromptu retort.
And there is a nice answer of Bion to Theognis' lines:*

> Men beaten down by need can neither talk nor do;
> their tongues are tied.

It runs: 'How do you manage to talk such rubbish to us when
you're a poor man yourself?'

Neither must we neglect opportunities for correction which 5
arise out of the context or associated remarks. The cantharis is
deadly, but doctors think its feet and wings valuable, and an
antidote to its poison. Similarly, in poetry, if some noun or verb
in the context takes the edge off the compulsion we feel to
interpret the passage in a bad sense, we should fasten on to it and
expound its implications. This is sometimes done with the lines:

> This is the privilege of unhappy men,
> to crop their hair and let tears fall from their cheeks,*

and with the lines:

> Such is the fate the gods give wretched men,
> to live in sorrow.*

Homer does not mean here that the gods doom all men
indiscriminately to a life of sorrow, but only the foolish and
thoughtless, whom he calls 'unhappy' and 'wretched' because of
the miserable and pitiable state to which their wickedness brings
them.

SOME EDUCATIONAL USES OF PHILOLOGICAL KNOWLEDGE

Thus there is another way of removing the suspicions attaching 6
to a piece of poetry, and giving a better interpretation. This is
based on the normal use of words. The young student should be
exercised in this more than in the study of what are called
'glosses'.* The latter is indeed a scholarly pursuit, and it is nice
to know that *rhigedanos* means 'doomed to a bad death' because
danos is the Macedonian for death, or that the Aeolians say
kammoniē for a victory produced by patience and endurance, or
that the Dryopes call their daimones *popoi*.* The other however
is genuinely valuable and essential.

If we are to profit from poetry and not be harmed by it, it is essential to understand how the poets use the names of the gods and of good and bad, what they mean by Fortune and Fate, whether these terms in their usage are univocal or equivocal, and so on and so forth. For example, the word *oikos** sometimes means 'house':

> to the high-roof *oikos*;

and sometimes property:

> my *oikos* is being eaten up.

*Biotos** sometimes means life:

> and dark-haired Poseidon deadened the point of his spear,
> robbing him of *biotos*;

and sometimes money:

> others consume my *biotos*.

Similarly, *aluein** is used sometimes for being distressed or at a loss:

> He spoke, and she went away *distressed*, and greatly hurt;

and sometimes for being exultant and joyful:

> Are you on *top of yourself* because you have beaten
> the beggar Irus?

*Thoazein** means either 'to be moved', as in Euripides:

> a monster *moving* from the Atlantic deep;

or 'to sit', as in Sophocles:

> Why *sit* you thus
> garlanded with suppliants' branches?

It is also a neat trick to accommodate to the subject in hand the use of words which, as we learn from the grammarians, acquire a different force in different contexts. For example:

> Praise a small ship; load your cargo on a big one.*

The word *ainein* normally means 'praise' (like *epainein* which we now use similarly of refusal); compare the common phrases 'that's fine!' and 'how welcome!' which we use when we do not want or do not accept something. So some say that the adjective *epainē* applied to Persephone means 'she whom we seek to avert'. p. 23

This difference and distinction in words should be carefully observed in matters of greater consequences and seriousness. The instruction of the young student may begin with the names of the gods. These are used by the poets sometimes because they are thinking of the gods themselves but sometimes because (with no change of word) they are referring to certain forces which the gods give or over which they hold sway. For example, when Archilochus says in a prayer:

O Lord Hephaestus, hear my prayer; be favourable to me and
  help me;
and give whatever thou dost give,

he is obviously appealing to the god himself. But when, in lamenting his sister's brother, who was lost at sea and unburied, he says that he could bear the trouble more easily

  if Hephaestus had worked on his head and lovely body,
    wrapped in clean clothing—

he means fire, not the god of fire.

Again, when Euripides says in an oath

      by Zeus amid the stars, by bloody Ares,*

he means the gods themselves; but when Sophocles says:

      Ladies, Ares is blind and does not see;
      he grubs up trouble with a pig's snout,

he means war; just as Homer means 'bronze' by Ares in the line:

      Sharp Ares split their dark blood by Scamander.*

There are many such examples. We should note particularly that the poets use the name 'Zeus' sometimes for the god, sometimes for fortune, often for destiny. When they say

      O father Zeus, who rulest from Ida,*

or

> O Zeus, who says he is wiser than thou?

they mean the god in person. But when they give the name Zeus to the causes of all events and say that the wrath of Achilles* 'hurled many valiant souls to Hades . . . and the plan of Zeus was fulfilled', they mean destiny. The poet does not believe that the god plots evil for man; he is giving a correct indication of the necessity inherent in events: if nations, armies, or princes behave wisely, success and victory are guaranteed them; if, like the characters in the *Iliad*, they fall into passion and error, and differ and quarrel among themselves, they are fated to make a bad showing, suffer turmoil and confusion, and come to a bad end:

> fated it is that man shall reap
> from his bad plans a bad return.

And, when Hesiod* makes Prometheus advise Epimetheus,

> Never accept gifts
> from Zeus of Olympus; send them away,

he is using the name Zeus for the power of fortune; it is the blessings of fortune that he calls 'gifts of Zeus'—wealth, marriage, office, all external goods, the possession of which is profitless to those who cannot use them well. This is why he thinks Epimetheus, a poor foolish creature, ought to be on his guard and cautious of good fortune, because he may be harmed and ruined by it.

Again, when he says

> Do not reproach a man with dire, killing poverty:
> it is the gift of the blessed immortals,

p. 24   he is calling the accident of fortune the gift of the gods, and saying that it is wrong to reproach those who are poor through bad luck; it is need accompanied by idleness, softness, and extravagance that incurs shame and reproach. The actual word 'fortune'* (*tuchē*) was not yet in use; but the poets were aware of the strength and—to human calculation—unpredictability of the irregularly and indeterminately moving cause, and therefore used the names of the gods to describe it—just as we use the adjectives 'supernatural' and 'divine' of events, moral qualities, speeches, and men.

Many apparently outrageous statements about Zeus are to be corrected in this manner: e.g.

> By Zeus's door stand two jars full of dooms,
> one good, one bad,*

and

> Zeus, enthroned on high, has not ratified the oaths;
> he wishes both sides ill. . .,*

and

> For then the beginning of woe rolled on
> for Trojans and Greeks, through mighty Zeus' design.

These passages are about Fortune or Fate—i.e. the element in causation unamenable to our calculations and in general outside our control. But where appropriateness, reason, and probability are present, we may suppose that the god himself is meant: e.g.

> The ranks of all the others he visited,
> but he avoided the troops of Aias son of Telamon;
> for Zeus was indignant when he fought a better man,*

and

> In great things, Zeus takes care for men;
> the lesser he leaves to other gods.

Other words also deserve attention, for they suffer changes and variations at the hands of the poets in many different situations. 'Virtue' (*aretē*) is an example. Virtue not only makes men wise, just and good in word and deed, but also commonly invests them with fame and power. Accordingly, the poets treat reputation and power as virtue (compare the names of the trees 'olive' and 'beech' homonymously for their fruit). So when the poets say

> The gods have put sweat in the way of virtue,*

or

> Then by their virtue the Greeks broke the phalanx,

or

> If we must die, it is honourable to die thus,
> bringing life to its close in virtue,

the young student should realize immediately that this is said of
the noblest and most divine quality in us, which we conceive as
rightness of reason, excellence of our rational nature, and a
consistent habit of soul. On the other hand, when he reads

> Zeus makes men's virtue wax and wane,*

or

> Virtue and glory go with wealth,

he must not sit back in wonder and amazement at the rich, as
though virtue were something wealth could buy, nor must he
think that the increase or diminution of his own virtue depends
on fortune; he must realize that the poet has used 'virtue' in the
sense of reputation, power, success, or the like.

Similarly, by 'evil' (*kakotēs*), they sometimes mean, in the
proper sense, vice or wickedness of soul: thus Hesiod:

> Evil you can have in abundance.

But sometimes they mean non-moral damage or misfortune: e.g.
Homer's

> For men grow old quickly in evil.*

Similarly, it would be self-deception to think that the poets mean
'happiness' in the philosophers' sense of 'complete possession or
acquisition of good things' or 'perfection of life flowing smoothly
in its natural tenour'. In fact they often (by catachresis) call the
rich happy or blessed, and power or reputation happiness.
Homer uses the words correctly in the line

p. 25

> So I do not reign amid this wealth in happiness;

so does Menander:

> I have much property, all call me rich;
> but no one calls me happy.

But Euripides produces great muddle and confusion when he says:

> I never want a happy life that's painful,*

and

> Why honour tyranny, happy injustice?—

unless, as I said, we follow the metaphors and catachreses carefully.

POETRY MUST REPRODUCE EVIL AND CONFLICT

Young men must be shown and reminded again and again that 7
the imitative purpose of poetry compels it to use its ornaments and splendours in handling the events and characters of its subject without abandoning the likeness to reality, since the attraction of imitation lies in its convincingness. Any imitation therefore which is not utterly neglectful of truth inevitably reproduces the marks of vice and virtue along with the actions concerned. Homer's art, for example, will have no truck with the Stoic doctrine that virtue has nothing bad attaching to it and vice nothing good, the ignorant man being in error in everything and the good man universally successful. That is what we are told in the schools; in real life, as Euripides says,

> good and bad are not to be found apart;
> there is a sort of mixture.

And even apart from considerations of truth, poetry prefers if possible to use varied and diversified material: emotional effect, paradox, and surprise—prime sources of both wonder and charm—are given to myth by variety, whereas simplicity lacks both emotion and poetical effect. This is why poets do not represent the same people as always victorious, prosperous, or successful. Indeed, they do not even treat the gods, when involved in human affairs, as free from passion or error. This is to safeguard the disturbing and exciting element in poetry from lapsing through the absence of danger and conflict.

This being so, we must ensure, when we introduce the young 8
student to poetry, that he is free from the prejudice that these

great and noble names were necessarily wise and upright men,
excellent kings, and patterns of all virtue and right conduct. He
will indeed come to harm if he thinks everything splendid and
gapes in awe, never feeling annoyance at anything he reads
and ignoring the protests of those who find fault with actions and
words like

> O father Zeus, Athena, and Apollo,
> would that no Trojan alive might escape from death,
> and no Argive either, so long as you and I
> dodge the destruction, and break, alone, the holy ring-wall
> of Troy;*

or

> I heard the piteous cry of Priam's daughter, Cassandra,
> whom treacherous Clytemnestra killed beside me;

or

To lie first with the concubine, to make her loathe the old man;
I was persuaded, and I did it;

or

> Father Zeus, no god is more baleful than thou . . .

p. 26   The young reader must not get into the habit of praising anything
of this kind, or displaying unscrupulous persuasiveness in
devising excuses and specious evasions for bad deeds. Poetry, he
must realize, is an imitation of the manners and lives of men, who
are not perfect, pure, and irreproachable, but involved in
passions, false opinions, and ignorance—though they often
indeed improve themselves through their natural goodness. This
kind of training and attitude in a young man exalted and inspired
by good words and actions and unreceptive of, and distressed by,
bad ones, will ensure that reading does no harm. The student
who admires everything and makes it his own, and whose
judgement is ensnared by the heroic names, will inadvertently fall
victim to many faults: it would be like imitating Plato's stoop or
Aristotle's lisp. There is no need to be cowardly about it, or
shiver or fall down and worship in superstitious awe; we must
accustom ourselves to commenting with confidence, and saying

'wrong' and 'inappropriate' as often as we say 'right' and 'appropriate'.

Consider for example the conduct of Achilles. He summons an assembly when the soldiers are ill. It is his own military distinction and reputation, of course, that particularly make him distressed at the lull in the fighting. But he has medical knowledge and realizes, after the ninth day* (the normal crisis period), that the disease is no ordinary one and comes from no common cause. He rises, and, instead of making a speech to the multitude, addresses advice to the king:

Son of Atreus, now I think we should turn and go home . . .

This is correct, decent, appropriate behaviour. But when the seer [Calchas] says he is afraid of the anger of the most powerful of the Greeks, Achilles no longer behaves so well; he swears that no one shall lay hands on Calchas while he lives, and adds 'even if you mean Agamemnon'. This displays neglect and contempt of the ruler. Then he becomes even more furious and grabs his sword with intent to murder—a wrong action from the point of view both of honour and expediency. His repentance follows:

> He thrust his great sword back into the scabbard
> and did not disobey Athene's words.

It is quite right and proper that, unable to eradicate his anger altogether, he controls it and subjects it to reason before doing anything irremediable.

Or take Agamemnon. In his words and actions in the assembly he is a ridiculous figure, but in the Chryseis episode more dignified and kingly. When Briseis is dragged off, Achilles

> wept and drew aside and sat apart from his comrades,

but Agamemnon puts the woman on board ship himself and hands her over, though he has not long before said that he thinks more of her than of his wife. Here is nothing shameful, no yielding to love. Note also what Phoenix says, after his father has cursed him because of the concubine:

> I planned to kill him with the sharp edge of bronze;
> but some immortal stopped my wrath, and made me think

of what the folk would say, and all the reproaches:
I did not want to be called my father's murderer.*

p. 27   Aristarchus excised these lines, alarmed by them; but they are
right in the situation. Phoenix is showing Achilles what anger is
like and what men dare do out of anger, unless they use their
reason and listen to soothing words. Phoenix also cites Meleager
as having been angry with his fellow citizens, but then pacified.
He rightly finds fault with the emotion, but praises, as both
honourable and expedient, Meleager's resistance, opposition,
control, and repentance. In this passage, the difference is
obvious. Where the intention is less clear, a distinction must be
made by drawing the student's attention in some such way as the
following.

   If Nausicaa's remark to the maids—

> I wish I had a husband like that
> living here; I wish he wanted to stay*

was made frivolously because when she saw the stranger
Odysseus she felt towards him like Calypso, because she was a
spoilt girl and now marriageable, then her forwardness and lack
of control deserve censure; but if she perceived Odysseus'
character from his words and admired his sensible conversation,
and so comes to pray for a husband like that rather than one of
the nautical gentlemen and good dancers of her own country—
then she deserves admiration.

   Again, when Penelope converses amiably with the suitors, and
they give her clothes and gold and other ornaments, Odysseus is
pleased

> because she took their presents and charmed their hearts.*

If it is her acceptance of presents and her greed that pleases him,
this is living off immoral earnings to a degree worse than
Poliagros in the comedy:

> O happy Poliagros,
> with his heavenly goat that brings in the money!

But if Odysseus thought he would have them more under his
thumb because of their expectations—they would be confident

and not see what was coming—then his pleasure and confidence are justified. . Similarly with his counting the treasure the Phaeacians left with him before they sailed away. If he was really afraid for the money

> for fear they had gone away with something on the ship,*

then indeed—given his desolate situation and the total uncertainty about his own fate—his avarice deserves pity or disgust. But if, as some say, he was uncertain whether this really was Ithaca, and thought the safe transport of the treasure an indication of the Phaeacians' good faith—they would not otherwise have kept their hands off the money if they had landed him, with no profit to themselves, in a country not his own—then he uses a perfectly sound argument, and we should commend his common sense. Some actually disapprove of his being put ashore like this, if it really happened while he was asleep. They say the Etruscans preserve a tradition that Odysseus was naturally sleepy, and bad company to most people for this reason. They approve it only if the sleep was not genuine—that is to say, if he felt ashamed to send the Phaeacians away without presents and hospitality, but was unable to conceal himself from his enemies if he had them with him, and therefore covered up his difficulty by pretending to be asleep.

If we point out these things to young people, we shall stop any tendency to deterioration of character, and encourage the pursuit and choice of the better course, because we unhesitatingly accord blame to the one and praise to the other. This is especially necessary in tragedies which contain plausible and unscrupulous speeches concerned with disreputable or immoral actions. When Sophocles says,

> From evil actions good words never come,

it is just not true. He himself often attaches smiling words and kind explanations to bad ways and atrocious deeds. As for his colleague,* you know how *he* makes Phaedra actually reproach p. 28 Theseus as though it was because of his infidelities that she has fallen in love with Hippolytus; and we have another example in the language assigned to Helen about Hecuba* in the *Trojan Women*, where she decides that it is Hecuba who really should be punished, because she was the adulterer's mother! The young student must beware of thinking this neat or smart. He must not smile indulgently at the ingenuity. The words of vice should be more detestable to him even than the deeds!

It is thus always useful to inquire into the reason for what is said. Cato as a child used always to do what his attendant told him—but he always asked why. There is no need to listen to poets as though they were lawgivers or tutors unless their subject stands up to examination—which it will if it is good. If it is bad, it will be seen as vain and futile. Now many people inquire acutely into the rationale and significance of lines like

> And not to put the pourer above the bowl
> while they are drinking;*

or

> The man who can reach another chariot from his own
> must thrust with his spear.

But they accept without question dicta on graver matters:

> It enslaves a man, however bold he is,
> to know a mother's or father's evil deeds;

and

> he who fares badly should have lowly thoughts.

Yet these sayings touch the character and cause confusion in life, because they produce bad decisions and unworthy opinions, unless we accustom ourselves always to ask *why* the man who fares badly should have lowly thoughts, instead of resisting fortune and raising himself above humiliation. And why, if I am the son of a bad, foolish father, but myself decent and sensible, should I not be proud of my good character? Must I be humbled and cast down because of my father's stupidity? If you react and resist like this, instead of bowing to every word as to a gust of wind, and if you remember that 'it is a lazy man who takes fright at everything that is said', you will soon be free of many of these false and unhelpful statements.

So much for the ways of ensuring that reading poetry does no harm.

EXPLANATORY NOTES

Plato: *Ion*

THIS is one of Plato's earlier and lighter dialogues. Socrates punctures the pretensions to knowledge of a professional reciter of epic poetry, and demonstrates the irrational nature of poetic inspiration and the absurdity of the poets' claim to useful knowledge.

1 *Asclepieia*: the festival of the healing god, Asclepius, at Epidaurus in the Peloponnese, the greatest centre of his worship. Games and musical contests were a feature of the festival.

rhapsodes: 'stitchers of songs'—the name given in Plato's time to professional reciters of Homer, such as Ion.

Panathenaea: an Athenian festival in honour of Athena, held annually in a lesser form, but every four years as a greater event.

Metrodorus . . . Glaucon: Metrodorus interpreted Homer allegorically; the others, so far as we know, did not.

Homeridae: a guild of reciters known in Chios (reputedly Homer's birthplace) by the sixth century, and claiming descent from the poet.

4 *Daedalus . . . Theodorus*: the first two sculptors are mythical figures (Epeus built the Wooden Horse), but Theodorus is a real person, a gem-engraver of the sixth century.

Olympus . . . Ithaca: the poets are again mythical; Phemius is a character in the *Odyssey*.

5 *Corybantic dancers*: participants in an orgiastic ritual dance, believed to have therapeutic powers in some kinds of mental disturbance.

dithyrambs: elaborate lyrics in complex metres, characterized by high-flown language and neologisms.

encomia: songs of praise, strictly of men or heroes rather than of gods, who are celebrated in 'hymns'.

hyporchemata: songs with dance accompaniment.

iambics: poems of invective were written in iambic metre. This was regarded as its original use, although it was also the metre of dramatic dialogue.

paean: a song in praise of Apollo.

6 *Odysseus . . . Priam*: Socrates is thinking of some specially powerful scenes in Homer. Odysseus on the threshold is in *Odyssey* 22; Achilles' advance comes from *Iliad* 22; the pathetic passages are the lamentations for Hector in *Iliad* 24.

8 *Nestor . . . Patroclus*: *Iliad* 23. 335 ff.

9 *Homer*: the following passages are: *Iliad* 11. 369, 24. 80; *Odyssey* 20. 35; *Iliad* 12. 200.

Pramnian wine: supposed to be a strong red wine.

10 *Melampodid*: i.e. a descendant of Melampus, for whose history see *Odyssey* 15. 223 ff.

12 *government . . . yourselves*: Ephesus was a member of the Athenian alliance for much of the fifth century, after the Persian wars. Its affairs were then largely controlled from Athens. Sparta is mentioned as the other major military power in Greece. Socrates counters Ion's excuses by naming a few people (of whom we know nothing certain) who *have* attained office at Athens, despite coming from other cities.

Plato: *Republic* 2. 376–3. 398

PLATO'S discussion of poetry in *Republic* falls into two parts. The first discussion is concerned with the educational dangers of poetry. Though the ostensible subject is the education of the ideal 'guardians' of an imaginary state, the points made have often been regarded as Plato's criticism of the poetical element in the actual culture of his time.

15 *Ouranos . . . upon him*: according to this primitive myth (Hesiod, *Theogony* 137 ff., 453 ff.) Kronos castrated his father Ouranos and swallowed his children.

a pig: the victim which had to be offered by everyone seeking to be initiated in the Eleusinian mysteries.

17 *by Zeus's door . . .*: *Iliad* 24. 527 ff. Cf. Plutarch (p. 209).
Pandarus: *Iliad* 4. 69 ff.

19 *in guise . . . of shape*: *Odyssey* 17. 485 f.

to the life-giving . . .: a fragment of Aeschylus.

21 *the dispatch of the Dream*: *Iliad* 2. 1–34.
he hymned . . . killer: again from Aeschylus.

22 *Rather would I . . . dead*: *Odyssey* 11. 489 ff. The following passages are all from Homer: *Iliad* 20. 64, 23. 103; *Odyssey* 10. 495, *Iliad* 16. 856 and 23. 100; *Odyssey* 24. 6.

23 *Cocytus, Styx*: fabled rivers of Hades, with significant names: 'Abhorrèd Styx, the flood of deadly hate . . . Cocytus named of lamentation loud' (*Paradise Lost* 2. 577).

24 *lying now on his side . . .*: *Iliad* 24. 10. The following passages are also from the *Iliad*: 22. 414, 18. 54, 22. 168, 16. 433.

25 *then unquenchable laughter...*: *Iliad* 1. 599.

   any of those...: *Odyssey* 18. 383.

26 *Sit quietly...*: *Iliad* 4. 412.

   You drunken sot...: *Iliad* 1. 225.

   the tables...: *Odyssey* 9. 8.

   the bitterest way...: *Odyssey* 12. 342.

27 *he then forgets*: *Iliad* 14. 294 ff.

   Ares and Aphrodite: *Odyssey* 8. 166 ff.

   He beat his chest...: *Odyssey* 22. 17.

   Gifts convince...: probably a line of Hesiod.

   Phoenix: *Iliad* 9. 575 ff.

   Achilles: the episodes referred to are in *Iliad* 19 and 24.

   You have wronged me...: *Iliad* 22. 15.

   disobedience...: *Iliad* 21. 130, 221 ff. The further references are to Achilles' behaviour later on, in *Iliad* 23 and 24.

28 *Theseus . . . Pirithous*: the two friends went down to Hades to attempt to kidnap Persephone.

   the gods' near relatives . . .: Aeschylus, *Niobe*. It is noticeable that Aeschylus, not the later and more sophisticated Euripides, is the source of so many of the tragic passages that Socrates finds objectionable.

30 *and he begged all the Achaeans...*: *Iliad* 1. 15–16.

31 *dithyrambs*: see p. 5.

32 *illness, love, or childbirth*: Plato is thinking of tragic heroines like Medea, Phaedra, or Niobe.

33 *horses neighing...*: cf. Plutarch, p. 198.

35 *the cobbler a cobbler . . .*: Plato is contrasting his imaginary city with democratic Athens, where a cobbler might well serve at sea, and farmers and others regularly sat on juries.

Plato: *Republic* 10. 595–607

THIS second discussion concentrates on the psychological and metaphysical reasons for regarding poetry as a dangerous illusion. It rests on arguments advanced in the intervening parts of the work, and was very probably written considerably later than Books 2–3.

41 *Homeridae*: see note to *Ion*, p. 1.

his generalship or advice: compare the argument of *Ion*, p. 12.

Creophylus: i.e. 'meat-stock'.

45 *men performing actions*: this is very close to the formulation of Aristotle, *Poetics* 1448ᵃ1, p. 52.

49 '*the yapping bitch* . . .': this and the following quotations are not known from other sources.

Aristotle: *Poetics*

INTRODUCTION

VARIOUS factors make the *Poetics* a work singularly easy to misinterpret and it is worth listing them: (1) Aristotle's thought, though generally exquisitely lucid, is never easy and never slack. (2) Some accidental features of its composition or its transmission have made the *Poetics* one of his most compressed and elliptical works. (3) Aristotle presupposed in his audience an acquaintance with the thought of Plato (see notes to pp. 53, 72, 83, 88) and also with the central concepts of his own logical and metaphysical theories as well as with the doctrines of the *Ethics* and *Politics* (see notes to pp. 59, 61, 69). (4) The *Poetics* envisages a variety of different interests in literature, the politician's, the poet's, the critic's; but the book is not written primarily for any of these, but rather for the philosopher. In other words, it is neither principally a defence of poetry, nor a treatise on how to write it, nor an enunciation of principles of literary criticism, though it has elements of all these: it is first and foremost a work of aesthetic theory, and the questions it poses are 'What is poetry, and what is the nature of our pleasure in it?'

ARISTOTLE'S THEORY OF AESTHETIC PLEASURE

Aristotle had a quite coherent theory of the nature of our pleasure in art. It starts from simple principles and ramifies everywhere; it explains his preferences in literature and it is the antithesis of Plato's, though it accepts some of the same presuppositions.

The basic premiss of Aristotle's aesthetic theory is stated in c. 4 of the *Poetics* and several times in the *Rhetoric*: it is that by and large human beings positively enjoy learning or understanding or realizing things (all of these being possible translations of his word *mathēsis*). Our desire to understand things is a natural desire like hunger, and its satisfaction is pleasurable, a 'restoration to a natural state', like eating (*Rhetoric* 1371 a 21 ff.). Our pleasure in art is a branch of this pleasure; the poet or the orator or the painter makes us see or understand things that we did not see before, and particularly he points out the relations and similarities between different things and enables us to say, in Aristotle's phrase, 'this is that' (p. 54 and several times in the *Rhetoric*).

This basic foundation of aesthetic pleasure explains many of Aristotle's further requirements in art. First and foremost, it justifies the general Greek belief, which Aristotle accepted and elaborately defends, that art is essentially 'representational', i.e. that *mimēsis* is necessary to it. Aristotle takes the relation between *mimēsis* and *mathēsis* to be a close one, both at the simplest level, where 'we make our first steps in learning through *mimēsis*' (p. 54), and at the infinitely more sophisticated one where the tragic poet makes 'general statements' analogous to those of the moral philosopher. At the lowest level, *mimēsis* is what Plato asserted it was at any level, mere copying, a parrot act that can be performed without any real knowledge of the act or object copied: even here, however, Aristotle implies that though we may not have knowledge before we engage in *mimēsis* we acquire knowledge by engaging in it. And at the higher level the tragic or epic poet, presenting individually characterized people in specific situations, makes us aware of moral facts and moral possibilities relevant to more than the situation he envisages.

If *mimēsis* is to produce the sort of realization that Aristotle demands of art at its best, a prime requirement is obviously truth. A poem or play that operates in the realm of fantasy can charm and rouse wonder, and Aristotle is as susceptible as anyone to the enchantment of the fantastic in Homer (pp. 83–4). Yet his judgement is against fantasy and given in favour of the more rigorous causal chain of tragedy, which, because it is presented to the senses and not just to the feebler imagination, cannot afford to follow epic into the area of the marvellous and the irrational.

Yet the realization must, to be in the highest degree pleasurable, also be sudden, and for this the prime requirement is surprise. A play whose plot, however truthful, is predictable will not give us the pleasure of sudden realization. This is the reason for Aristotle's insistence on the unexpected and a second reason for his preference for the complex form of tragedy, which is defined with reference to surprise turns (*peripeteiai*) and recognitions. As he says several times in the *Rhetoric*, it is juxtaposition that best makes us aware of opposites, and the sudden reversals of fortune in complex tragedy most powerfully bring home to us the truths that the poet is stating.

For both these reasons Aristotle regards complex tragedy as the *entelecheia* or full realization of the essential nature of poetry. It is the form that makes us realize most truth fastest and therefore provides in greatest measure and concentration the pleasure that a work of art can provide. The same criteria are deployed not only to judge between or within literary kinds, but also in evaluating details of style; it is, for instance, the requirements of *mathēsis* that determine the high estimate Aristotle gives to metaphor (p. 80).

THE DEFENCE OF TRAGEDY

Whatever may be true of other arts, tragedy operates on a consciousness heightened by intense emotion, and specifically by the two emotions of fear and pity. The discussion of these two emotions in *Rhetoric* 2. 5 and 2. 9 shows them closely related; essentially they are roused by the same kind of situations, but fear is self-regarding and pity other-regarding. Aristotle's statement that tragedy rouses fear in the audience therefore implies that he takes for granted a remarkable degree of identification between the audience and the characters represented, as we can see from the statement in *Rhet.* 1382 b 30 ff.: 'No one feels fear if he thinks nothing is likely to happen to him, or fear of things he does not think would happen to him or of people he does not think likely to harm him, or at the time when he does not anticipate harm'.

A by-product of the stimulation of these intense emotions is their *catharsis* (p. 57). This cryptic phrase has attracted more attention than it deserves, but the theory concealed by it is nevertheless important. In the tenth book of the *Republic* Plato had attacked *mimēsis*, and particularly tragedy, on two counts, the first that it does not present us with truth, the second that it stimulates emotions that a good man tries to suppress. Aristotle's answer to the first charge is to be found in the *mathēsis* doctrine, and especially in c. 9 of the *Poetics*. Plato had claimed that an instance of *mimēsis* has less reality than a particular, which in turn has less reality than the *idea*. Aristotle replies that the statements of the poet, so far from being inferior to statements of particulars, are more comprehensive and more philosophical (p. 62); if he were thinking in Platonic terms this would amount to saying that the object of *mimēsis* is not the particular but the *idea*. Of course he does not say any such thing, as he did not believe in substantive *ideai*; but the implication was drawn by later Platonists. The answer to Plato's second charge is contained in the reference to *catharsis*.

Some light is thrown on the concept by a passage in the *Politics* (1341 b 32 ff.), where Aristotle discusses the kinds of music that the legislator should approve. One of them is cathartic music, the highly exciting and clamorous music used in the rites of Bacchus and other orgiastic cults; it was an established therapeutic practice to use such music as a kind of homoeopathic cure for religious hysteria. Aristotle goes on to suggest that something analogous happens in the case of the tragic emotions of pity and fear, and promises a further discussion of the concept in the *Poetics*.

The reference in the *Poetics*, unprovided with the explanation promised in the *Politics*, has provoked the most various interpretations. The most promising line is that put forward by H. House, *Aristotle's Poetics* (London, 1956), pp. 100 ff.; he takes *catharsis* in its medical sense of the production of a right balance (a 'mean'), and interprets the concept of 'mean' in Aristotle's own sense. When we consider what degree of emotion is 'undue', we take into account not merely the quantity of emotion but its objects and its circumstances (*Nicomachean Ethics* 1106 b 18 ff. 'One can feel fear, confidence, desire, anger, pity . . . both too much and too little, and in both cases wrongly; but the mean is attained when we feel them at the right time, at the right objects, towards the right people, for the right reason, in the right way'). Aristotle's answer to Plato seems to be that tragedy presents us with objects (great and good men suffering terrible fortunes) that are proportioned to the degree of emotion they arouse. So far from encouraging a vicious indulgence in emotion on any and every occasion, tragedy gives us an imaginative apprehension of a degree of suffering normally beyond our ken and helps us to make an appropriate response to it.

It is important that this purely defensive move does not commit Aristotle to either of two erroneous aesthetic positions common both in antiquity and later times. *Catharsis* is not something the tragic poet aims to produce. His aim is defined (p. 68) as 'to produce the pleasure springing from pity and fear via *mimēsis*'; *catharsis* is a therapeutic by-product, not something the poet either does or should intend. But just as Aristotle can therefore avoid the Scylla of taking the poet to have a duty to improve his audience's morals, he equally shuns the Charybdis of denying that poetry has any moral effect. Tragedy is not trivial, and it does alter our moral attitudes, by enlarging, however fleetingly, our imaginative understanding.

51 *The genus*: the genus that Aristotle proceeds to divide is not *mimēsis* in general, but the variety defined by the media, '*mimēsis* in speech, harmony and rhythm, separately or in combination'.

in others . . . voice: the reference is to sounds, not necessarily articulate, made by human vocal organs, e.g. direct mimicry of the bird-call kind.

52 *Those which do use speech*: in the following section too Aristotle seems to use a not-*x*/*x* method of division and considers first the arts that do not use music and dancing and next those that do.

has as yet no name: the objection is double: (*a*) the whole mimetic art that uses speech but not music and dancing has no name; (*b*) its two species, prose and verse, have no names. Lobel reasonably conjectures: 'The art that uses only speech by itself and that which uses verse . . . have as yet no names.'

similarly . . . 'maker': the point is sophistical: both on Aristotle's criterion of *mimēsis* and on the ordinary language criterion of verse, Chaeremon belongs to the generic class 'poet', but ordinary language can find no specific term for him parallel to 'hexameter-maker'. The previous argument is no better, since in his *On the Poets* Aristotle commends Empedocles as 'Homeric and stylistically excellent, particularly in his use of metaphor' (a prime poetic merit, p. 80). Aristotle is not over-scrupulous in this argument for the necessity of *mimēsis*.

rhythm . . . verse: 'rhythm' here means 'dancing', while 'song' is a combination of all three of the media isolated earlier, 'verse' a combination of rhythm and speech.

people doing things: for Aristotle the word means 'people performing responsible and morally characterizable actions'.

or else . . . are: the second distinction (idealized, caricatured, realistic) is a refinement on the first, perhaps an afterthought.

53 *differ as . . .*: text defective.

sometimes in narration . . . things: one might also interpret '(i) sometimes in narration, either becoming someone else, as Homer does, or speaking in one's own person without change, or (ii) with all the people. . .'. The threefold classification given in the translation accords with Plato's view (*Rep.* 392 d ff.), and, more importantly with Aristotle's own insistence on the uniqueness of Homer (pp. 55, 81, 83, 84).

54 *when their democracy was established*: early in the sixth century.

Chionides and Magnes: the first known poets of Attic comedy, very little later than Ephicharmus.

55 *The development of pre-dramatic poetry*: the series hymns–Homer–tragedy is unhistorical, as the great poets of encomium (Simonides, Pindar, Bacchylides) were later than Homer. The series invectives–Homer–comedy is even worse; not only was the great invective poet Archilochus later than Homer, but the invention of the iambic trimeter was attributed to Homer in the *Margites*.

high actions: the translation is borrowed from Milton (*Paradise Regained* 4. 266); the word is translated 'good' (e.g., p. 52) or 'noble' (p. 57) when used of persons.

58 *of the verse-parts*: i.e. of the dialogue parts.

59 *the end and aim of human life*: commonly assumed by the Greeks to be *eudaimonia*, an assumption that Aristotle accepts; the word is often rendered by 'happiness', here by 'success'.

what the rest of the tragedy is there for: Aristotle is talking in terms of his own theory of explanation; in this teleological explanations ('final causes') are of more than one kind. Though one sort of 'final cause' is the answer to the question 'What is the purpose of *x*?', another is the answer to the question 'For the sake of what in *x* is the rest of *x* there?' (e.g. one final cause of a knife is cutting and another is the cutting edge). The argument here plainly shows that plot is the 'final cause' of tragedy in the second sense. The purpose of tragedy is not plot, but is stated on p. 68, 'the poet's job is to produce the pleasure springing from pity and fear via *mimēsis*'.

the principle of life: the 'principle of life' renders *psychē* ('soul'), which has the same relation to the living body as plot to tragedy; it is what the rest is there for as in (*a*), and it is what the living body essentially is, as in (*b*).

60 *'mimēsis of intellect'*: cf. p. 75.

a work is potentially a tragedy: others interpret 'a tragedy can do its job' (cf. pp. 88–9). But here the point seems to be a different one; though an actual, fully realized performance of a tragedy demands spectacle, the poet has done what he has to do when he has produced a text that is potentially a tragedy. Its staging is not something that belongs to the poet's art.

Closer analysis of plot: Aristotle is not yet talking about what is necessary for a good plot; that topic begins on p. 66. This section concerns the essential nature of tragedy and considers the minimum characteristics a plot must have if it is not to be positively defective.

The essential characteristics . . . action: the four essential characteristics are not on a level; the first three are defined in terms of the last. The kind of order, amplitude and unity in question are all explained in terms that invoke probable or necessary connection.

61 *as they say . . occasion*: text corrupt, meaning uncertain.

just as the one . . . such-and-such: the analogy is drawn from logic. For example, some of the statements to be made about a coffee-pot will define it as a piece of crockery, those plus some more statements will define it as a coffee-pot; but a great many statements that are incidentally true of it ('It was washed up today') only detail its life history and do not define it as a member of any species.

62 *this is what poetry aims at*: to grasp the intellectual power and the refinement of Aristotle's analysis here, one must remember that to the Greeks Oedipus was just as much a historical personage as Alcibiades, i.e. they saw no obvious difference between 'Oedipus did *a*' and 'Alcibiades did *a*'. The distinction between what a poet means when he says 'Oedipus/Alcibiades did this' and what a historian means by an identical statement is by no means easy to arrive at. Aristotle sets high standards for both historian and poet. The historian's job is truth to fact: he must not suppress the fact that does not fit in nor bridge the gaps in his evidence with plausible

conjecture presented as fact. The poet tells truth of a different kind, because he cannot say anything without his audience's taking it to be relevant to the picture they assume he is presenting, and that picture is an investigation of moral possibilities. That is why Aristotle regards poetry as more like philosophy (or like science); its statements, though in form the same as the historian's, are taken to be statements of the greatest generality that its subject-matter allows. Of course, bad historians (like many ancient ones) or bad poets (like the authors of modern 'faction') fall below these standards.

63 *defective*: conjectural; the manuscripts have 'simple', which is irrelevant in the context.

64 *such plots*: those where things happen unexpectedly but because of each other.

one that is continuous . . .: one that has probable or necessary connection.

in the way described: in a way involving surprise.

it seemed that he would comfort: or 'came with the intention of comforting'. However, the construction used is the same as in the Lynceus example, where it was certainly not Lynceus' intention to be put to death. The frustrated expectation seems to be felt by the audience, not by the characters.

Lynceus: lost play by Theodectes.

65 *anapaestic dimeter . . .*: the anapaestic dimeter is a marching metre, normal in chorus entries, the trochaic tetrameter a running metre appropriate to a hasty choral entry. Cf. A. M. Dale, *Collected Papers* (Cambridge, 1969), pp. 34 ff.

66 *So it is clear . . . families*: Aristotle's thought in this section is illuminated by the discussion in *Rhetoric* 2. 9 of the emotions that expel pity. Among them is 'justified indignation'. In the *Eudemian Ethics* (1233 b 25 ff.) this emotion is said to have several aspects, pain at the undeserved misfortunes of the good, pain at the undeserved good fortune of the wicked, pleasure at the deserved misfortunes of the wicked; these three aspects correspond to the three cases Aristotle here excludes. 'What satisfies our human feeling' (*to philanthrōpon*) seems here to be the opposite of the 'morally outraging' (*to miaron*).

Aristotle clearly has some difficulty in reconciling the need to avoid 'justified indignation' with the requirement that the characters of high poetry should be good. To do so he invokes *hamartia* as the cause of their misfortune. In the context two things are necessary, that the tragic figure should in some sense be responsible for his fate (to avoid the first case), and that his fate should nevertheless be worse than he deserves (to avoid the third case); i.e. a *hamartia* here is 'a going wrong that is venial'. In the *Eudemian* and the *Nicomachean Ethics* acts can be venial if done in ignorance or under the influence of an irresistible passion; the same act done coolly or with full knowledge would be a crime. See further T. C. W. Stinton, *CQ* 25, 1975, pp. 221 ff.

67 *those who censure . . . mistake*: they make the same mistake as the 'some people' mentioned above and below, those who prefer a happy ending for the good.

most tragic: 'most tragic' means 'best at arousing pity and fear'.

69 *again in the* Helle . . .: Aristotle is here clearly commending a situation that leads to a happy ending for the good, and the passage is therefore in downright contradiction with the censure of the happy ending on p. 67. Bywater is probably right in taking the two paragraphs from 'Well, one cannot interfere . . .' to '. . . giving her up' to be a later addition made by Aristotle himself to his own text and enshrining a change of mind.

not suitable for a woman . . .: cf. *Politics* 1.5 and 1277 b 21 ff., for the difference between the virtues of men and women, even when their virtues are called by the same name.

Menelaus in the Orestes: his cowardice in 682–715. G. F. Else rightly argues that this and the other examples given are, when we can check them, 'unnecessary' because they do not contribute to the action of the play, which would be unaffected whether they were there or not.

70 *the mimēsis of character*: this is the reading of the sixth-century Syriac translation and is the only one that allows all this chapter, except the last sentence, to deal with character. The rest of the evidence for the text has 'should arise from the plot itself'. If this is right, we must suppose that the bundle of practical hints for playwrights that occupies chapters 16–18 and interrupts the orderly development of the treatise begins with this sentence.

outside the tragedy: cf. p. 84.

Digression on various topics . . .: the discussion of excellence in tragedy, which proceeds from plot (cc. 13–14) and character (c. 15, but cf. note on *mimēsis* above) to the representation of intellect (c. 19) and verbal expression (cc. 19 ff.), is suspended, and we have three chapters which nobody would have planned to put where we find them, though they are indubitably Aristotelian.

71 *the Bath episode*: the recognition by Eurycleia in *Odyssey* 19.

the 'voice of the shuttle': Philomela told her story by weaving, as her tongue had been cut out.

we have the argument . . .: Electra does not use this dubious bit of reasoning to help her recognize Orestes; he recognizes her because he hears her producing it in lines 164 ff. Her recognition of him is 'manufactured by the poet', i.e. he simply declares who he is (219) and also produces tokens (225 ff.).

72 *there is a hypothesis . . .*: if this is a hypothesis entertained by one of the characters and means 'If he truly says that he will recognize the bow that he has not, since his arrival in Ithaca, seen', a character might falsely infer 'He is Odysseus'. The false inference is the fallacy of inferring the antecedent from the consequent, p. 83.

this [false inference] . . .: text and interpretation are a matter of speculation.

That is why . . . degenerate: the manuscripts have 'That is why poetry is the work of a genius or a madman', in conjunction with which the next clause must be interpreted 'for the genius is by nature adaptable, while the madman is beside himself'; if this is right Aristotle is placidly assenting *en passant* to Plato's account of poetic *mania* (*Phaedrus* 245 a), though that account can hardly be reconciled with the demands that he himself makes on the poet at this point. This attitude is, to say the least, less to be expected than that of tacit dissent from a Platonic paradox, and one may happily share the doubts of Castelvetro, Dryden, and Tyrwhitt.

75 *In poets apart from these*: to a modern reader the failure to take Aeschylus into account is notable. One may remark also that Aeschylus is thought to have composed a trilogy on the main action of the *Iliad*, something derisively mentioned only as an absurd possibility on p. 74.

As I have dealt . . .: at this point the same line of the argument is resumed (see note to p. 70).

Its sections are . . .: except on p. 59, Aristotle in c. 6 confined the *mimēsis* of intellect to the speeches containing demonstrative arguments and general maxims. Here he includes the use that the characters in a poem make of persuasive language more widely defined.

76 *three subdivisions*: in modern terminology: vowels, fricatives, and stops.

77 *Different . . . nouns*: to avoid repetition, the discussion of poetical style covers all kinds of high poetry, choral lyric and epic as well as tragedy. The compound words in the first classification are

particularly suited to choral lyric, while many of the decorative elements in the second classification are epic rather than tragic.

decorative terms: this term is not defined and discussed below. A papyrus fragment, perhaps of a work by Aristotle's pupil Theophrastus, seems to deal with ornamental epithets ('blazing steel', 'bright gold') after a discussion of metaphor akin to ours.

78 *'Here my ship . . .'*: Homer, *Odyssey* 1. 185.

'Odysseus . . .': Homer, *Iliad* 2. 272.

'drawing . . .': Empedocles (frr. 138, 143); the reference in the second is to a bronze bucket.

'Ares' cup': Timotheus, *PMG* 797.

'the sunset of life': Plato, *Laws* 770 a.

'sowing . . .': from a choral lyric or a tragic chorus.

arētēr: the word is used three times by Homer.

A 'lengthened word': the terms in this and the following two sections are epic. To explain them nowadays we invoke comparative philology, but Aristotle thinks of poetic licence.

79 *dexion*: a fatuous and un-Aristotelian remark on the division of nouns by gender is here omitted.

as much as one liked . . .: Aristotle here quotes two hexameters in which Euclides parodied Homer's occasional irrational lengthening of short syllables.

80 *'being little . . .'*: Homer, *Odyssey* 9. 515. *oligos* in the sense of 'small' is here regarded as a dialect term: in Attic it means 'few'. *outidanos* does not belong to prose at all, while *asthenikos* is decidedly prosaic as most of the words terminating in *-ikos* were not only of recent formation, but associated with philosophical and scientific discourse; *aeidēs* also seems to be used only by philosophers and medical writers.

'putting down . . .': Homer, *Odyssey* 20. 259. *mochthēros*, in the sense of 'distressed' or 'distressful' or as a term of moral condemnation, does belong to high poetry; but its use of things like chairs, to signify that they are 'in a bad way', is confined to Attic colloquial speech.

'the shores shout': Homer, *Iliad* 17. 265. *krazein* of human bawling is no more or less prosaic than *boan*, with which indeed it is sometimes linked as a synonym by the orators: but *boöōsin* is a 'lengthened' word, for which Attic would use *boōsin*.

use in conversation: Aristotle adds examples: archaic forms of pronouns, anastrophe of prepositions (putting them after their nouns).

iambic verse: the metre of tragic dialogue, which in Aristotle's view should largely confine itself to the same resources as impassioned prose.

81 *middle parts*: the plural, as distinct from the 'middle' of tragedy (p. 60), allows for epic's greater extension.

he did not undertake . . .: in the *Iliad*: there seems to be a reference back to the discussion of the unity of the *Odyssey* on p. 62. 'Whole' here as there implies 'unified'.

82 *the same species as tragedy*: cf. p. 73. 'Simple' here corresponds to what should probably be 'spectacle' there.

And in addition . . .: F. Solmsen, *CQ* 29, 1935, 195, was probably correct in arguing that a series of remarks about the qualitative parts (here enclosed in double brackets) has been superimposed on a straightforward discussion of the species of epic.

above mentioned . . . guide: p. 61.

the ancients: the phrase delicately veils the name of Homer, the only one of the older epic poets to produce very long compositions.

83 *but Homer . . . character*: the doctrine in this section seems at variance with the view that plain narrative is a variety of *mimēsis* (p. 53). The same sort of exaggeration of the small part played in Homer by direct narration seems to occur in Plato, *Republic* 393 a.

Bath scene: see note to p. 71.

84 *this sort of irrationality*: Sophocles seems to have been aware of this irrationality, and to have tried to palliate it by attributing to the royal house of Thebes and to the chorus an instinctive distaste for the public discussion of unpleasant subjects (91 f. Creon, 637 f. Jocasta, 678 f., 685 f. the chorus).

Criticisms of Homer . . .: this discussion is extremely difficult and compressed, presumably because it is an epitome of the six books Aristotle wrote on *Homeric Problems*.

85 *an impossibility*: though Aristotle takes an impossibility as an example, he could equally well have chosen something irrational, morally damaging, or self-contradictory (p. 88).

Answers derived from basis (a): the first three answers here are various ways of dealing with the charge that what is said is not true, the fourth with the charge that what is said is not as it should be, i.e. is morally damaging.

86 *Answers derived from basis* (b): the charges answered are, as one would expect, of very diverse kinds: answer (7), for instance, copes first with a supposed irrationality, then with a supposed self-

contradiction ('How could Dolon run fast if he was deformed?'), then with something supposed morally damaging.

88 *contrary to technical correctness*: i.e. involving ignorance of, for instance, botany or zoology: cf. p. 85. An offence against 'the art of poetry itself' would be an indefensible example of one of the other four.

The statement of the opponents of tragedy: the position here stated is largely that formulated by Plato in the *Republic* (393 ff.) and the *Laws* (658 f.).

Horace: *A Letter to Augustus*

THIS 'epistle' (2. 1) was written by Horace to the first of the Roman emperors around 15 BC. The grandness of the addressee, who is virtually regarded as a god in the introductory lines, has its effects on the poem, but like Horace's other Epistles it is often oblique and humorous, with transitions hard to analyse and a tone that is often difficult to pin down.

For edition and detailed commentary see C. O. Brink, *Horace on Poetry* iii (Cambridge, 1982).

91 *Liber*: the Roman equivalent of Dionysus, Greek god of wine. Horace treats Liber and the other divinities mentioned (including Hercules, 'the hero who crushed the dread Hydra', as one of his Labours) as heroes who won their way to heaven after death.

the Alban Hill: the Muses, normally associated with Greek mountains like Helicon (p. 105), here speak on Monte Cavo, south-east of Rome.

the Tables: the Twelve Tables, the earliest code of Roman law, traditionally drafted by a board of ten (*decemviri*) in 450 BC. Horace continues with further allusions to the remote past: treaties with locals in the regal period, books kept by the priests with records of ritual, and oracles.

On that principle: i.e. such analogical arguments could be used to lead to absurd conclusions. Olives have no stones because nuts have none (so too nuts have no shells); we are supreme in the arts because we are masters of the world.

Achaeans: grandiose term for the Greeks.

92 *Heap*: if I take things away one by one, when does it stop being a heap?

turn out: Ennius wrote in his *Annals* that in a dream Homer's soul had become his by the process of metempsychosis (popularized by the sixth-century 'philosopher' Pythagoras). Horace appears to mean that a poet so inartistic shows little sign of worrying about living up to so grand a genealogy. In what follows, Horace implies that the praise given to all early Roman poets is misplaced.

93 *Hymn*: the archaic chant of the Salii priests (instituted by the early king Numa), unintelligible to Horace's contemporaries.

her wars: in the early fifth century BC.

southernwood: an aromatic shrub, much in favour in ancient medicine.

94 *Genius*: i.e. the individual's tutelary spirit.

Fescennines: Fescennine verses were traditionally ribald lines sung at Roman weddings.

Saturnian: the common verse of early Roman poetry.

95 *Punic Wars*: the Hannibalic war ended in 201 BC. Horace alludes to early tragedians like Pacuvius and Accius.

*Dossennus:*i.e. dolt.

knights: rich Romans, below senatorial rank.

Corinth: sacked by Rome in 146 BC.

96 *Apollo*: the new library on the Palatine Hill in Rome, built by Augustus.

Boeotian: Athenian malice made the stupidity of their northern neighbours, the Boeotians, a byword.

97 *I*: Horace now puts himself in the position of Augustus, recipient of unwanted poetic attentions.

Horace: *The Art of Poetry*

HORACE'S *Ars Poetica* (not his own title) is an 'epistle', like the *Letter to Augustus*, with which it shares many themes. Its technical material is indirectly descended from Aristotle's *Poetics*, but its humour and allusiveness make it something quite different from a versified treatise on tragedy. Leading themes, bewilderingly intertwined, include consistency, unity, propriety, the debt of Rome to Greece, and the need for 'art' and for moral commitment. The poem's ideas, and their brilliant phrasing, gave it a long and wide influence.

For edition and detailed annotation see C. O. Brink, *Horace on Poetry* ii (Cambridge, 1971).

98 *my Piso friends*: Horace addresses a father and two sons, of uncertain identity.

the man who is paying for the picture: the picture is commissioned by someone who has made a vow to a god and repays it by putting up a votive tablet on his safe return from a voyage (cf. 'expression of a vow fulfilled', p. 100).

School of Aemilius: a training establishment for gladiators.

99 *Cethegi in their loin-cloths*: i.e. primitive Romans.

100 *Lines unequally yoked in pairs*: i.e. elegiac couplets, formed of hexameter and the shorter pentameter.

Banquet of Thyestes: Thyestes, son of Pelops, had his own sons served up to him by his brother Atreus (cf. the reference to 'wicked Atreus', p. 102).

Chremes: a common name in New Comedy. Horace thinks especially of irate fathers. Telephus and Peleus come from Euripides.

knights and infantry of Rome: i.e. the entire Roman people, assembled in the theatre. For the knights, see note to p. 95.

101 *It is hard . . . unsaid*: i.e. to invent names and circumstances for a general theme is undesirable; if you object that the known myths are hackneyed, the remedy is in the treatment of them in a new way.

Tell me . . .: the first words of Homer's *Odyssey*.

Antiphates . . . Charybdis: the various tales in *Odyssey* 9–12.

from the twin egg: i.e. from the birth of Helen.

103 *five acts*: this precept is not Aristotelian, but Menander seems normally to have composed his comedies in five acts, separated by choral interludes.

Satyrs: Horace now discusses the so-called Satyr plays, which featured Silenus and satyrs in burlesque episodes of myth. Such a piece was commonly performed as a fourth play after three tragedies.

104 *Davus . . .*: more names from New Comedy.

Fauns: Roman equivalent of the satyrs.

A long syllable . . . the trade: Horace humorously gives some very elementary metrical instruction. Greek trimeters have the basic scheme: $\cup - | \cup - | \underline{\cup} - | \cup - | \underline{\cup} - | \cup -$ whereas the corresponding old Latin *senarius*, used by Ennius and Accius, admits spondees also in the second and fourth feet.

105 *Old Comedy*: represented mainly by Aristophanes.

Children of Numa: i.e. Romans. Numa was the second king of Rome.

Helicon: mountain home of the Muses.

Anticyras: hellebore, proverbially a cure for madness, came from Anticyra in central Greece.

106 *a hundred parts*: 12 unciae = 1 as; 5 unciae = quincunx; ⅓ as = triens; ½ as = semis.

107 *Sosii*: booksellers.

109 *Aristarchus*: the great Alexandrian scholar marked spurious or doubtful lines in Homer with the sign which Horace here attributes to the good critic.

Tacitus: *Dialogue on Orators*

IT is uncertain when Tacitus wrote this dialogue on the decay of oratory at Rome; but the dramatic date is under the emperor Vespasian, probably AD 74. Maternus, seen in the early pages as a poet rejecting the materialist values of oratory, is given the last word, magisterially putting forward the thesis that the Empire was unfavourable to political eloquence of the type that flourished under the Republic. He thereby refutes both the claim of Aper that modern oratory was at least as good as that of the past, and the view of Messalla, an admirer of the ancients, who lays the blame on a faulty educational system. The work, a masterpiece of characterization, is inspired by the dialogues of Cicero, and differs greatly in style from Tacitus' historical writings. But it brings a historian's perspective to a question that much exercised critics in the first century (see especially 'Longinus' c. 44).

For English commentary see W. Peterson's edition (Oxford, 1893). For the problems raised see R. Syme, *Tacitus* (Oxford, 1958), 100 ff.

111 *Cato*: the story of the suicide of the younger Cato during the Civil Wars naturally gave scope for anti-imperial sentiments. The same was true of the myth of Thyestes, son of Pelops, who had his children served up to him by his brother Atreus, and of the story of Domitius (whether Lucius or Gnaeus Domitius Ahenobarbus, both relations of Cato).

115 *centumviral court*: court concerned with testamentary and other civil cases, which grew important under the Empire (see also p. 139).

119 *Virgil's 'sweet Muses'*: Georgics 2. 475.

120 *write safeguards into my will*: it was safest to leave money to the Emperor himself.

your brother's: M. Aquillius Regulus, notorious and violent orator.

121 *Cicero's* Hortensius: a lost exhortation to philosophy, a famous and influential work.

122 *a hundred and twenty years*: but the figures given add up only to 118.

123 *'Attic'*: allusion to a literary dispute of Cicero's last years. Cicero was criticized as too 'Asian' in contrast with the restraint of the fifth-century Attic orators (for whom see p. 128) and their later imitators.

124 *speeches against Verres*: Cicero's famous prosecution of a governor of Sicily in 70 BC. Tullius and Caecina were defended by Cicero on less important charges.

126 *'wheel of fortune'*: In Pisonem 22.

'boar-sauce': cf. *Verrines* 1. 1. 121. The Latin is a pun, and could also mean 'Verrine justice'.

esse videatur: 'may seem to be', a form of the common cretic + spondee (– ◡ – – –) clausula.

130 *your ancestors*: Messalla may have been related to (M. Valerius Messalla) Corvinus, an orator several times mentioned in the dialogue.

132 *he relates*: Brutus 304 seq.

133 *Peripatetics*: the philosophical school founded by Aristotle, just as Plato founded the Academy.

134 *the wide spaces of the Academy*: Orator 12.

136 *'schools for shamelessness'*: De Oratore 3. 94. This was in 92 BC.

suasoriae: declamations where pupils 'advised' historical, mythological, or fictional characters at critical points of their lives.

controversiae: declamations where pupils spoke in the character of litigants, or their advocates, in imaginary law-cases.

judges . . .: there is a lacuna here, perhaps quite long. When the text resumes, Maternus is the speaker.

139 *third consulship*: 52 BC.

140 *prosecuted and defended*: all five were defended by Cicero.

'Longinus': *On Sublimity*

THIS book is attributed to 'Longinus', long supposed to be a well-known statesman and critic of the third century AD. Internal evidence, however, suggests an earlier date, probably some time in the first century. About a third of the book is lost, because of damage to the one manuscript through which it survives, and the course of the argument is not altogether clear.

The influence of 'Longinus' was at its height in the eighteenth century, following Boileau's famous translation (1674).

See W. R. Roberts (Cambridge, 1899, 1907) and D. A. Russell (Oxford, 1964) for modern editions with commentary.

143 *Postumius Terentianus*: unidentified.

Caecilius: Caecilius of Caleacte (*c.* first century BC) was an influential critic, but most of our knowledge of his views has to be inferred from 'Longinus'' refutation.

144 *profundity*: we translate *bathous* (= 'depth'), but the conjecture *pathous* ('emotion') may be right. The English word 'bathos' perhaps acquired its meaning from a misunderstanding of this passage.

Demosthenes: Oration 23. 113.

145 *restrain . . . proper song*: the speaker is Boreas (the North Wind), the writer Aeschylus.

Hence . . . same: The writers criticised in this passage, apart from Gorgias, are from the Hellenistic period, in which classicizing critics (like our author) saw no good.

146 *Panegyricus*: Isocrates wrote the *Panegyricus* in the 380s. Its polish and technical mastery were famous. The Spartans conquered Messenia in the eighth century.

Athenians captured in Sicily: in the disastrous expedition against Syracuse (415–413 BC), which had been preceded by the mysterious vandalizing of the statues of Hermes in the city, an event which caused great scandal.

147 *maidens*: the word *korē* means both 'girl' and 'pupil'. Xenophon replaced it by *parthenos*, which means unambiguously 'maiden'.

Drunken sot . . .: *Iliad* 1. 225.

Plato: the passages quoted are from the *Laws* (741c, 778d), Plato's last and stylistically most eccentric work.

Herodotus' description: 5. 18, an account of the entertainment of a party of Persians in Macedonia. The 'excuse' offered recalls the principles of interpretation we see also in Plutarch (p. 199).

149 *Xenophon*: the importance of Xenophon in later times rests partly on his simple and (apparently) imitable style, partly on his manly moral tone.

emotion: in the mutilated form in which we possess the book, this is nowhere discussed as a separate issue, and this fact has given rise to many speculations. The long missing passage in ch. 9 probably held the clue.

Aloadae: the impious Otus and Ephialtes, *Odyssey* 11. 315–17.

150 *Ajax's silence*: Ajax (*Odyssey* 11. 563) turns away from Odysseus in

Hades without speaking (as Dido does from Aeneas in Virgil's adaptation, *Aeneid* 6. 450 ff.).

Parmenio . . .: Parmenio said that if he were Alexander, he would stop fighting, and, Alexander retorted 'So I would, if I were Parmenio'.

Strife: Homer (*Iliad* 4. 440 ff.) describes Strife as having her head in the sky and walking on earth. So Longinus means that Homer too is a colossus of cosmic dimensions.

Mucus . . . nostrils: [Hesiod] 'Shield of Heracles' 267.

151 *As far as . . . horses*: Iliad 5. 770–2.

And . . . gods detest: a conflation of *Iliad* 21. 388 and 20. 61 ff. (Similarly, the last passage on p. 151 ('The high hills . . .') is a conflation of *Iliad* 13. 18 ff. and 20. 60. Illustrative quotations in common use were not necessarily exact.)

152 *the lawgiver of the Jews*: many have thought that this passage is spurious, on the grounds (1) that a pagan author would be unlikely to know Genesis, (2) that the passage interrupts the argument. But neither ground holds; it is even possible that Caecilius, who was said to be a Jew (Plutarch, *Cicero* 7), may be the source. In the eighteenth century, the quotation gave a lead to a literary approach to biblical texts (R. Lowth, *De Sacra Poesi Hebraeorum*, 1753). See S. H. Monk, *The Sublime* (1935), 33.

O Father Zeus!: Iliad 17. 645 ff.

rages like Ares . . . mouth: Iliad 15. 605 ff.

153 *There lies . . . dear son*: spoken by Nestor, *Odyssey* 3. 109 ff.

154 *To me he seems . . .*: Sappho fr. 31, often translated into English (e.g. by Ambrose Phillips, *Spectator* 229, with critique by Addison). Imitated by Catullus (51).

Arimaspea: this lost poem was attributed to Aristeas of Proconnesus, a prophet of Apollo supposed to have travelled deep into central and northern Asia in the seventh century BC. The Arimaspi were said to be a one-eyed race who fought with the griffins for gold (cf. Herodotus 4. 27, *Paradise Lost* 2. 944).

155 *He fell . . . only just*: Iliad 15. 624 ff. The contrasting passage is from Aratus (*Phaenomena* 299).

Archilochus . . . Demosthenes: we do not know what is meant about Archilochus, though several extant fragments of his poems relate to storms and shipwreck. The passage of Demosthenes is the famous description (*de corona* 169) of the panic at Athens when news came one evening that Philip had taken Elatea (339 BC).

157 *Republic*: 9. 586 a (adapted).

158 *Pythia*: the theory that the prophetic frenzy of the priestesses at the
oracle of Delphi was due to inhaling a vapour was widely held in
ancient times, but seems to be simply a philosophical theory of
inspiration, with no basis in fact.

'this strife . . .': *Works and Days* 24.

159 *Mother . . . to me*: Euripides, *Orestes* 255–7. This passage and the
next (*Iphigenia in Tauris* 291) refer to Orestes' vision of the Furies
who pursue him.

160 *whips flank . . .*: *Iliad* 20. 170.

Phaethon: Euripides' *Phaethon* (extant only in considerable fragments)
told the story of Phaethon's marriage and how his mother revealed
to him that he was the son of the sun god, Helios. He asks to be
allowed to drive the sun's chariot, and disaster follows. Our
passages are from the messenger's speech reporting his death.

Ye Trojans . . .: perhaps from Euripides' *Alexandros*. We do not know
the context, and Longinus' point is not clear from these few words.

Seven against Thebes: 42 ff.

161 *Lycurgus*: Aeschylus wrote a play on the fate of the Thracian king,
Lycurgus, who refused passage to Dionysus on his march to India.
Euripides' *Bacchae* tells a similar story of the unbelieving Pentheus,
King of Thebes.

Sophocles: the references are to the closing scene of *Oedipus at
Colonus* and perhaps to the appearance of Achilles' ghost in the lost
Polyxena.

Let me go . . .: Euripides, *Orestes* 264–5.

Suppose you heard . . . end of him: the passage is from Demosthenes
Against Timocrates (*Or.* 24. 208).

162 *Chaeronea*: Philip's victory in 338 BC.

The next topic: we expected 'emotion' (cf. 8. 1 and Introductory
Note).

Demosthenes: 18. 208.

163 *Eupolis*: in *The Demes* (produced 412 BC) Eupolis introduced heroes
of the past (here Miltiades, the victory of Marathon) commenting
on current events. The lines parody Euripides, *Medea* 395 ff.: 'No,
by the mistress whom I honour, no one shall grieve me and not
suffer for it'. Dr Johnson (*Life of Dryden*, World's Classics p. 299)
greatly admired this discussion of the Marathon oath.

165 *Or—tell me . . . spots*: two passages of Demosthenes are meant:
Philippics 1. 4 and 44.

Herodotus: the break in the text prevents us knowing what passage is meant, but 7. 21 would meet the case: 'What nation did Xerxes not lead out of Asia? What water did not dry up with their drinking, save only the great rivers?'

Xenophon: *Hellenica* 4. 3. 19.

Eurylochus: in *Odyssey* 10. 251–2.

Against Midias: Demosthenes 21. 72.

166 *the normal sequence*: a few words are probably missing here.

167 *Herodotus*: 6. 11.

168 *polyptoton*: the occurrence of the same word in various inflections.

The innumerable host . . .: source unknown, and text uncertain.

Sophocles: *Oedipus Tyrannus* 1403 ff.

Hectors . . .: again an unknown line (from a tragedy).

169 *'No Pelopses . . . blood'*: Plato, *Menexenus* 245 d, not cited elsewhere in extant parts of this book. The author may of course be alluding to another of his works.

The whole Peloponnese . . .: Demosthenes, *de corona* 18.

Phrynichus: this early tragic poet produced his unfortunate play in or soon after 494 BC. (Plays might sometimes be about contemporary events, like Aeschylus' *The Persians* (472 BC).)

Xenophon: *Cyropaedia* 7. 1. 37.

Homer: *Iliad* 15. 697.

Aratus: *Phaenomena* 287.

170 *Herodotus*: 2. 29.

'You could not tell . . .': *Iliad* 5. 85.

'Hector shouted . . . spot': *Iliad* 15. 346 ff.

Hecataeus: the story of the children of Heracles, who fled to Trachis after his death, but were sent away by the king, Ceyx, at the bidding of Eurystheus.

Against Aristogiton: (Demosthenes) *Oration* 25.

171 *Penelope*: *Odyssey* 4. 681 ff.

Funeral speech: i.e. *Menexenus* 236 d.

Xenophon: *Cyropaedia* 1. 5. 12.

172 *Herodotus*: 1. 105.

Plato: *Laws* 801 b.

173 *filly*: (i.e. a girl) translates a conjectural supplement, and the author's point is not clear.

Herodotus: 6. 75, 7. 181.

'*Vile flatterers . . . good*': Demosthenes, *de corona* 296.

174 *Xenophon . . . Plato*: *Memorabilia* 1. 4. 5 ff. and *Timaeus* 65 c–85 e. The following passage is made up of extracts from *Timaeus*, not in order or in context.

175 '*It is not easy . . . drink*': *Laws* 773 c–d.

176 *Erigone*: the story of the poem was the death of Icarius (killed by shepherds to whom he had given wine which they believed to be poison) and the suicide of his daughter Erigone. It was a learned Alexandrian work, concerned to show the origin of an Attic ritual. There is an extant version of the same story in Nonnus, *Dionysiaca* 47. 34–264.

177 *account of Leto*: in the lost *Deliacus*. The funeral speech, to which 'Longinus' also alludes, is extant (*Oration* 2).

Phryne . . . Athenogenes: the defence of the courtesan Phryne, known from fragments, was very famous: the Athenogenes speech, which deals with a contract for the purchase of slaves, survives in a papyrus.

178 *so long as . . .*: a line of the 'epigram on the tomb of Midas', ascribed to Homer.

Colossus . . . Polyclitus: while it is debated whether or not the 'Colossus of Rhodes' or some other large statue is meant, the reference to Polyclitus' Doryphorus indicates the fame of this statue (known from Roman copies) as an example of beautiful proportion.

179 '*Unless . . . them*': Demosthenes (?), *Oration* 7. 45.

Panegyricus: see on p. 146. The passage cited is §6.

180 *Thucydides' account*: 7. 84.

Herodotus: 7. 225.

181 '*untouched . . .*': an often quoted line of Euripides (from the lost *Stheneboea*). In the original it is Love that makes a man a poet.

the decree: i.e. the decree making provision for war after Philip's seizure of Elatea (*de corona* 188).

182 *Heracles*: Euripides, *Hercules Furens* 1245.

183 *And . . . them all*: the passage is from Euripides' lost *Antiope*. The comment turns on certain sound-effects in the Greek: *perix helixas* and *petran drun*.

184 *Herodotus*: 7. 188, 191, 8. 13.

Theopompus: this passage described the expedition of Artaxerxes Ochus against Egypt in the middle of the fourth century.

185 *Xenophon*: *Memorabilia* 1. 4. 6.

186 *Homer*: *Odyssey* 17. 322–3.

187 *'Best to let these things be'*: Euripides, *Electra* 379.

Dio of Prusa: *Philoctetes in the Tragedians*

THIS short essay is *Oration* 52 in the collected works of Dio of Prusa, a successful sophist with philosophical leanings who flourished around the end of the first century AD. For a good general account of his work, see C. P. Jones, *The Roman World of Dio Chrysostom* (1978).

In this essay he gives a conventional view of the differences between the three great tragedians, as illustrated by their treatment of the story of Philoctetes. Sophocles' play (the latest of the three) survives: the other two are lost, but Dio himself (*Oration* 53) gives a paraphrase of the prologue of Euripides' play, which may be quite close to the original.

190 *Eurybatus . . . Pataecion*: proverbial rogues (Aeschines 3. 137, 189: Plato *Protagoras* 327 d).

Eumaeus and Penelope: *Odyssey* 13. 429 ff., 16. 172 ff.

191 *virtue*: see Horace, p. 103.

He licked the jar . . .: from an unknown play of Aristophanes.

Plutarch: *On the Study of Poetry*

PLUTARCH (*c.* AD 45–*c.*120) was the most versatile Greek writer of his age. Moralist, philosopher and biographer—his 'Lives' are indeed a 'world's classic'—he occasionally touches on topics of literary criticism, usually when they impinge on education. In this treatise he follows the tradition of moralizing criticism of the classical poets set by Plato (pp. 14–50), but comes to a more positive conclusion. Instead of forbidding the reading of poetry, he shows how it can be made harmless by accurate interpretation or looking for a deeper meaning. To this end he deploys considerable scholarship as well as ingenuity. The outcome is an important book for anyone who wishes to understand how the Greek classical heritage was received in the Hellenistic and Roman world.

Many of the quotations in this book are from works that do not survive; we do not give references for these, though they are to be found in the standard collections of fragments of tragedy or lyric. We give the first part of the book only.

192 *Abaris . . . Lycon*: these are dialogues by popular philosophers of the school of Aristotle (fourth–third century BC), which included colourful myths.

Cleandros: since Marcus Sedatius' son has a Greek name, we may assume that the father is a Greek-born Roman citizen, like Plutarch himself (L. Mestrius Plutarchus). The boys are probably now about 10.

193 *Many drugs . . . the wise*: Odyssey 4. 230, Iliad 14. 216.

Ithacan sailors: Odysseus blocked their ears with wax so that they should not hear the Sirens' song (*Odyssey* 12).

Epicurus: Epicurus said 'Set sail and get away from education of every kind'—meaning the traditional studies of grammar, rhetoric, and mathematics.

Lycurgus: Iliad 6. 130.

Plato's expression: Laws 773 d.

194 *Metre . . . word-order*: Plutarch enumerates the formal characteristics of poetry: his enumeration is slightly odd, since 'trope' strictly includes 'metaphor'.

Socrates: Plato, *Phaedo* 60a ff.

Empedocles: Plutarch accepts the position of Aristotle, excluding didactic works from the category of poetry (p. 52). Nicander's poem on 'Animal venoms and their remedies' is an Alexandrian didactic poem (second century BC) by a prolific poet, on whom Plutarch wrote a special monograph (not extant).

195 *Poseidon*: see p. 151.

he who sang . . .: see Plato (p. 21) above.

Make haste . . . hereafter: Odyssey 11. 223.

196 *He put . . . abandoned him*: Iliad 22. 210.

Zeus . . .: Iliad 4. 84.

God . . . a house: see Plato (p. 17) above.

and . . . White Rock: Odyssey 24. 11.

Do not . . . unburied: Odyssey 11. 72. The following quotations are from *Iliad* 16. 856 and 22. 362 and Euripides, *Iphigenia at Aulis* 1218.

197 *Socrates' disavowal*: Plato, *Phaedo* 96b ff.

Thersites: the ugly man of the people, caricatured in Homer (*Iliad* 2).

198 *If we* must *do wrong . . .*: Euripides, *Phoenissae* 524. The second quotation is from an unknown tragedy, the third from an unknown comedy.

199 *Paris's . . . battle*: Iliad 3. 380.

He spoke a sweet . . . Odyssey 6. 148. The following quotations are also all from Homer: *Iliad* 2. 189, 1. 24, 1. 225, 1. 223, 23. 24.

200 *Bad deeds . . .*: Odyssey 8. 239, followed by *Iliad* 8. 198 and 4. 104.

allegory: Plato (p. 16) used the word *huponoia*.

201 *cestus*: Aphrodite's magic girdle 'in which were all her charms' (*Iliad* 14. 214).

changes of clothes. . .: *Odyssey* 8. 249, followed by 8. 492.

So that . . . me: *Iliad* 15. 32.

202 *You know . . .*: *Iliad* 7. 358, followed by 6. 138, *Odyssey* 6. 46, *Iliad* 24. 525.

203 *Pindar*: Isthmian 4.52, followed by 7. 47.

204 *Epaminondas*: national hero of Thebes, who led his country during its brief hegemony over Greece (371–362 BC).

205 *Theognis' lines*: ll. 177–8. Bion (of Borysthenes) is a cynic moralist of the third century BC who must have quoted and criticized the lines of Theognis, who does in fact complain of the excesses of wealth and thus reveal himself as poor.

This is the privilege . . .: *Odyssey* 4. 197.

Such is the fate . . .: *Iliad* 24. 525.

'*glosses*': cf. Aristotle (pp. 78, 86: 'dialect words'). The word *glōssa*, 'tongue', comes to mean 'unintelligible sound', and so 'foreign word': in later usage, 'gloss' means the interpretation of such a word.

popoi: this is an explanation of an exclamation, *ō popoi*, common in Homer.

206 *oikos*: the passages cited are: *Odyssey* 5. 42, 4. 318.

Biotos: the passages cited are *Iliad* 13. 562, *Odyssey* 13. 419.

aluein: the passages cited are *Iliad* 5. 352, *Odyssey* 18. 333.

Thoazein: the passage from Euripides is from the lost *Andromeda*, that from Sophocles is *Oedipus Tyrannus* 2.

Praise a small ship . . .: Hesiod, *Works and Days* 643.

207 *by Zeus . . .*: *Phoenissae* 1006.

Sharp Ares . . .: *Iliad* 7. 329.

O father Zeus . . .: *Iliad* 3. 276.

208 *the wrath of Achilles*: Plutarch quotes the opening lines of the *Iliad*.

Hesiod: *Works and Days* 86: the following passage is 717.

'*fortune*': it was observed that Homer did not speak of 'fortune' though most later poets did.

209 *By Zeus's door . . .*: see Plato (p. 17), from whom Plutarch clearly takes the quotation.

Zeus, enthroned . . .: *Iliad* 7. 69, followed by *Odyssey* 8. 81.

The ranks . . . man: *Iliad* 11. 540.

The gods . . .: Hesiod, *Works and Days* 289, following by *Iliad* 11. 90 and a quotation from a lost play of Euripides.

210 *Zeus . . . wane*: *Iliad* 20. 242, followed by Hesiod, *Works and Days* 313 and 287 (Plutarch wrote a commentary on *Works and Days*, and the frequency of reference to it is due to this special interest in a fellow Boeotian).

For men grow old . . .: *Odyssey* 19. 360, followed by 4. 93.

211 *I never want . . .*: Euripides, *Medea* 603 followed by *Phoenissae* 552.

212 *O father Zeus . . . Troy*: *Iliad* 16. 97, followed by *Odyssey* 11. 421 and Iliad 9. 452 and 3. 365.

213 *the ninth day*: *Iliad* 1. 53: 'nine days the God's arrows went about the army, and on the tenth Achilles called the people to assemble . . .' The following passages are from the opening scenes of the *Iliad*.

214 *I planned . . . murderer*: *Iliad* 9. 458. These lines are not in the manuscript tradition of Homer, but are known (and therefore included in modern editions) from this passage of Plutarch. They were not, as Plutarch's evidence shows, in the edition of the great Alexandrian scholar Aristarchus; but that he was 'alarmed' at the immoral sentiment is only Plutarch's conjecture.

I wish . . . stay: *Odyssey* 6. 244.

because . . . hearts: *Odyssey* 18. 282.

215 *for fear . . . ship*: *Odyssey* 13. 216.

his colleague: i.e. Euripides, whose *Hippolytus* is about this story. Plutarch refers here not to the extant version, but to an earlier one.

Hecuba: *Trojan Women* 914 ff.

216 *And not . . .*: *Works and Days* 744, followed by *Iliad* 4. 306, Euripides, *Hippolytus* 424, and a fragment of a lost play of Euripides.

INDEX OF PROPER NAMES

American Literature

British and Irish Literature

Children's Literature

Classics and Ancient Literature

Colonial Literature

Eastern Literature

European Literature

History

Medieval Literature

Oxford English Drama

Poetry

Philosophy

Politics

Religion

The Oxford Shakespeare

A complete list of Oxford Paperbacks, including Oxford World's Classics, OPUS, Past Masters, Oxford Authors, Oxford Shakespeare, Oxford Drama, and Oxford Paperback Reference, is available in the UK from the Academic Division Publicity Department, Oxford University Press, Great Clarendon Street, Oxford OX2 6DP.

In the USA, complete lists are available from the Paperbacks Marketing Manager, Oxford University Press, 198 Madison Avenue, New York, NY 10016.

Oxford Paperbacks are available from all good bookshops. In case of difficulty, customers in the UK can order direct from Oxford University Press Bookshop, Freepost, 116 High Street, Oxford OX1 4BR, enclosing full payment. Please add 10 per cent of published price for postage and packing.